MW01156838

LAS VEGAS IS MY BEAT

Las Vegas

Is My Beat

by Ralph Pearl

with a Foreword by Jack Benny

Lyle Stuart, Inc., Secaucus, New Jersey

DEDICATION

This book has to be dedicated wholly to my wife, Roz. Because of her incessant bickering and constant acts of violence on my defenseless body (which she chained to my typewriter), I finally was able to finish *Las Vegas Is My Beat*. True, there were moments when I would have gladly poisoned her to avoid my literary obligations and stray off to the more pleasurable things in life. And some day I could be sorry I didn't do away with her. That cruel awakening may come when I've seen the book reviews, heard from the public, and examined my royalty statements.

Contents

Preface

One of the legendary characters of this Show Capital of the World is supreme storyteller Myron Cohen, who has been a regular in the Las Vegas entertainment picture for the past quarter of a century. In this city without clocks or conscience, Myron Cohen is as important as Disneyland is to the small suburb of Los Angeles known as Anaheim.

I've always believed my living and working here for twenty years without climbing walls is a psychiatric miracle. So whenever I'm asked by visiting newsmen to explain the minor miracle of my surviving all these years in face of the numerous temptations and hurdles, I always tell them a favorite Myron Cohen story.

The story has to do with a salesman who visits a small town and shacks up with the mayor's wife. Suddenly they hear a key in the door and the mayor's voice. "My God," the wife screams, "that's my husband. Go hide in the bathroom!"

But the mayor, a suspicious bastard, spots a cigar burning in the ashtray and knows it's not the brand his wife usually smokes. So he searches through the premises, his wife tagging along and assuring him there's nobody in the house. His Honor finally storms into the bathroom, rips aside the shower curtain, and finds the unclad salesman cowering there.

In a snarling rage, the mayor asked the question men have asked from time immemorial: "What the hell are you doing here?"

The salesman replied, "Listen, everybody's gotta be some place, no?"

As far as I am concerned, "some place" has been Las Vegas for more than twenty years. I've watched more than just high-salaried stars perform from behind the footlights of Strip hotel showrooms. I've seen plenty of the sordid side of humanity—those who fell by the wayside after gaming, boozing excesses hopelessly aiming at impossible targets.

Las Vegas doesn't have a monopoly on shattered lives and suicides. Race tracks, dog tracks, and pleasure palaces around the world have done equally "good" jobs of keeping our population from exploding.

Las Vegas is where I write a daily show-business column for the Las Vegas *Sun* and do a nightly television show. That I haven't been a casualty thus far is easy to explain. I get sick to the stomach when I bet more than a dollar and lose. I can't stand the taste of booze, and have never smoked in my life. As the comics would put it, "Three out of four ain't bad."

I've watched several colleagues, medicos, and barristers—not to mention a few top business executives—try to live like weekending, high-rolling swingers. They're long gone from here and earning their livelihood in less tempting environs.

Rubbing elbows over the years with the likes of Mitzi Gaynor, Danny Thomas, Johnny Carson, Sammy Davis, Jr., Tony Newley, Don Rickles, Elvis Presley, Mike Douglas, Barbra Streisand, and all the other stars has been a considerably more pleasant task than selling haberdashery in a Manhattan shop or picking underripe oranges in a California grove.

True, I wish I could have done something about the location of Las Vegas. Sticking it in a hollow just outside of Death Valley wasn't the happiest thing that ever happened to a town. It's not as ideally located as the happy little villages around Lake Tahoe or Malibu Beach. The burning heat of the summers and chilling frost of the winters, plus what seems to be a constant blowing of sand several months a year, haven't made Las Vegas my dream "getaway rendezvous."

As a matter of fact, the desert and its dryness have inflicted me with an itching skin and a warped sexuality that make me the talk of all the parties in this town. And before you start linking me up with a page out of the Kinsey Report, let me explain that my "warped sexuality" stems from the constant flickering of billions of neons night and day, the clanging of slot machines, and the blasting of musical instruments in my ear for twenty years.

As Myron Cohen says, "Everybody's gotta be some place," and that "some place" for me is right here in Las Vegas.

But the mere fact that "Everybody's gotta be some place," is not enough reason for me to be writing a book in this cynical, surly vein. Several relatives, and some of my friends in show business seem to feel I owe an unpayable debt to Las Vegas for allowing me to exist all these past twenty years in its neon bosom while making a fairly good living as a columnist and TV newsman.

George Jessel was even more explicit when I told him I had already finished *Las Vegas Is My Beat*. Despite my urgent argument that I'm not really a pariah in Las Vegas because I'm merely depicting it the way I see it, Jessel probed deeply into his vast storehouse of stories to fit every occasion.

"Naturally, you're gonna write the book, and I'm sure it'll

be very well received by the public and by Las Vegas itself. However, lemme tell you the story of the little bird which I've been re-telling for the past twenty years," said Jessel. "Naturally, it has a moral which just might apply to your situation.

"A little bird once got caught in a heavy snowstorm. His beak, wings, feet, and eyes froze immediately in that blizzard. Right away the bird began figuring he's gonna freeze to death. But along came a huge cow, saw the poor little bird laying in the snow, and immediately dropped a large pile of shit on him. It proved to be a lifesaver for the bird. The shit was warm enough to thaw out the frozen bird, who came back to life and began chirping happily. Unfortunately, he chirped so loudly that it attracted a miserable old wolf nearby who pounced on the poor little bird and ate him up.

"Now, there are three morals to the story," continued the number one storyteller in the nation, who slumped slightly as he told the story because of the weight of the numerous medals on his USO-decorated chest.

"Always remember, Ralph, being shit on isn't so bad. But being pulled out of shit isn't so good either. However, when you're up to your eyes in shit, always remember one thing: DON'T SING!"

Foreword

Las Vegas columnist Ralph Pearl has asked me to write a
piece about him for his new book *Las Vegas Is My Beat*,
which I will read just as soon as it's released by the publisher,
Lyle Stuart. (I hope it will be a gift.) I'll go a step farther and
say I'll even *purchase* a copy of Ralph's book, if forced to, because he's a guy who really *knows* Las Vegas and has written
about that incredible town most interestingly—and provoca-
tively—for twenty years.

Back in the early Fifties, many of my colleagues in this
business—Danny Thomas, the late Sophie Tucker, Jimmy
Durante, and the late Joe E. Lewis—tried to convince me to
play Las Vegas. I kept saying no because I felt it wouldn't
give me prestige—just lots of beautiful money. Then I got
sick at the thought of the huge salaries being paid Sophie,
Danny, Jimmy, and Joe.

Finally in 1957 I signed with the Flamingo Hotel and
opened there later that year. I'd read some of the columns by
Ralph Pearl of the Las Vegas *Sun*, and he struck me as a
fearsome little fellow at that portable of his. But fearsome or
not, he was constructively critical. As I opened that night at

the Flamingo, I saw Pearl sitting owlishly at ringside, dabbling at the tablecloth with his pencil.

It was then I remembered Danny Thomas kidding me about Ralph after I'd signed that Flamingo contract. "Don't worry about Ralph Pearl," said he. "He's very fair. He once gave his own mother a nasty review when she opened in the *Folies Bergere* at the Tropicana." It wasn't so funny when I stood behind the footlights trying to remember my first line in a Las Vegas café.

Luckily, everything turned out fine, and I'll be celebrating my sixteenth year in Las Vegas in 1973. As for Ralph Pearl, he's rough and tough, but he can be a positive pussycat sometimes. Read his book. You're bound to like it!

JACK BENNY

1. Land of the Boozers, Losers, and Lovers

The huge orange ball, low in the Las Vegas sky, started sinking behind the brooding, purple mountains. And as darkness descended over this modern valley, a cascade of millions of neon lights brightened the sunless heavens. It was a sign that would prepare thousands of pleasure-seekers for another evening of fun and games in the Show Capital of the World.

And if you happened to be watching the sky from the Strip-side windows of the plush Caesars Palace, above the tenth floor, then you had to see the bizarre sign on the highway which read, "Cash Your Pay Checks at the Mint Hotel for Double Payoffs!" There was absolutely nothing on that billboard that told the prospective paycheck holder his chances for a double payoff were as hopeless as Twiggy's titties.

Below the gaming casinos that never close, nasal, monotonous exhortations of the croupiers pleaded with the gamers to "Get your bets down, folks. They're coming out a winner every time." These selfsame croupiers conveniently forget to note that eight out of ten times "the winner" is the house.

Not too much later this evening a goodly number of these

gaming gents will start straggling away from the tables completely "tapped out." They'll walk away muttering to the high heavens for divine guidance toward a new bankroll. And if that miracle fails, then they'll beg the Almighty to provide them with one helluva fine alibi to explain the empty wallet to the wife.

Those more optimistic, however, placate themselves by vowing there'll be another time when the dice, the wheel, or the pasteboards will be more favorable to them.

But now it's time to start the evening. So I go out into the night, staunch and freshly laundered to slay or maybe just maim a few dragons. My first stop this Saturday night is Caesars Palace, where all the action seems to be. A gent by the name of Frank Sinatra is holding out in the showroom.

Neither he nor any of us knows that it'll be Frank's last appearance as a performer or even a guest in Las Vegas. It's only three nights before his classic hassle with Palace gambling boss, Sandy Waterman, that'll soon break in newspapers as far away as the *Cairo Bugle* and cause Frank to vow that he'll never darken a Las Vegas dice table or the town again.

Now I'm elbowing my way through the gaming casino here at the Palace with much difficulty. The tables are jammed with sweating ivory and pasteboard speculators. Others are queued behind them waiting for one to step away so they can jump in.

Money is changing hands so rapidly that I'm wondering if it'll mar the ink on Uncle's new currency going into circulation for the first time that night. As always, the gaming bosses are standing off and watching this currency carnage. They rub their hands gleefully together because much more of the money is going into those handy black boxes under each gaming table than into the pockets of the gamers.

As usual, it's turning out to be a most profitable night for the house. It needs to be. The Palace has a budget that hits the mark at $36 million annually.

The Palace has to take in roughly $100,000 a day just to keep its doors open. They've done more than that since the hotel opened in 1966. However, some other hotels aren't that lucky—especially those in the Howard Hughes chain, which have been in the red constantly. More about that later.

So, I'm on the outer fringe of the casino now, and a boss greets me warmly. Sometimes on a cold, rainy Monday he'll be grumpy as hell, as business slumps considerably, but tonight he practically kisses me on the mouth, the stubby cigar stuck in his jaw notwithstanding.

"Ralphie, boy," he lies, "you look terrific. How is Roz and the kids?" So I tell him, "How can I look terrific when I've got this boil on my jaw, a three-day growth of beard, and I've been suffering four days of constipation?" He listens while talking to a customer. "Hey, glad to hear it. How's Roz and the kids?" Again, patiently, I explain that we have no kids. "As for Roz, she's suffering from a nasty sinus condition and a $20 hair styling that didn't work out."

"Great, great," screams the gent, "give them my love."

But I know how to get him to listen. "Hey, Ike, you guys are really gonna make it tonight. Look at those hundred-dollar chips all over the dice tables." Ike's face has already fallen several inches into his pot belly, covered conveniently by a white-on-white silk shirt. He has listened.

Large tears start forming in his icy gray eyes. He starts to wring his hands as a big tear slobbers down his paunchy jowls. "Jesus, kid, we're not doing that good. Don't let all the action fool you. We'll be lucky to break even tonight."

And that's the very least I can wish for all you people heading this way. "Break even, won't you?"

Las Vegas: A polygamous, orgiastic, and world-famous money machine constantly being threatened by a slim gathering of native Las Vegans, mostly Mormon, who vow one day to outlaw the legalized gaming with all its attending vices by voting it out of existence in a referendum.

But they'll never do it.

Evil or otherwise, this gaming economy has a death-hold on everyone—even those who scream they'd like to vote it out one day. Las Vegas has become a way of life not only for those who make a living out of its carnivorous practices, but for those many millions who come here annually to do a bit of "spring cleaning" on their wallets.

There are even those, I've heard it whispered in the dead of night in dark alleys, who come here for the climate and to catch up with the many stars working the hotel showrooms. But don't go by me. I predicted that Howard Hughes would never invest in Las Vegas.

I will readily agree at this early moment, when the portable is fresh and snippy, that prostitution is the oldest profession in the world. But coming up fast on the inside rail have to be gambling, boozing, and a combination of the choice kinds of lechery that go with them.

It comes all dressed up here in a most spectacular show-case with nary a single, solitary "danger ahead" sign any-where. It's now up to not only the millions of tourists but also the steady locals what sort of "high tab" they'll have to pay for their fun. And kiddies, many a soul has paid and paid and paid.

The latest consensus (July, 1972) has more than 300,000 people living in Clark County, with 165,000 in Las Vegas, twenty-five percent of them being Mormons—who came here more than ninety years ago. It's a matter of record that some wealthy Mormons have contributed heavily in financing some of the Vegas luxury hotels—especially in the Fifties. But they rarely participate in the luxuries of drinking and gambling.

18

However, they don't fight the Las Vegas economy, which is now a billion-dollar industry. The Mormon Church considers it all as being legal. They also know that, if legalized gaming were ever shut down, Las Vegas would become a ghost town. Investing their millions in this Show Capital of the World has paid back heavily for them. And, as a Mormon leader told me once, "We can go to Mexico, but it doesn't mean we have to drink the water there."

Then he proudly emphasized the fact that Las Vegas has more than 150 churches, two synagogues, and almost two hundred Boy Scout troops. He said nothing about the hookers, hustlers, and whores (there's a difference) who ply their wares in the gaming casino hotels. They, of course, are the necessary evils in an industry which took in more than $450 million (after taxes) from almost 950 gaming tables and 20,000 slot machines.

Despite the sugary ads noting the "loosest slots and record number of jackpots," the average club keeps more than ninety percent of the coins fed those insatiable "one-armed bandits." If you've watched the average slot player, he or she can hit a dozen jackpots but, when it comes to quitting time, they usually walk away minus not only the many jackpots but also the original investment.

The cautious, statistical-minded Las Vegan will point out that Vegas consumes nineteen billion gallons of water a year. And considering that the town gets less than four inches of rain a year, depletion of the water table has caused the town to sink three feet in the past twenty years! Antigaming forces here gloatingly tell you, at that rate, Las Vegas will be swallowed up by the earth in less than a million years! And they can't wait to see it happen.

EARLY DAYS IN LAS VEGAS

Back in the late 1870's the Meadows of the Las Vegas Valley were first conquered by the Mormon pioneers, who had been sent in droves to convert and tranquilize the Indians. But it was an unsuccessful crusade, because the Indians wouldn't accept the Gospel of Jesus Christ. Those who stayed, on orders from Mormon leader Brigham Young in Salt Lake City, built the town of Las Vegas. They also determined to conquer the Indians by teaching them how to raise melons, potatoes, corn, and wheat.

What was even more important, the Mormons built a fort in the Meadows (Las Vegas) not only to protect themselves from warring Indian tribes, but also to protect the U.S. mail as pioneers traveled westward toward the Coast.

The adjoining hills were rich in silver ore, so many came to the Meadows to prospect for the metal. Soon gold and silver strikes were made within thirty miles of Las Vegas, as well as in the town itself. The news spread, and Las Vegas became the hub of many wagon trains and prospectors. As was to be expected, soon came construction of the railroad and an enormous expansion in and around Las Vegas.

And though many have taken credit for discovering Las Vegas, it really had to be our own Uncle Samuel who played a vital part in taking it from almost complete obscurity to world prominence. It all happened in the late Twenties when a couple of lawmakers from California, Swing and Johnson, passed a bill to erect Boulder Dam in Nevada.

Construction on the Dam began in 1933. Twenty-five miles away sleepy, dusty Las Vegas and its four thousand residents broiled under the wicked summer sun and swallowed sand the other windy months. The most entertaining moments in Las Vegas came when the train from Salt Lake City thundered through early in the day, then came through again late in the night back from Los Angeles.

The town itself in those early years was a frowsy procession of broken-down stores and a few visitors availing themselves of the privilege of playing faro, roulette, 21, fantan, and keno without being apprehended by the law. In short, it was legal to play those games in Nevada. If you had happened to get lost between Los Angeles and Chicago, you'd have found Las Vegas in the early Thirties a replica of a Randolph Scott, Tom Mix, or Hoot Gibson silent movie set.

The smart set, either from the West Coast or coming in from the East, usually wound up in Reno, where the hotels and the gaming casinos were elegant and the ladies of the evening "reasonable."

But back in Las Vegas things began stirring in those early Thirties. Thousands of migratory workers were coming in from all over the nation to help build the Dam. Boulder City was erected to help the workers, but many got into their old jalopies and drove the forty minutes to nearby Las Vegas to shop and gamble and visit some of the brothels.

And as the traffic between Boulder City and Las Vegas increased, so did the prosperity in Vegas. More stores began popping up where once stood cow pastures. Some of the construction workers even moved to Las Vegas and went into other lines of work after leaving the Dam project.

No longer did the residents have to stand in the depot waiting for the afternoon special from Salt Lake City to roar through. Now there were other modes of entertainment. Some of the gambling halls were hiring "fancy lady singers from Chicago and New Orleans to entertain the gaming folks."

A downtown section of Las Vegas was named after General John Fremont, the sturdy gent who wandered through a section of land then known by the Spanish missionaries as The Meadows in the Eighties. So Fremont Street became the hub of all the commerce, politics, and general excitement.

Clara Bow and her boy friend, Rex Bell, driving east from Hollywood toward Salt Lake City, where one of her pictures was opening, stayed in Las Vegas a couple of nights. Bell became so enamored with the town he wound up buying a 350,000-acre ranch there. Not many years later, Rex married

Clara and both settled on the ranch. Bell prospered mightily, while Clara began ailing. Bell became lieutenant governor of Nevada in the early Fifties, then died suddenly while campaigning for the governorship several years later.

And in the years Rex and Clara spent as Nevada residents they had many of their Hollywood pals—John Gilbert, Clark Gable, Kay Francis, Charles Coburn, Errol Flynn, Norma Shearer, and the Barrymores, John and Lionel—stay with them on their ranch.

The Dam became an enormous attraction as many hundreds of thousands visited this incredible structure from every part of the nation and the world. Las Vegas was now ready for the big time. Small hotels were popping up downtown every week as the cow paths slowly gave way to concrete and "two-story high rises."

Who ever heard of the Strip in those days? When you left downtown in the direction of Los Angeles, it was all wooded area with a narrow two-lane, unlit highway. Then, in the spring of 1941 a couple of sharp gents—one the veteran Las Vegan, Jim Cashman, the other a Palm Springs and L.A. hotel man, Tommy Hull—decided to build a fancy hotel in that wooded area.

"We'll call it El Rancho Vegas," said Hull, "and within a matter of fifteen years you'll see a whole row of hotels on this Strip." Cashman grunted impolitely, but agreed with a roar, "On that you can bet your bippy."

Twenty-eight years later in Hollywood a couple of Las Vegas lounge entertainers struck it rich with a TV series titled *Laugh-In*, which featured bippies among other things.

But Hull and Cashman started the Strip with the El Rancho Vegas, which was later to be made internationally famous by a gent with crooked legs, an incredible thirst, and a terrific café act, Joe Everglades Lewis. The Hollywood stars came a bit more frequently to El Rancho Vegas even though

Joe E. Lewis wouldn't start there until later in the Forties.

About a year later the Last Frontier Hotel, now known as the Frontier Hotel, was built a mile further on the Strip. And these two hotels were the forerunners of a billion-dollar gaming and tourist economy that would eventually become a mecca for the nation.

BUGSY SIEGEL

Shortly after the Last Frontier opened its doors early in 1942, a violent little mobster, Benjamin "Bugsy" Siegel, came on the scene with his flashy clothes, toothy smile, and the murderous drive which had made him chief executioner of Murder, Inc., back in New York City. Associated with him were such infamous characters as Jack Dragna, Mickey Cohen, Al Capone, Lucky Luciano, and Meyer Lansky.

Despite Siegel's highly publicized career in murder, narcotics, and other fancy endeavors, he had many friends among the Hollywood movie stars on the West Coast, who wined and dined "The Bug" regally whenever he paid a visit out there.

It was on one of those trips to the West Coast that Bugsy one day in March of 1942 stopped off to take more than a curious look at the "small gambling" activities going on in Las Vegas. Sure, by now there was a fancier, more popular gaming industry flourishing in Reno, "The Biggest Little City in the World." But it wasn't as accessible to the Hollywood stars as Las Vegas, which was less than three hundred miles away.

So, there was Bugsy Siegel wandering about the few streets in downtown Las Vegas, getting his expensive alligator shoes and fancy duds muddied up. He walked in and out of many of the store clubs, which not only featured blackjack, craps, and faro, but also took bets on all race tracks in the nation.

23

The results and payoffs of the races came over a special wire service which was controlled by Al Capone, a business associate of Bugsy's.

Siegel walked into the most flourishing club, met the owners, and told them he was cutting himself in for a tidy interest in the club starting right now. He also explained, in case there was any doubt in their minds, about his ownership in the race wire, which the clubs could not do without.

Bugsy Siegel became a partner as of that moment.

By 1944 the gaming industry awakened to the enormous possibilities of the quiet, unpublicized "Strip" several miles south of the downtown hustle and bustle. And while dispossessed lizards, gophers, and prairie dogs looked anxiously on, Benjamin "Bugsy" Siegel started making his major move away from the toughies and touts downtown to the elegant Strip, where only two hotels prospered (slightly)—the Last Frontier and El Rancho Vegas.

"The Bug" had definitely decided downtown wasn't for him and his associates back East and down in Miami. He rushed to Los Angeles and the comfort of his suite at the Beverly Wilshire Hotel in plush Beverly Hills. Making himself comfortable, Siegel grabbed the phone and called Meyer Lansky in Miami Beach.

"Meyer, you ain't seen nothing like it," Siegel bellowed into the phone. "I'm talking about Las Vegas. No, not the race books downtown, but the fancier places that could be on the Strip about four miles away. This could be the biggest thing we got. It's a license to steal. It's all legal, legal." His voice began cracking under the strain. "Let's have a meeting right away, Meyer. I'll meet you and the rest of the boys in New York tomorrow."

Unfortunately, at the meeting Siegel's enthusiasm wasn't shared by the other members of the "corporation." As a matter of fact, several of them graphically told "The Bug" to go back to Las Vegas, get caught in one of those Las Vegas sandstorms, and disappear for all time. But in their blacker than black hearts they ruefully had to admit that Siegel had a bonanza in the desert—provided it was handled properly.

Lansky hesitated. After all, the mob already had strong control in a couple of joints downtown as well as all the gaming and extra assorted vices on the West Coast from the movie studios to the waterfront. But "Bugsy" had a vision. He had spoken with Del Webb, who was ready to construct anything Siegel decided he wanted on the Strip.

A few days later, when Siegel was back in Las Vegas, Lansky gave him the green light to go ahead and find a suitable lot on the Strip for a gaming casino hotel. But Meyer went into his fancy bed that night in Miami hoping that a sandstorm in far-off Las Vegas would blow his temperamental partner into the wilds of Utah for keeps.

Back in Las Vegas the exuberant Siegel bounced off the walls with happiness at Lansky's go-ahead signal. And if you had happened to be driving along the road leading straight through the middle of Las Vegas the next afternoon, you would have seen the hatless leader, clad in a fancy "Pietro" suit from the finest tailor in Beverly Hills and wearing dark glasses, plowing through the sands of a huge empty lot while three of his loyal "followers" brought up the rear.

They were strictly city fellows, not the kind of enterprising gents with pioneering blood who'd dare to be found even dead in a vacant lot in Las Vegas with sand all over their clothes, and in their eyes, ears, and mouth.

Heshie, "the Masher," kept muttering under his breath as he followed the boss, "He's gotta be flipping his lid. Suddenly he's become a real estater." The other bodyguard had a more cheerful attitude. "Leave him alone. He likes to play wid sand." That was Moishe, the "Mauler." He had been with Siegel for years, and the boss could do no wrong.

That left the dubious one, "Brass Knuckles" Bernie, who had been transferred much against his will from Miami to

Las Vegas. Strictly a Pisces who enjoyed water, not desert, "Brass Knuckles" had brooded ever since he got the job with Siegel. He was most disconsolate.

"Listen, take my advice. Let's shoot the boss and leave his body in the sand here. Who's gonna find it? Then we can all go back to Miami." But his suggestion was never executed because at that moment "Bugsy," about thirty feet ahead of the others, let out a shrill cry. He had his hands high in the air and was waving them hysterically. The scene was no doubt much like that when Cortez wallowed about in the Florida swamps and discovered Miami Beach.

Siegel was screaming, "Over here. Over here." His $300 gabardine coat was waving in the wind. His sparse hair was standing straight up on his skull. Bugsy Siegel was a truly Messiahlike figure on that sandy, windy lot.

Now Siegel was solemn. He pointed in a majestic arc all around him, and said, "Boys, this is where I'm gonna build the goddamn biggest, fanciest gaming casino and hotel you bastards ever seen in your whole lives."

"Brass Knuckles" was aghast. "You're shitting us, boss. Say it's a joke." Siegel shook his head vigorously. Then he began loping through the heavy sand and dirt, kicking it in all directions as he ran like a bereft gazelle in heat.

Believe it or not, Siegel wasn't running around aimlessly. What he was doing was breaking ground in his own unortho-dox fashion. He just couldn't wait for the proper ceremonies a month away.

There were many things Siegel had to do to build a luxury hotel, which would feature gambling and top-name stars in the showroom. But first he had to pick a name for his "brain child." So, while his enforcers stood off in the corner of his suite at the Last Frontier Hotel, Siegel went into deep thought. His handsomely scarred countenance took on a pained look. Now he began scribbling on the pad before him, then scratching it out. Finally after ten minutes of this, Siegel looked up triumphantly. "I think I got a name for my hotel. Whadd'ya call those crazy long-legged birds we see when we go to the races at Hialeah Park?"

Moishe, "the Mauler," had a bright look on his face. He was the educated member in the room. He had gone through the eighth grade in grammar school before he launched his career picking pockets in crowded Brooklyn movie houses.

"I know what them are, boss. Them's flamencos."

Siegel eagerly accepted the hard-to-come-by information. "Great. That's what we'll call the hotel, the Flamenco."

But "Brass Knuckles" Bernie differed, even though he couldn't match the extensive schooling background of Moishe, "the Mauler."

"Moishe is a schmuck. He don't know what he's talking about," said Bernie. "I never went to no schools, Benny, but I know about those boids. They're flamingos, not flamencos." Then giving Siegel and Moishe looks of contempt, he said, "A flamenco's a Greek food."

Siegel had passed his first and easiest hurdle, the naming of the hotel. The name was going to go up in blazing letters thirty feet high, "The Flamingo Hotel."

Whether or not he knew it, Siegel was uttering a profound statement when he told his trio of "advisers" that afternoon in his hotel suite, "And it'll be the first of many hotels to come here in the next fifteen years."

Benny Siegel, the boy from the ghetto of Brownsville in Brooklyn, whose mother wanted him to be an accountant, "maybe even a lawyer," would be a martyr in the town he turned into an instant gold mine. He wouldn't be around to see its enormous growth as "The Show Capital of the World."

While Bugsy was building the hotel, he suddenly ran out of money, and was told so by one of the contractors. The following morning Bugsy took off for New York and a meeting with some of his associates. Meanwhile he told the crew to keep on the job. "I'll be back in a couple of days with enough dough to keep you guys going."

A man of his word, Siegel returned to Las Vegas lugging two heavy satchels that dragged almost down to the floor. Calling in the contractor, he dumped the contents on the rug while the builder's eyes bulged. Lying on the carpet of Bugsy's makeshift Flamingo Hotel office was a pile of green currency that looked like crumpled spinach. There was $400,000 on that floor—just enough money to finish the building of the Flamingo.

It was, of course, the forerunner of a billion-dollar industry with many swanky hotels to follow. But, as with almost every pioneer, few appreciated Siegel's vision. His associates in Miami and New York weren't thrilled about Bugsy's Flamingo Hotel in Las Vegas. What had started out as a million-dollar project in the desert was now way over three million.

These were post-World War II years, and the cost of building was sky high. But that didn't matter to Siegel. He was paying triple time to the crew for working on Sundays and after hours. He paid five times the usual amount for everything that went into the hotel. Naturally, the cost kept zooming upward.

And, of course, the boys back in Miami Beach, lolling at the race tracks or in their cabanas, swore to dismember Bugsy Siegel joint by joint if he didn't cease and desist spending their hard-earned money. Even his guardian angel, Meyer Lansky, threatened to bury him in a choice plot adjoining the Flamingo Hotel swimming pool. Siegel would be interred face down just in case he tried digging his way out.

Other Siegel partners vowed that he must be lining his own pockets. No one, they declared, could go through money so fast without leaving any traces. Bugsy, of course, had answers to such skepticism. "Sticks and stones may break my

bones, you crummy bastards, but woids will never hoit me."
That's how much he knew!

The Flamingo Hotel finally opened on December 26, 1946, with the gaudy opulence of a top hoodlum's funeral. Spotlights lit up the sky, while traffic from all sides of the highway converged, creating a hopeless snarl.

Inside the hotel, it looked like a Hollywood movie premiere without the movie. Tons of fresh flowers had practically inundated the gaming casino. VIP's from the movie industry and the underworld rubbed elbows. Striding all over the place like a proud papa was Bugsy himself. He wore a pink carnation in his fancy black tuxedo and glad handed anybody and everybody.

It was his day to howl even though he had already heard ominous rumblings from Cabana seventeen in Miami Beach that he had to go. And that gent in Miami Beach wasn't referring to a vacation trip to Hawaii for Siegel.

Jimmy Durante, who had been hired to star in the showroom, watched it all with great bewilderment and some amusement. So, when Siegel grabbed him and began asking what he thought of the flowers, Jimmy cracked, "Benny, da place looks like a cemetery wid dice tables and slot machines."

Though the word was already out that Siegel's days were rapidly coming to a close, he still had a chance to escape with his life if the casino began paying off. Unfortunately, it did just the opposite, a rare procedure for a gaming casino in Las Vegas. The losses at the Flamingo mounted. And Bugsy didn't help it along any by bringing plane loads of movie stars and columnists from Los Angeles, who consumed tons of food and expensive whiskey on the house.

On the morning of June 20, 1947, Siegel, plagued by his associates and steadily rising losses, flew to Los Angeles to spend a couple of days with his mistress, Virginia Hill, in her

29

plush home at 820 Linden Drive in Beverly Hills. He knew he'd get an encouraging word or two from Virginia because she had always encouraged him to build the Flamingo.

Before Siegel arrived at the house, Virginia had been notified by "proper sources" to get the hell away from that vicinity because a premature July 4th fireworks celebration was going to take place soon. Hence, Siegel spent most of the day and evening alone except for his man, Al Smiley, who stayed in the house to keep him company until Virginia returned from her "shopping trip."

He never saw Virginia again. Later that night, as Siegel sat sprawled on a chaise longue watching television, he sipped beer from a can, with his shoes off and his pants opened at the waist for more comfort.

And while he lolled and half dozed, several shadowy figures scurried outside the house near the hedges trying to get a bead on Siegel through the living room window. And when they got him in their gun sights, they let him have it with a barrage that startled half of Beverly Hills.

Nine of the bullets slammed into him hard enough to hurl him halfway across the living room—some in his head, others in his chest and belly. The next day the newspapers around the country ran a page one picture of the notorious Bugsy Siegel, soaked in his own blood and lying half off, half on, a chaise longue. The desert entrepreneur had paid a high price for his unwise business decisions.

It stood to reason that the next day his associates in Miami Beach and New York—also in Arkansas and Las Vegas—would mourn his loss. Some of them who had threatened him constantly for weeks had great big tears in their eyes as they wailed about Siegel's having been their dearest friend and partner. A couple of gaming gents in Las Vegas stopped casino action for a full five minutes the day of the funeral.

That last move would have really touched the sentimental

Bugsy. However, his abrupt departure proved to be nothing more than a minor interlude in the Las Vegas saga.

Siegel's death had many repercussions throughout the underworld, as several syndicates started playing footsie with the reigning Lansky faction trying to undo the numerous financial wrongs existing at the Flamingo.

One repercussion was that a nice elderly Jewish lady in Brooklyn heard about the Siegel killing in Beverly Hills and immediately put in a phone call to her son in Las Vegas. Though it was a matter of life and death, my mother explained, she wasn't going to talk more than the prescribed three minutes.

I was to get the hell out of Las Vegas as fast as I could. Even though Siegel had contracted his fatal lead poisoning almost three hundred miles away on the West Coast, she could tell it wasn't a healthy climate.

However, it didn't take Siegel's assassination or my mother's advice to sour me on Las Vegas in those early summer months of 1947. I had already made up my mind that Las Vegas was strictly for dice and blackjack prospectors who didn't give a damn about sweltering to death during an average 114-degree summer day. Not only that, a newspaperman in Las Vegas in those days was about as necessary as a kosher restaurant in the Vatican.

"What kind of a place is that Las Vegas anyway?" screamed my Jewish mother from faraway Brooklyn. "All kinds of bums live and work there," she pleaded. "There are bad girls there and all kinds of drunken people who gamble."

The day I left Las Vegas, determined never to return to an environment of bad girls and gambling all around me, I couldn't forget some of the last words of wisdom I'd heard from Bugsy Siegel during the months the Flamingo was nearing completion.

Rubbing a nail file over his carefully manicured cuticles,

he looked out of his window at the Flamingo one day, and said wistfully, "Kid, this is gonna be the world's greatest resort town. Wait and see." (I didn't put too much stock in that far-fetched prophecy after he died, because he had also told me that he had consulted a mind reader who assured him he would live to the ripe old age of eighty-two.)

Continuing to look out the window, Bugsy pointed to a stretch of wasteland just across the street from the hotel. "Buy yourself half an acre of that property and some day you'll be living off the fat of the land," he said.

Following his gaze, I screamed, "What half acre? All I see is lots of sand blowing." At that moment a raging sandstorm had all but hidden everything on that side of the highway. Fifteen years later a fellow by the name of Kirk Kerkorian would buy seventy acres of that sand-swept land across the street for $900,000, and in 1969 realize $7 million from Caesars Palace, the hotel which now stands on that spot.

If I had taken Bugsy's advice in 1947, it would have meant stealing $50,000 somewhere to buy that land. In those days—and it's not much different today—I would have had problems raising $500, let alone $50,000.

Years later I wondered why I never asked Siegel to come up with a down payment that would have gotten me part of that property. The man who always said, "The bullet with my name on it hasn't been made," might have made me a tycoon.

As I walked out of Caesars Palace on the land Bugsy Siegel had told me to buy, it all came back in a rush. The hoodlum who had been spawned in the ghettos of Manhattan and Brooklyn had seemed to guess wrong too many times and had paid with his life. But Bugsy Siegel would always be a living legend in Las Vegas, because his predictions and vows about its becoming a world-famous resort had come true.

After Bugsy's death and my mother's phone call, I stayed away from Las Vegas for almost five years doing free-lance magazine writing with a thousand others in Hollywood. Though I was starving amidst the orange blossoms and movie studios, a fat little Jewish lady couldn't have been happier far away in her Brooklyn home. However, her happiness was short-lived.

I returned to Las Vegas early in 1953.

WEDDING CHAPELS AND HOT DOGS

Flying toward Las Vegas from the west, you look down at night and see what resembles a series of illuminated bugs on a black surface. Almost seventy-five percent of the business Las Vegas enjoys comes from Los Angeles and environs, some three hundred miles away.

Naturally, Las Vegas hasn't endeared itself to the hapless millions (twenty million yearly) who try to break the bank. But that's as likely as Raquel Welch's becoming a nun, or some of the spectacular nude girlie shows being endorsed by the Daughters of the American Revolution.

Come what may, it seems likely that millions will continue to storm these gaming strongholds annually, ever hopeful, ever masturbating in their absolute futility. And from time to time, a loser will slink away muttering, "That's it. I'm cured. I'll never come here again." Don't you believe it! No matter how mortally wounded he may be in his wallet, there's always tomorrow and a possibility for a new bankroll.

The mere fact that you point out the many multimillion-dollar palaces all around him, then explain that they are built from the steady losses of gamblers like him, means nothing. That applies to the *other* loser.

Over in the far end of the casino is a fat, sweating little man who has been toiling over the dice table for several hours. He has been trying to mount a winning streak all in vain. Now he's out about $4,900. A couple of hours later he's in the red about $12,000. So far it has been a hopeless struggle with the unconscionable ivories. But suddenly our fat little man starts to win and win and win.

His beady eyes light up. This is it! The dice are doing everything but jump into his pocket. He can do no wrong. Three hours later he has gotten back almost all his $12,000. Suddenly he stops shooting, gathers up all his chips, and staggers to a nearby cashier's window to cash them in.

"How'd you do, Charley?" asks a pal with the typically sallow expression of a loser. "Fine, fine," says our sweating little hero bouncing happily toward the exits. "I broke even!"

Ask the average native in Las Vegas about his town, and he'll glow happily about its being a greater resort than Acapulco, Palm Springs, Puerto Vallarta, and Lake Tahoe all rolled into one. I'm not that naïve. Furthermore, I figure such a brash utterance could get me sued for libel by the Chambers of Commerce from the cities just mentioned.

Having lived here as man and boy, in that order, for almost twenty years, I find it almost imperative to get away from here at least once a month to preserve whatever sanity I've got. The tourists aren't kidding when they say, "Gee, I love to spend weekends here, but I wouldn't like to live here."

To date I've covered approximately ten thousand opening-night shows in the big showrooms and another five thousand acts in the adjoining lounges in this Siberia of booze, broads, blackjack, and lavish entertainment. And except for an advanced case of hypertension, ulcers, and rapidly declining manhood from constant confrontation with the fleshy, sick-eyed chorines, I'm in pretty good shape.

Outside on this world-famous "Strip" are million-dollar neon signs fronting the hotels to the point of vulgarity. That seems to be the name of the game in Las Vegas: Drape everything in neon even if it's a lousy little shoe store or wedding chapel.

And since weddings are made easy to perform, there are more than fifty of these shops for quickie, reasonable-priced hitchings. One of them is down the street from the Sahara Hotel and is called "Cupid's Wedding Chapel." Naturally, a huge neon sign in front depicts a chubby little cupid, arrow and all, blinking on and off to the point of utter distraction— if you happen to have a store or an apartment near there.

A large sign in front reads, "Free wedding information inside." So you go inside and find a space the size of three phone booths—just enough room for the couple, a marrying Justice of the Peace, and a witness or two. Hidden snugly in an overhead crevice is a speaker that blares out a tinny off-key wedding march during the ceremony.

Wedding chapels take up almost four pages in the Las Vegas phone book's yellow pages. A typical ad reads, "We arrange everything for a beautifully blissful wedding . . . including flowers, rings, and recordings. Free transportation and credit cards accepted gladly."

Across the street from "Cupid's Wedding Chapel" is a thriving hot dog stand doing a landslide daily business. Some of its patrons are newly marrieds who had gourmet feasts on their agenda, but had played the tables and wound up "gourmeting" at the hot dog stand.

The owner of the hot dog stand? He once had a substantial interest in a Strip hotel, a fancy home in Malibu, and an assortment of mistresses that would have dazzled even Frank Sinatra in the days when Francis had to rely on Wheaties to keep up his strength because of the round-the-clock starlets breaking down the doors in his Sunset Boulevard and Palm Springs pads.

Then the hot dog entrepreneur decided to do a bit of "casual betting" on the dice tables. Within two years he had "casually" gambled away his Strip hotel interest, an apartment house, and just about everything else he had. A few years later he got a chance to buy into this hot dog stand with a strong financial assist from one of his Strip cronies.

Money now began flowing into the coffers, and the ex-Strip hotel big shot was able to look the world, Las Vegas, and his creditors in the eye again. No, you haven't guessed how this story ends. He doesn't sell the stand and gamble away the proceeds, which would be a logical conclusion here in Las Vegas.

However, you wouldn't be too far off if that's what you guessed. Standard Oil bought his location, tore down the hot dog stand, and put up a fancy service station. Having learned many valuable lessons from his costly splurge of yesteryear, the gent invested his money in a new hotel that had just gone up—the Royal Nevada—on the Strip.

The Royal Nevada Hotel went into bankruptcy a little more than a year after it opened. And my unfortunate friend never recovered from that fiasco. He died from a heart attack.

A compulsive gambler is a sick, dangerous guy who'll even put his kids on the line when he runs out of money. Comics aware of that streak in many gamblers crack, "I lost my kids on the pass line, but that's okay because I went home and started making a batch of chips."

The gaming fever also exists among the upper-strata kind of guy who is in big industry. Once he gets that infectious "crap dust" in his lungs, you can bet your tushie he'll go all the way—even if it means speculating with the firm's dough.

But what is even more aggravating and ulcer-forming is the compulsive gambler who never knows when to call a halt. He can be $10,000 ahead or way behind, but he continues unabated in his furious assault on the green felt tables.

If he's ahead $10,000, he will tell you he'll quit as soon as he gets $15,000 ahead. Naturally, the gods of chance frown on his arrogance, and he ultimately walks away minus the ten grand and plus a hollow feeling in the pit of his stomach, not to mention the hollow feeling in his wallet where once resided $10,000.

That type of loser is not uncommon, because he never stops dreaming of the day he'll get all his money back from the Las Vegas tables, plus a hefty bankroll. This is the "greed psychology" of gamers in Las Vegas. The owners build more and more multimillion-dollar hotels on such illogic.

BOBBY PASCAL

More than $450 million finds its way into the little black boxes under the gaming tables annually. Yet, it's amazing how many of those millions are carelessly wagered—and lost—because the tourists and locals are utterly ignorant of the basic principles of the game they're trying to beat. Mind you, even a careful knowledge of the games won't guarantee winners. But at least you're giving the house a run for your money. Then, of course, there's the matter of hysteria by the big-rolling tourist. He wants to walk away at least a thousand percent ahead of his original investment.

Yet, these same wealthy people, who operate prominently in the business world, would gladly take a 10-percent profit in their businesses every week in the year for the rest of their lives and be content. It's only when they get behind a gaming table that reason leaves them. Here they want to make at least $10,000 for an initial capital of maybe $500. I've seen scores of those guys and gals get as far as $50,000 ahead, yet drop it all back because they had set unattainable goals before quitting.

So, that takes me to a pal of mine who used to work as a correspondent here in Las Vegas for a Hollywood trade newspaper. His name was Bobby Pascal, and I refer to the gent in the past tense because he completely dropped out of sight back in 1955 after trying to break some of the gaming casinos on the Strip in a five-day (and night) period.

Bobby was a scraggly gent in his late forties who always looked like he could use a solid, seven-course meal topped off with a big Havana cigar and some fancy liqueur. Unfortunately Bobby never got past the stage of eating sparingly and inexpensively—except when he was covering a show in a Las Vegas hotel. Then he wined and dined like the gent he always wanted to be. Working in a gaming town for Bobby was like the late Joe E. Lewis taking a job in a Haig and Haig distillery in Kentucky as a whiskey taster.

Bobby was an inveterate, fundless crapshooter. As long as he had to survive on a lousy newspaper salary, he couldn't get hurt too badly. After all, he could always walk into a Strip hotel and load up on the fanciest food as the guest of the inn's press agent. But it became dangerous when Bobby came face to face with a fairly large bankroll. And that's exactly what happened in late 1955.

The Riviera Hotel had opened its doors earlier that year. An English gent associated with the hotel at that time was most appreciative when Bobby introduced him to a showgirl from another hotel. The Londoner immediately gifted Bobby with three crisp, brand-new, hundred-dollar bills. And from that moment began the saga of one Bobby Pascal.

For four years here in Las Vegas Bobby Pascal nurtured great, luxurious dreams of one day hitting the casinos for a tidy bankroll. Then he would leave Las Vegas immediately, if not sooner, and buy a villa—or is it a chalet?—in Switzerland. And when he got tired of the villa, or the chalet, he could always fly over to Paris or Rome, maybe even for a quick weekend in Las Vegas to tease the other working fourth-estate slobs with his affluence and easy living.

Actually, it wasn't too far-fetched a dream. Bobby was the kind of a gambler who could go all the way. He had that ice-water-in-the-veins kind of gaming fever once he got into the casino. The dice or the croupiers could never intimidate him. And if he ever mounted a fairly good winning streak, the boys in Las Vegas would really watch some tidy fireworks. After all, as a correspondent in Vegas, hadn't he watched hungrily and agonizingly as some jerk with a bankroll picked himself up a much larger wad because the dice rolled his way?

So, why couldn't he, Bobby Pascal, get that kind of a break—if he could ever get his hands on "real playing money"?

And now the time had come for Bobby Pascal, a guy who never had more than a hundred dollars in his hands at one time, to make his move.

Invading the Riviera casino with the $300 clutched tightly in his grubby fists, he started a winning streak that's still the talk of the town among us old-timers who watched for many hours while Bobby was winning.

That first outing was a success. Bobby won more than $4,500 with his $300 bankroll. He stopped to change his underwear in his downtown $15-a-week motel, then rushed back to the Strip, but this time to a room in the Sands Hotel. No longer timid and always trying to hide the frayed cuffs of his $25 sports jacket, Pascal the Potent jammed up to one of the dice tables at the Sands, stared coolly at one of the players, Frank Sinatra, then threw two $500 bills on the table. "Gimme ten black chips," he told the dealer, while several elderly ladies gasped and a few younger ones giggled.

In a matter of four hours, Bobby had supplemented his bankroll of $4,500 with an additional $15,000. He left his small fortune in the cashier's cage at that casino, got a receipt for his money, then went back to his room and threw up on the carpet. His fantasy of a Swiss chalet was becoming more and more of a reality. So he slept for three hours, got up and put on his other jacket and trousers, and headed back to the Sands Hotel dice tables.

Many old-time professional gamblers still say it was an incredible spree. Bobby just couldn't lose. No matter where he gambled, the dice and the cards seemed to curl up and cry for help, while the casino bosses also began curling up and crying for help. But some of the wiser gaming tycoons didn't carry on too badly. All they worried about was that Bobby might quit with a large bankroll and not give the casinos a chance to get it all back.

Now, five days later, the transformation of Bobby Pascal had been positively revolutionary. His bankroll at the moment was $70,000. Once a shy, poverty-stricken guy looking for a quick buck, he was now being wined and dined and adored by everybody at the Riviera Hotel—where he now lived. They had given him a penthouse suite. The generosity of the Riviera Hotel management had a method to its madness: They intended to keep Bobby and his bankroll, won mostly on the Riviera tables, as close to them as possible, so they could get another crack at it.

Even though several of Bobby's old buddies begged him to quit while he was ahead and put at least part of his $70,000 into a real estate venture, he was too obstinate—also too drunk—to listen. The management had sent up dozens of bottles of Scotch whiskey and brandies, and Bobby had done a remarkable job of emptying them into his thoroughly oiled interior. Lady Luck, who had spat on him wickedly for almost forty years, was now beaming on him for a change. And he loved every winning moment of it.

That chalet in Switzerland was getting closer by the minute. The harder his buddies pleaded, the more Bobby insisted that he had set a $100,000 goal for himself. "And I don't have too much farther to go for those big hundred C's," gloated Bobby, who was feeling absolutely no pain. He hadn't been sober in more than a week. Even his hair hurt.

One buddy was explaining to Bobby, "The Fremont Hotel is in construction downtown. Let me invest $50,000 of your winnings in this hotel, and you'll be pissing on the world for the rest of your life." Bobby grinned crookedly. Now even his teeth felt soft. Plutocracy was just around the corner. All he needed was one more good night's winnings on the tables, and Switzerland would be next.

And who could tell him that he was wrong? His suite was littered with Uncle Sam's greenback currency. Practically all the maids in the hotel fought to get up to the top floor to clean Bobby's suite, because they knew it meant at least a $50 tip. The night before, in the casino, a cocktail waitress had faithfully supplied Bobby with drinks every ten minutes and, when her eight-hour shift was over, she was $3,000 richer from the thoroughly drunk and overly generous Bobby. So, can you blame the girl for wanting to work overtime? By the end of the evening, she was being forcibly shoved out of the casino so another girl could start her own shift.

Sunday morning, after a hectic session of dice shooting that had started early the day before, Bobby lay stretched out on his satin-quilted king-sized bed. He now had $87,000! He took a cold shower and some stay-awake pills. A local Cadillac dealer was coming this morning with a $7,500 runabout, and Bobby wanted to be awake to accept it and pay the gent with seventy-five crisp hundred-dollar bills. A real estate agent from Beverly Hills was flying in to pick up a $25,000 down payment from Bobby for that chalet in Switzerland.

The phone rang twice within twenty minutes. The first call was from the local Caddy dealer, "Bobby, I'm just getting over the flu and, since it's also Sunday, let me deliver the car personally bright and early tomorrow morning. Okay?" Call number two: A frantic real estate agent was calling from Los Angeles, "Mr. Pascal, the airport here in Los Angeles is completely fogged in. All planes are grounded and nobody knows when it'll lift. However, I'm driving out and will be in Las Vegas in six hours—with the deed!"

So Robert Pascal, Esq., a man who rose from poverty to affluence in four days and some hectic nights, went to sleep.

"Wake me at four," said Bobby to the operator in the hotel. "And, baby, I'm sending down a little something for you. Go out and buy yourself a dress." Then he peeled off a hundred-dollar bill, slipped it into a hotel envelope, addressed it to the phone operator, and sent it down with a bellhop, who got himself a sawbuck for his efforts. Then Bobby slept.

Precisely at four, a charged-up, devoted phone operator awoke Bobby. He dressed, loaded all of his suit pockets with hundred-dollar bills, then proceeded down to the gaming casino for another session at the tables—this time the blackjack tables. This could be the day he reached the $100,000 mark. After that it would be a romp in luxury and broads.

He had it all figured out. The chalet in Switzerland actually cost $55,000. So, after the down payment of twenty-five "big ones," Bobby would have ten years to pay it out.

As he toyed with the cards at the blackjack table, he suddenly realized that the $7,500 Caddy wouldn't fit in with his plans to leave the country. "Oh well, I'll buy it and give it to Perry _____, the Riviera gent who started me off on this road to luxury five days ago with that $300." He also decided that the first thing Monday morning he'd call a boat company in Los Angeles. He had always dreamed of owning a boat.

After a remarkable five-day splurge of phenomenal luck at the tables, Bobby had to giggle. He had just lost $3,000 at blackjack. So what? He wandered over to the dice tables. Within the next twenty minutes, Bobby dropped another $8,000. Now he was slightly irked. He would have to buckle down and win at least $25,000 if he expected to reach that $100,000 goal.

Bobby played far into the night. The action was blood-curdling, the damage irreparable—to Bobby.

Then it was Monday morning. The hustle and bustle of weekending tourists was over, and a peaceful lull had descended on the Strip hotels as the money-hungry bosses in the casino cages counted up the heavy profits. As for Bobby Pascal, he was getting ready to vacate his swanky penthouse suite on orders from the hotel management, who wanted him "the hell out of there in ten minutes because a good customer from Chicago is checking in." Meanwhile several maids were removing traces of Bobby Pascal's orgiastic spree—expensive Havana cigar stubs and empty champagne bottles.

Now Bobby, his green complexion clashing with the pink draperies over the huge windows, gingerly fingered five ten-dollar bills. That's all that remained of the huge $87,000 Pascal bankroll of only eighteen hours earlier. Also missing was the notorious Lady Luck, who'd been shacking up with Bobby all during his splurge on the casino banks.

There wasn't too much for Bobby to pack. Just a couple of sport shirts, his toothbrush, and a thoroughly neglected tube of toothpaste he never seemed to get around to using. And as he headed for the door, he longingly sneaked a look back over his shoulder. On the rumpled bed and its satin spread lay a travel folder, "Switzerland—the Alps." Even the fog in Los Angeles had plotted against Bobby Pascal. If only the real estate guy had gotten into town last night as he had promised. . . .

"That guy" never got out of Barstow, California. His car suffered motor trouble just on the outskirts of that desert town, and the garage people told him to forget about Las Vegas and his appointment until the following day.

So, what about the local Caddy dealer? He arrived bright and early (but not early enough) behind the wheel of Bobby Pascal's Caddy, parked it out front, then went in to hear the bad news. He had arrived eighteen hours too late.

However, he got a better break than the realtor. A gent from Syracuse, New York, was just cashing in winnings of more than $16,000 when he ran into the Caddy dealer on the way out of the hotel. A hurried conference, a bit of haggling, and the winner handed over $7,200 to the local dealer, then stepped into his brand-new Caddy. But he's a rarity in the Las Vegas gaming halls. Few things are bought from winnings because the average gamer is fashioned after Bobby Pascal, a dreamer walking barefoot on a street littered with broken glass.

Bobby has been long gone from Las Vegas. But there's nothing unusual about that. Eventually they all leave town—one way or another. Sometimes they return, much the worse for wear, but just as confident as ever about starting a new streak. As for Bobby, one day the scraggly gent, much older and certainly not the wiser if he returns to test his luck again, will show up—probably dragging an anemic bankroll behind him.

He'll try again and again to put a gaming casino out of business. He'll even settle for a big win, like maybe $25,000. But that's like the trout trying to outsmart the angler. Sure, some get away. But the majority stay and help the owners build bigger and fancier hotels here in Las Vegas.

And if Bobby ever returns, I hope I'm still here to greet him.

JIMMY HOFFA, "LAS VEGAS BANKER"

Among the early supporters of legalized gaming was a gent by the name of James R. Hoffa, who had just replaced Dave Beck as the International Teamsters Union president after Beck had gone to jail. He was sent up because, as Joe E. Lewis used to put it so aptly in his café heyday, "He got caught with his duke in the tambourine." And a bright fellow by the name of Robert F. Kennedy was the lad who caught him in that awkward stance. The late Bobby Kennedy was then a chief counsel ferreting out improper activities for a U.S. Senate committee.

Jimmy Hoffa, now the big boy with the only key to the Central Pension Fund strongbox, began handing out massive loans to several of the Strip hotel owners. It wasn't that the few greedy hotel owners needed the money; they were already making it hand over fist while stuffing goodly sums away in numbered accounts in far-off Swiss banks. This was their way of conveying to the boys at the Internal Revenue Service that things weren't too good at their hotel—that there was need for financial assistance from Hoffa.

Another reason for the huge loans, which were taken at the six-percent interest rate, was for "expansion," a thoroughly vague term. The hotel boss, after getting the loan, would start expanding his news counter, snack bar, and umbrella stand in the far counter of the lobby.

I'm not about to delve into the books of all the hotels and other businesses in Las Vegas that got large loans from the pension fund. Suffice to say, Hoffa and his abundant coffers spread the green currency liberally over the Las Vegas landscaping to the tune of maybe $100 million up to and including 1972.

I met Jimmy Hoffa several times during his many visits to "his money" here in Las Vegas. We never exchanged more than our views on the state of the weather and the condition of our health. However, one night in 1965 I ran into Jimmy as I was leaving the Stardust Hotel. The owner of the hotel, Moe Dalitz, had once gotten a huge loan from Hoffa and his pension fund for $6 million.

Instead of once again nodding and discussing the nippy, below-45-degree weather, I decided to get real gabby. "Jimmy, how about getting a loan from your pension fund?" He stopped and started grinning because I, too, was grinning.

"You see, I'm building on to my mobile home and need a few extra dollars, like maybe a hundred, to get the job done." I quoted Jimmy an absurdly low figure so he wouldn't think I was serious. Hoffa went along with the rib.

Still grinning broadly, Jimmy said, "I'm sure I can put

through the loan, Ralph. What kind of collateral can you offer?"

About eighteen months later James Hoffa went to prison.

A mourning period was observed in some Las Vegas Casinos when James R. Hoffa was convicted and sent to jail for practically the same reasons as had landed his predecessor, Dave Beck, in the clink. In early 1972, Hoffa was released, and hotel owners in Las Vegas rejoiced.

2. Las Vegas, Las Vegas, That Wonderful Town

JOE E. LEWIS

Though Broadway had its "Roaring Twenties," I prefer to remember a far more exciting, robust era in the world of entertainment right here in Las Vegas during the Fifties, when a battered man by the name of Joe E. Lewis, the star of El Rancho Vegas, had the town and the millions who came here in his hip pocket. He was easily the greatest café comic who ever played a fancy saloon.

It was a stormy, colorful decade that ended on a sad note early in the spring of 1960 when El Rancho burned to the ground. To this day the reason for this mysterious blaze is not known. But about Lewis, the legendary King Klown: He played to the boozers and losers, the elite from the mob and snobbery lane.

A Joe E. Lewis opening night at the El Rancho in Vegas wasn't another chore for me but an event I looked forward to with much anticipation. Even though Joe and I had been close friends for more than thirty years, he always looked at me with distrust because I was a teetotaler. And when he was drunk, which was usually from the hours of eight in the evening until the same hour the next morning, he would put his arm around me and say, "You silly bastard, if only you knew what you were missing." Then he'd down a double Scotch with the ease of a growing schoolboy swallowing a glass of milk.

Sitting in the old, slightly broken down El Rancho Vegas, which had a character all its own, I'd watch Lewis come staggering out of the wings to the tune of "Chicago, Chicago."

He'd be clutching at a tall glass of his favorite mouthwash, Ambassador Scotch, and wobbling in a manner that threatened to drop him into the laps of the ringsiders. And as the band played and the crowd roared affectionately, Joe would take a sip or two of the life-giving liquid, look at the crowd, then mutter, "Please forgive me for drinking onstage. But it's something I like to do while getting drunk."

To heckle Lewis meant a fate worse than death—as when a lady, almost as drunk as Joe and sitting at ringside, began carrying on a conversation with Joe in a voice that could be heard out in the gaming casino. Joe gave her a nasty look, then cracked, "Listen, lady, I don't go to your counter at Woolworth's and bother you while you're working, do I?"

Joe would begin singing one of his famous parodies, and only a handful of his close friends and associates knew that he was suffering the tortures of hell. Sick from advanced diabetes and bleeding ulcers, Joe would forget his aches and pains as he listened to the roaring laughter of the audience.

In his famous, slurring speech, which was an aftermath of that day back in Chicago in the late Twenties when a Chicago mobster cut his throat and left Joe for dead in a pool of his own blood, Joe would start off in a rollicking mood.

"It's good to be back at the Ranch again and working for Beldon Katleman. The last time I was here, Beldon held over my money and let me go. But that's okay, I'm always glad to come back to visit my money here." From time to time Joe

48

would sip from his drink. And when he did, the people roared, because that was the image Joe E. Lewis had created. But on one of those nights he didn't tell them he was sipping iced tea.

That night Joe was in agony. And the fact that he had been boozing it up all those weeks hadn't helped his condition. Sure, Joe knew that he mustn't drink with severe bleeding ulcers and diabetes. But there were a lot of things Joe E. Lewis knew that he should not have been doing but he did. He dared the grim reaper constantly as he went into the hay with a pretty young chick. It was a devastating parlay: Diabetes, ulcers, and alcohol could lead to a possible coronary.

Joe got more laughter when he sipped, then told the audience, "This is ice tea, no fooling." What a clown, that Joe E. Lewis, pretending it was tea! He was making a big concession to his doctor, who was down front watching him intently.

Sitting at ringside also was Ed Sullivan, the famous deadpan TV host, and his wife Sylvia. Joe spotted Ed and cracked, "That's Ed Sullivan sitting there, ladies and gentlemen. He lights up a room just by leaving it. I remember Ed for many years, especially when he used to be a greeter at Forest Lawn Cemetery. But he had to give up the job because it turned out to be too dangerous. They tried to bury him three times."

Now the dinner show was over and Joe staggered offstage, to be met by his doctor inquiring about his condition. Joe waved him off as the doctor yelled, "Don't forget, Joe, stay off the whiskey for the next few days." Joe nodded, then got lost at a dice table. Five minutes after the dire admonition from his medic, Joe hailed a cocktail waitress and ordered his favorite booze. A worried pal at his side asked him, "Do you have to, Joe?"

"Christ, yes," growled Joe. "If only just to get the taste of the goddamned iced tea out of my mouth." Then Lewis

49

began shooting dice until El Rancho Vegas owner, Beldon Katleman, came up to tell him the midnight show was about to start.

A man with an incredible constitution, considering his ailments and the way he abused his body, Joe E. Lewis went onstage, still holding a drink—this time real booze. His eyes were now almost closed from fatigue and pain, but as long as he could stand, he could perform—and brilliantly.

Holding onto the piano with one hand and the drink with the other, Joe gave his long-time friend and accompanist, Austin Mack, the sign. Then he began singing his most-requested parody, "Sam, You Made the Pants Too Long," from the original "Lord, You Made the Night Too Long," which had practically lost its identity since Lewis introduced his parody.

Joe had just finished a couple of hesitating choruses when he suddenly began backing away toward the wings. He stopped singing and concentrated mainly on getting off that stage because he was in the throes of a diabetic coma! Only when he got into the wings did he collapse completely into the arms of his doctor. Lewis was in a local hospital for more than a week, then was flown to Los Angeles, where he was operated on for his bleeding ulcers. Part of his stomach was removed in the process.

Three months later Joe was back in El Rancho Vegas and telling his howling disciples, "Lemme tell you about my operation. The doctor removed a shot glass from my gut. I don't know how the hell it got there because I'd been drinking from the bottle the past six months! Anyway, it's good to be back here at El Rancho Vegas. Beldon Katleman must have gone to great expense to remodel the bar and put in all new drunks."

Lewis was not only almost indestructible, but funnier than he'd ever been after he added the hospital routine. He could recover from almost anything but heartbreak, which he suffered poignantly when Martha Stewart and he broke up their quickie marriage. But that was the way Joe wanted it. Another shock was when the El Rancho Vegas Hotel, his home and bar away from home and bar, burned to the ground in the spring of 1960.

Sure, he went to work at the Flamingo Hotel for the next couple of years, but it wasn't the same. "The drunks aren't the same as they were at El Rancho Vegas," Joe used to tell me between shows. "This is a girls' finishing school compared to that sawduster of Beldon Katleman's. I feel like a guy working in a bank—with his fly open."

I remember one night, after doing his midnight show, when Lewis went on the town with a young blonde Hollywood starlet. Eight hours later, thoroughly exhausted and an $8,000 loser, not to mention that he was completely boozed up, Joe was being driven back to his suite at the Flamingo by the blonde doll.

As the car drove slowly toward the entrance, a drunken Joe opened the door, stepped out, and landed on his ass. That saying about God always protecting drunks had a lot of truth to it. As he lay there, several employees of the hotel rushed out and took him back into the hotel, then called his doctor.

Except for torn cartilages in his left leg and a lot of bruises, Joe was in good shape. He missed the show that night, but the next night he came back hobbling on a cane, then rested on a high stool, where he did his act.

In his best whiskey-soaked grumble, Joe came onstage to the familiar tune of "Chicago, Chicago, That Wonderful Town." Then, looking down at his leg, he croaked in that world-famous voice, "I know you're wondering about the cane. So, I'll tell you what happened. Yesterday afternoon I went over to Dean Martin's house to play some checkers with Dino. We drank some hot chocolate, then put on some Lawrence Welk records. That's when I spotted this spider on the ceiling, and, without thinking, tried stepping on it. That's how I happened to hurt my leg."

This was the real Joe E. Lewis arising briefly from those gloriously nostalgic El Rancho Vegas days. A year later Joe went into retirement, and Las Vegas has never really recovered. But in September, 1970, I came up with the idea of a testimonial dinner for Joe E. Lewis here in Las Vegas at the Riviera Hotel. It had been long due, this tribute to "Mister Las Vegas of Show Business."

He, more than any other star (and that includes Frank Sinatra, Dean Martin, and Danny Thomas by their own admission), deserved that signal honor for truly making Las Vegas the "Show Capital of the World." And they turned out from all professional walks of life that September 13th to honor Joseph Everglades Lewis. Probably the most nostalgic moment of the entire affair came after more than three and a half hours when Joe, more dead than alive, staggered to his feet and did another parody like in his heyday at El Rancho Vegas.

Sung to the tune of "My Way," Lewis brought instant tears to the eyes of every one of the one thousand people there that night when he croaked, "And now I've reached the end . . . this is the final curtain." Nine months later he was dead.

After sneering at the Grim Reaper many times in his hectic sixty-nine years, Joe Everglades Lewis had drunk once too often from his cup of lustful pleasure, lapsed into a diabetic coma, and died on June 4, 1971. The man, who had defied medical science for years after his throat was cut by Machine Gun Jack McGurn's hoods almost forty-five years earlier in a Chicago hotel, had finally reached the end of the line.

BIG JAKE, THE LANDLORD

He was like no other landlord you ever met. His name was Jake Gottlieb and he owned the Dunes Hotel property. And that's about as fancy a tenant as you can get when you realize that the rent Jake collected was in the neighborhood of $750,000 annually. So Jake was quite concerned about his tenants and their enterprises.

Every night he would toddle into the casino, step gingerly over the ropes enclosing "the pit," and then spend a few moments with the casino bosses. And after he had paid his respects, Jake would toddle back to his suite in the hotel and mark off another day on his calendar. The reason Jake Gottleib toddled was that he carried 260 pounds on a squat five-foot, three-inch frame. And being in his late sixties, Jake wasn't in what you would call the pink of condition.

One night he went into the hotel on his regular "good will" mission, started stepping over the ropes by the dice tables, caught his heel, and toppled heavily to the floor. The impact rattled the dice and shook the foundation as he lay there. He was seriously hurt. As he lay there moaning, both eyes closed, a dozen Dunes Hotel employees ran to his side while others ran to get the house doctor.

It was the kind of sight you see only in Las Vegas—a huge man on his back in the midst of the gaming tables while the action continued unabated. One frustrated blackjack player, stepping away from the table after losing, almost tripped on the fallen Gottleib, while an army of slot machine players ten feet away gave him sidelong, slightly sympathetic glances. A couple started in Jake's direction, then changed their mind as others waiting for the machines started edging toward them.

Through all this by-play, Jake Gottleib, his face ashen, his breathing labored as in the throes of death, kept his eyes shut. And while a doctor made his way over from elsewhere in the hotel, out of the casino cashier's cage came the credit manager. Leaning down in his most solicitous manner, he asked Jake how he felt. Jake merely moaned.

Then the casino credit manager got down to business. "Listen, Jake, I just got a call from Goldberg of Kansas City.

He's in the hotel and wants $10,000 credit to gamble. Shall I give it to him?"

For the first time since Jake had crashed to the floor, he opened his eyes. He went on moaning as he thought for a few moments. Then he said, "Goldberg of Kansas City? Yeah, he's good as gold. Give him the money." After which Jake closed his eyes and resumed moaning until the doctor reached his side.

Except for a severe shock to his nervous system and a broken leg, Jake Gottleib weathered that storm. He was laid up for more than three months, but the day came when he managed to wobble down to the gaming pits once again.

What hastened his recovery is the news that was brought to his bedside that "Goldberg of Kansas City" had blown the $10,000 he borrowed from the hotel on the dice tables but two weeks later had paid the debt in full.

As a matter of fact, the nurses attending Jake swear they heard him humming pleasantly for days afterward.

KIRK KERKORIAN

Kirk Kerkorian, the son of an Armenian fruit peddler from Harpoot on the Turkish border, has been the most colorful Las Vegas tycoon in the history of this town. And that includes the Wilbur Clarks, the Del Webbs, and even old now-you-see-him, now-you-might Howard Hughes.

Head of Western Airlines and MGM Studios in Culver City, California, Kirk sold his interest in the huge International Hotel in 1971 to the Hilton chain. But before the year was over, he broke page one nationally with the story that he was returning to Las Vegas to build a $75-million Grand Hotel on the site of his shuttered Bonanza Hotel property just across from Caesars Palace on the Strip. Opening date would be in 1973, he announced.

Kirk, a living, breathing Horatio Alger "rags to riches"

hero in every sense of the word, was once again an integral part of the Las Vegas economy. This eighth-grade grammar school dropout may have made old Horatio drool in his mausoleum, because Kirk would have given the paperback writer his greatest novel of all time. And it would have been the gospel truth.

When his International Hotel opened in July of 1969, Kirk sat in a booth in the showroom well back from ringside. He had given strict orders that he wanted absolutely no publicity from the stage. However, his orders didn't apply to his friend, movie actor Cary Grant, who faced the two thousand people in the room that opening night, then said, "Kirk, I know you hate this sort of thing, but I want everyone here to see the guy who made this most spectacular hotel possible. Get up and take a bow."

Kirk rose quickly, took a speedy bow, and then slouched deeply back into his booth behind his wife, Jean, and two young daughters, Tracy and Linda. Later in the evening, the star of the show, Barbra Streisand, came onstage, looked in a bewildered manner all around the place, then cracked, "Shows you what a guy can do with a G.I. loan."

She wasn't too far wrong. Kirk Kerkorian had started his illustrious career way back in the early Thirties in Fresno, California, by operating a steam car wash. It obviously was not the kind of work he cared too much about, and Kirk closed it down. Then he went into the ring, because his older brother, Nish, was already a professional prize fighter in small clubs on the West Coast.

Kirk fought thirty-three fights, during which he developed not only a violent dislike for anything so physical but a slightly squashed nose. Still not having found what he was looking for, Kirk borrowed $12,000 from his older sister Rose, and started an air service, with unscheduled flights between Los Angeles and Las Vegas, also New York. While in the car-wash business, Kirk had taken flying lessons. And now they would pay off, because this was going to be it for K.K. The aviation business was his cup of tea.

Twenty-one years later Kirk Kerkorian merged his Trans-International Air Lines with Trans-America Corporation and came away with a $90-million profit. That wasn't too bad for a kid who had sold newspapers on the streets of Fresno and dreamed about one day being able to have his own business, a wife and kids, and maybe a $5,000 profit at the end of each year.

From that moment on, the sky was really the limit for K.K.'s lucrative endeavors. He scooted between Las Vegas, New York, London, and other European cities in his fancy white DC-9, a $4-million job that took him everywhere at the slightest hint that a deal could be consummated. And when things got too tangled and he felt as if he'd had it, then he and wife Jean and the kids would board his 145-foot yacht in San Diego, a $900,000 seafaring playground, and take off for ports unknown.

Though almost every part of Kirk's life has been written about in newspapers and magazines, it remained for Kirk himself to come up with the most priceless, hitherto unrevealed true story about him and his older brother, Nish, who now owns and operates a fancy restaurant in Las Vegas known as "Nishon's."

When both Kirk and Nish were youngsters (Nish fourteen and Kirk ten), they lived in a poor section of South Los Angeles because Papa Kerkorian was having problems getting and keeping odd jobs around Los Angeles. One summer day it was sweltering in town, and the boys decided to take off for the beach in far away Santa Monica.

They arrowed in on Mama K. in the kitchen, and managed to get thirty cents from her for emergency bus fare in case they had trouble grabbing free rides to and from the beach.

Bolting out of the ramshackle tenement house, which should have been condemned long before the oft-moving

Kerkorians settled there, the lads headed for a bit of sunshine, fresh air, and the sandy beach at Santa Monica. Nish, the older, clutched the thirty cents by keeping it in his fist in his pants pocket. Once on the road that led to the beach, they planted themselves at the strategic traffic light and waited for a charitable motorist.

The wait was brief, because chugging toward them was a battered truck steered by a most happy driver, who pulled over so they could catch up with him. No, the boys didn't mind sharing the back of the truck with a pile of vile-smelling blankets and rags that had to have come from a slaughterhouse.

What did it matter? The truck went right through Santa Monica. Nish and Kirk didn't have to walk more than a hundred yards before jumping into the welcoming blue-green waters of the Pacific. The water helped wash away the foul odor that had crept into their clothes and hair. And they had managed to hold onto the thirty cents.

This had to be the most glorious day for Nish and Kirk Kerkorian. But, as they bounded out of the surf, they began experiencing belly rumblings. It was a familiar sensation to them. They were hungry. But they had thirty cents. In a matter of seconds they ran to the nearest hot dog stand on the beach and were soon gulping down hot dogs and root beer.

"Who needs bus fare?" yelled Nish. "We'll get a ride back, right?" Then they plunged into the water, utterly at peace with the world, because the hot dogs and root beer had filled that aching void in the Kerkorian bellies.

Four hours later the belly rumbling returned. Now it was time to get the hell out of Santa Monica and head home for mama's specialty, shish kebab. It was a once-a-week treat, since the old man wasn't working regularly and the Kerkorian finances were nothing to talk about.

Sandy, bedraggled, sunburned, but happy, the boys headed for the highway, thumbs ready for motorists who'd take them back to South Los Angeles and a waiting supper.

But they were in for a rough time. Since it was around five o'clock, motorists were rushing home from work and in no mood to stop for a couple of tattered, sunburned kids waving a torn towel at them.

So they decided to start walking, stopping almost every ten feet to look over their shoulders for the welcome sight of a motorist slowing down to pick them up. And the more they walked and looked, the louder that rumbling sounded in their stomachs.

Kirk suddenly came up with a helluva scheme. "Nish, I know how we'll get a ride. Why don't you lay down here at the side of the highway, and I'll try to wave down a car and tell the guy you're sick or something?"

Nish cuffed Kirk sharply on the side of the head. "You crazy? One of those bastards'll probably drive right over me. You lay down, and I'll wave down a car."

The result was a dead heat, and soon the brothers Kerkorian were walking and looking over their shoulders again. The "laying down" idea had been shelved by a unanimous vote of two.

By now they had walked almost five miles, and little Kirk was dragging. Nish stuck a strong bracing right arm around him, and they continued walking. "That's Culver City up ahead," said Nish. "If we don't get a ride there, we'll rest for a half hour."

And that's what happened. They didn't get a ride, so they plunked themselves down on a fancy bench just a few feet away from the main entrance of the world-famous MGM movie studios.

The aches and pains in their bone-weary bodies disappeared momentarily as they looked through the bars of the huge entrance gate to the studios. Within the gate Nish and Kirk saw strange people in Arab, Western, and early-Twenties garb going their separate ways.

58

This was their fairyland, the place where Clark Gable, Spencer Tracy, Robert Montgomery, and the Barrymores—John, Lionel, and Ethel—made movies. Now the youngsters slid off the bench and inched their way to the closed entrance gate. Peering through the solid metal bars, they started yelling at the top of their lungs, "Hey, Gable, hey Tracy," over and over again.

It brought an instant response from a burly movie security guard, who came charging up to the gate waving a cudgel at them and ordering them to get the hell away from the entrance. The boys, tried and true symbols of a ghetto, stoutly resisted authority. They promptly told the red-faced guard certain pertinent facts about his ancestry, which raised considerable doubt about whether or not his mother and father had been married at the time he was born.

Almost apoplectic at the gall of these dirty-faced urchins taunting and screaming at him, he once again raised his cudgel threateningly. By that time, the boys were climbing up the gate, all the time yelling spitefully. That was one way of relieving themselves of the frustrations of hunger and the lack of free rides back home.

Rushing over to the gate, the guard rapped their knuckles with his stout piece of hickory. Kirk and Nish let out a scream of pain and instantly climbed down from the gate.

Licking their skinned knuckles like wounded little animals, they took off down the highway as the guard started opening the gate to grab them. Within a couple of minutes, they put a respectable distance between themselves and that monster with his cudgel.

Many years later, Kirk was telling me this story as he and I shared a couple of seats on a commercial airliner to New York City. It was one of the rare times Kirk wasn't availing himself of the comfort of his $4-million DC-9, which was in the Culver City Airport hangar for repairs.

And as we flew high over the Rockies on our way to New

York, he for a board meeting with members of MGM, I for a meeting with my family in Jackson Heights, New York, the story of two Armenian urchins trying to climb the huge gates of MGM in Culver City was truly a "Believe-It-Or-Not" that would have tickled the late Robert L. Ripley.

As the boss of MGM reminisced about that afternoon in front of the gates of the company he acquired, he showed me the knuckles on his right fist. A slight scar spread across two of them. Kirk was grinning. "I wonder if that sonofabitch still works for us at the studio."

THE POOR SOUL

He was such a cheerful, happy soul. We'll call him John Frobl, but that's not his real name. Coming all the way from Muskegon, he was taking his first vacation in twenty years in Las Vegas. As the owner of a small plastic factory, John Frobl could hardly contain himself as he strolled the grounds of the Last Frontier Hotel in 1947.

"Last night I saw Jimmy Durante at the Flamingo. I ate mighty well, had a couple of martinis and the biggest piece of cream pie you ever saw. And all it cost me was $3. Later in the casino back here at the Last Frontier I played dollar blackjack for several hours and dropped another $70, but it still was a super evening of fun and pleasure—even though I had to get up a couple of times during the night to take some Alka-Seltzers."

The best thing poor John Frobl could have done at that happy moment was pack his belongings and a cactus plant he'd bought for his wife, and go back to Muskegon. But he didn't, and thereby hangs the tale. I shared a room at the Last Frontier with an old Brooklyn buddy, Herman Milton Greenspun, next door to John Frobl. So we and he got quite chummy. Herman Milton Greenspun later became an enormous power in Las Vegas as the publisher of the Las Vegas

Sun. What was even more fantastic, six years later I became his columnist on the newspaper. But let me tell you more about Muskegon's John Frobl.

John became the slave of the gaming halls. Soon his bets soared into the $100-a-pop category at the dice and blackjack tables. At first, he was a pleasant, cheerful loser. And every night at five he would put in a long-distance call to his wife and two daughters back in Muskegon, then promptly return to the demon tables, which had him thoroughly mesmerized.

Now he was no longer the congenial Midwestern business tycoon on a vacation. He was a steely-eyed, nervous loser who had fallen victim to the strange, metallic click of the ivories banging against the dice table and the slap, slap, slap of the pasteboards on the blackjack table.

Gone was his once-immaculate appearance. He was wearing the same striped shirt for the third day. It was spotted with food and sweat stains. His eyes were slightly bloodshot, and the grayish stubble on his face was at least two days old. In short, the poor guy looked terrible. He was a loser. No longer did he greet Greenspun and me congenially, or tell us those awful, humorless stories.

In the hole about $30,000, Frobl started gambling recklessly in order to get back his losses. Otherwise how could he go back to Muskegon? The most Frobl had ever lost at games of chance in the regular Saturday-night poker sessions with the boys had been $25, and his missus had scolded him severely afterward. He dreaded to think what she would say now that he had blown a lifetime of savings in one hectic week at the Vegas tables.

It had become utterly embarrassing to face him, and we tried avoiding him by slipping out of the door quickly and turning out of sight. However, late one night as I made the rounds of the clubs, I saw his poor, sallow countenance in the glare of the overhead lights at the dice table. Inching closer and standing behind other gamers, I saw that John Frobl was down to the $10 class. Only the day before he had been betting $500 on the line and taking the numbers for $250 a pop. Now, he was grinding.

A chatty croupier told me, "Your friend from Muskegon really went to the shithouse last night. He lost about $20,000 and later tried to sell his watch for $50 to one of the bellhops. He came back a half hour later with $20 minus his watch, put it down on the 'Pass Line,' rolled the dice, and crapped out on the first roll."

Before falling off in a troubled sleep that night, Greenspun and I talked about Frobl and how his unsuspecting wife and daughters were facing poverty by way of the Las Vegas gaming tables. Since Frobl's room adjoined ours, I could hear him pacing the floor during the night. I made a mental note to talk to him in the morning.

At about four o'clock that morning, Greenspun and I were knocked out of bed by a blast that shook the ceiling and almost dropped the chandelier on our heads.

Since the atomic blasts at Yucca Flats wouldn't start for another eight years, I could only account for such a blast at such an ungodly hour in the desert flat lands of Las Vegas by assuming that Bugsy Siegel, who had recently opened the luxurious Flamingo Hotel down the Strip, had bombed the Last Frontier Hotel to get rid of a strong competitor.

Greenspun and I rushed out of the hotel room, he in his pajama bottoms, I in his pajama tops. The sight that greeted us made me retch. The door to Frobl's room had been almost blown off its hinges. Acrid smoke pouring from his room burned our eyes and nostrils. It smelled like gun smoke.

And there on the bed, half off, half on, was a pile of human rubbish that had once been a happy, prosperous industrialist, father, and husband, John Frobl. Much of his head had been shot away. His brains hung from the ceiling like some gruesome, ancient piece of Oriental art.

Jimmy Durante and the late champ,
Rocky Marciano.

In the late 50's, Eddie Fisher and his Debbie Reynolds tell Ralph Pearl on his television show "we've never been happier in our lives." Six months later Eddie left Debbie to marry Elizabeth Taylor.

The good-looking kid with the "prison stripe" jacket is Elvis Presley back in '55 when he was making his first appearance in Las Vegas at the New Frontier Hotel. The author is making like his tailor.

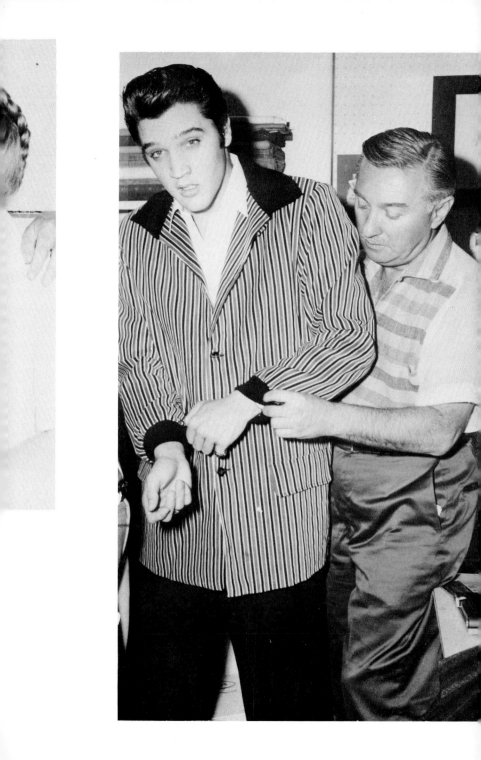

The late Wilbur Clark, who gave the
Desert Inn world recognition while
showcasing the Inn for boss Moe
Dalitz and associates.

The late Jayne Mansfield and her then-husband Mickey Hartigay, celebrating their sixth anniversary.

The late Gus Greenbaum, Riviera Hotel boss, killed in his Phoenix home in '58 with wife.

Ben "Bugsy" Siegel, who started gaming on the Strip in '47 with the Flamingo Hotel. He got blasted in July of that year in Beverly Hills.

Meyer Lansky, Mr. Big of the Las Vegas gaming industry from '47 on.

John Frobl had found a way to end his losing streak at the gaming tables.

The note on the dresser was pinned down with a water container, and it read, simply, "Tell my family I just crapped out once too often."

ED SULLIVAN AND CAROL BURNETT

She opened with the Ed Sullivan Variety Show at the Desert Inn very early in the Sixties without billing at a salary of $500 a week, which was the most she had been able to get since she started in show business a couple of years before in the East.

Looking like a scarecrow in a sexy gown, the girl came onstage after a brief introduction from Sullivan, then proceeded to stop the otherwise boring revue with her version of "I'm in Love with John Foster Dulles." Surprisingly, the girl had a great singing voice and a greater flair for offbeat comedy.

Sullivan wasn't overly pleased the next day when I devoted the entire column to Carol Burnett and said, "She is undoubtedly headed for stardom. There are moments in Carol's act when she cavorts about the Desert Inn stage in a manner that reminds me of the inimitable Charlie Chaplin himself."

Ed sent me a note the next day which simply read, "Dear Ralph: I knew I should have fired you when I had the chance back in the Thirties. Love, Ed Sullivan."

But that's an entirely different story.

In the Thirties Ed Sullivan was one of the better sports columnists in the business. He wrote daily for the *New York Evening Graphic,* a gruesome, grisly, daily tabloid which concentrated on murders, sex crimes, and divorces. Labeling the *New York Evening Graphic* merely as a tabloid was like describing Meyer Lansky as an "undesirable citizen."

The *Graphic* was published by an eccentric, Bernarr McFadden, who existed on nuts, herbs, and seeds. In those days he was looked upon as a wealthy crackpot with weird ideas about health and diet. Today he should be acclaimed as the "George Washington of the health food fad."

I was a copy boy on that newspaper. One of my chores was to pick up Ed's sports column and rush it down to the composing room. I never rushed it. I'd go straight to the men's room, lock myself in one of the cubicles, then proceed to read Ed's column about such sports heroes as Babe Ruth, Jack Dempsey, Bobby Jones, Paavo Nurmi, and Johnny Weissmuller.

That night when I got home and met with the boys on the block, I'd overwhelm them with my inside information about their favorite figures. The *Graphic* folded soon afterward, and Ed went over to the New York *Daily News.* I went back to school.

Many years later here in Las Vegas, specifically in 1955, I invited the visiting Ed Sullivan to guest on my TV show and introduced him as "A man who's now a giant in TV. However, if it wasn't for this columnist, me, Ed might have still been a sports writer in New York. I told him to get in on the ground floor with television."

Ed's eyes popped. He hadn't recognized me as his former copy boy back at the old *New York Graphic.* Ed burst into laughter, an occurrence that wouldn't happen too many times in his life.

In the summer of 1971, Carol Burnett, making one of her rare nitery appearances in Las Vegas, sat poolside with me reminiscing about the "good old days" when she was starving in Manhattan trying to break into show biz.

"I'll never forget when my agent told me he had arranged for me to work in the Ed Sullivan Variety Show at the Desert Inn in Las Vegas. I almost fainted from malnutrition and joy. He had asked Ed to pay me $750 a week, but Ed balked and wanted to pay me only $350 a week. We finally settled for $500. But it didn't really matter. I would have worked for spit in those days just to be able to get that Las Vegas exposure, and on an Ed Sullivan show yet!

"Naturally, whatever success I have had in this business, I attribute to my Las Vegas date, also to the groovy review you gave me then. It was only about five years later, after lunching with Sullivan in New York, when I learned that Ed had almost turned thumbs down on me after my agent popped him with that original $750 offer. Ed told me then the only reason he didn't get another singer was that time was running out, that he didn't have the time or patience to go shopping about for another, lesser-priced singer for his Las Vegas show.

"I have to wonder where I'd be today . . . probably selling hosiery in Macy's, if Ed hadn't taken me to Las Vegas with him."

FRANK SINATRA AND THE "CLAN"

Of the more than ten thousand shows I've seen in Las Vegas, there's no question as to the most exciting night in a showroom during those twenty years I spent accumulating ulcers, acid stomach, and nervous tension.

The show which stood out in bold relief from all the other great shows was that time in January of 1960 when Frank Sinatra, already established as a power outdrawing any other star in Las Vegas, came into the Copa Room of the Sands Hotel with his "Clan." It was publicized as far away as the Kremlin as Sinatra and his "Summit Meeting at the Sands." The Sands press agent instantly sent highly publicized wires to Eisenhower, Churchill, and Khrushchev inviting them to Frank's "Summit Meeting."

The "Clan," made up of Dean Martin, Joey Bishop, Sammy Davis, Jr., Peter Lawford, and their "leader," Sinatra, then proceeded to cut up in a manner which easily moved the Sands Hotel foundation at least three inches.

Tourists and locals in town during that three weeks looked on enviously as they watched from outside. Only VIP's were able to get reservations.

Though the boys had a basic act, it never worked out that way because all of them except Peter Lawford were veteran café laughmakers and highly experienced with the ad lib. Twice nightly during that three-weeker, almost every big star in show business made a visit to the Copa Room and eventually, whether they wanted to or not, wound up on the stage at the mercy of Sammy, Joey, Frank, Dean, and Peter.

The word "riotous" is used often by Las Vegas night-club critics and columnists, but it began to take on a true meaning only when describing the psychopathically funny antics of the "Clan." Dean would suddenly disappear from the stage, but you'd hear him speaking from his chest mike, "Hey, where the hell's the toilet back here. I gotta go real bad."

Suddenly Frank Sinatra would dash over to a slightly bewildered Sammy Davis, Jr., his one good eye popping nervously because he wasn't sure what would be happening to him at the hands of Frank and Dean. Sinatra would pick him up bodily as though he were a bundle of laundry, then rush to the mike.

"Ladies and gentlemen," then Frank would hold up Sammy, "I want to thank all of you for giving me this valuable NAACP trophy." Then, dashing away from the mike while the audience roared, Sinatra, still carrying Davis in his arms, dashed over to a prominent gent sitting at ringside, and dropped his "trophy" in his lap. The prominent gent? None other than Senator John F. Kennedy of Massachusetts, and already being touted for the White House.

Sammy Davis, Jr., looked up into Kennedy's face and meekly said, "It's perfectly all right with me, senator, as long as I'm not being donated to George Wallace or James Eastland." More howling. Joey Bishop and Peter Lawford, who was Kennedy's brother-in-law, rushed over to Kennedy and "retrieved" Davis, then rushed him out of the Copa Room. Minutes later they came back onstage, but without Sammy. Both had sad expressions. So it was natural for Frank and Dean to ask, "What happened to the 'trophy'?" Joey Bishop: "We played it on the hard eight and lost." Believe it or not, there were many moments during this madness when Frank, Dean, Sammy, Joey, and Peter tried sticking to the original format of the show. But that was almost as impossible as trying to get the always inebriated Dean Martin to walk a straight line.

It was all a great big romp and, after the opening night, people were offering as high as $100 to get a reservation to that show.

Sure, Frank, Dean, and Sammy got to sing songs, but neither of them ever succeeded in finishing a ditty without getting heckled into hysteria before the end of the song. I would have to believe that the "Clan" was the first group in show business to start racial humor by using Sammy Davis, Jr., as a foil for their K.K.K. clowning.

One night Kim Novak, then a big movie star from Columbia Pictures, was brave enough to sit at ringside. Before that show was half over, Dean and Frank got her up onstage and proceeded to unravel her from the top of her fancy coiffure to her open-toed shoes. Little Sammy Davis, Jr., tried coming to her "rescue" several times, but he eventually wound up stuffed in a large umbrella stand onstage by Frank.

It ultimately led to that fiery romance between Sammy and Kim which almost destroyed everyone connected with it.

But about the "Clan" during that three-weeker. It was the most profitable three-weeker for the Sands casino in the history of that hotel. The high rollers from all over the nation had absolutely no problem getting in to see that show as often as they wished. And whatever seats were left over went to other VIP's outside the gaming strata.

Since catching shows in Las Vegas has always been a

chore for me rather than a pleasure, I never see a show more than once, and that's on opening night. However, I made an exception for Sinatra and the "Clan." I saw that show six times during the next three weeks. And the only reason I didn't see it ten more times was that I was too embarrassed to come in because the Sands Hotel help might get the idea I liked catching shows.

SPENCER TRACY

The late, great movie actor Spencer Tracy only came to Las Vegas three or four times in his entire professional lifetime. But I can never forget one of those times, when he and I sat in the bar at the Sands Hotel. He had just finished making a movie from the immortal Ernest Hemingway novel, *The Old Man and the Sea*, which dealt with the adventures of a tenacious, gentle old coot in a tiny Mexican fishing hamlet. Except for several other male characters in that picture, that was the cast.

In talking with the great man of the flickers, I couldn't help but tell Spencer about my utter devotion to Hemingway and every book he ever wrote.

Tracy, his shaggy white mane lying unevenly against the sides of his heavily wrinkled countenance, grunted several times without missing a sip from his favorite rye and barley concoction, which he held firmly in his gnarled, wrinkled fist. Obviously he wasn't overwhelmed, at least not as fiercely as I was, by the literary genius of Ernest Hemingway.

The only thing that could cause him to miss a sip or two would be the sudden swooshing by of a heavy-breasted cocktail waitress. And many of that skimpily clad species managed to pass our table often when they found out it was Spencer Tracy sitting there as gloomy as a rainy day in Carson City, the fair capital of the state of Nevada.

He answered my numerous questions in ten words or less.

At that, he seemed to be doing me a favor by sitting there and talking with me. But, as a long-time Tracy fan who would dribble at the slightest bit of celluloidal pyrotechnics by Tracy, I was grateful just to be there.

For more years than I care to remember, I've rubbed elbows, tummies, kneecaps, and tushies with the greatest names in show business. Sometimes I was impressed. Other times some "big names," who were nothing away from the spotlight and their press agents, bored me. However, when Spencer Tracy came along, not only was I impressed, I forgot to go to the bathroom, even though I was hurrying there when I spotted Tracy.

But about our conversation concerning *The Old Man and the Sea.* I began prattling like a giddy high school boy about Tracy's role in the movie, as well as my passion for Hemingway's writings. Tracy had just downed a double Scotch in one gulp and was diluting it with a huge swallow of beer when I asked, "So tell me, Mr. Tracy, who plays the feminine lead in this Hemingway picture with you?"

Suddenly Tracy began choking over a large mouthful of beer that seemed to have gone down the wrong way. His eyes began bulging and tearing while he wheezed and spit and choked trying to regain his normal breathing.

I sat there wondering how to lead off my sensational page-one scoop about the sudden demise of Spencer Tracy in the Sands Hotel bar. That could be one helluva story. Tracy dead from swallowing a shot glass. However, he managed to clear his throat and wipe his wet eyes, nose, and mouth. Then he glared at me with a fierce hatred.

"You did say you've read everything Hemingway ever wrote. Right?" He was sputtering in uncontrolled rage.

"Yes," I timidly answered, wondering what his near-tragic demise from a Schlitz had to do with Hemingway. I didn't have to wait long for the answer.

"Did you know that in his book, *The Old Man and the Sea,*

69

there were no female characters?" I gulped, got up, and walked out into the mad evening traffic hoping to get run down. How could I have made such a horse's ass out of myself in front of my number one movie hero?

What plagued me most, I knew goddamned well there were no females in that book. It had just been a slip of the tongue. Or as some comics would put it, "My eyeteeth didn't see what my tongue was saying at the time."

I never saw Spencer Tracy again, though he did send me a note about six months later wondering what my reaction had been to *The Old Man and the Sea*, which had just been released nationally.

Tracy and Hemingway are long gone now, but I can't read a Hemingway novel or see an old Spencer Tracy movie on television without grinning nostalgically and remembering that night in the Sands Hotel bar with my movie idol—a crusty, cantankerous gent who'll never have an equal on the silver screen.

THE FABULOUS "MISTER ELL"

Since this was in the late Fifties and a man by the name of Fidel Castro with his tattered group of loyal followers was a harmless threat, I prepared to shove off for Havana on a press junket to attend the opening of the Riviera Hotel there. It seemed that every big movie, sports, café, and political name had also been invited for that royal bash.

I had managed to make several trips a year to Havana because there were several gaming casino hotels there, three of which were owned by Las Vegas syndicate owners. Sure, many of us with the press knew all about the greedy, mercenary habits of Cuban Dictator Batista. We also knew that Cuba as a whole, but Havana in particular, enjoyed an annual billion-dollar tourist bonanza.

Much had been written about the ultra-swanky Riviera

Hotel, which was owned by the mob. Not only were the celebs there en masse, but also many high-rolling Las Vegas hotel owners. And where there are gaming tables, high rollers, and stars, you're bound to find ladies of the evening (who will be identified from here on as hookers for brevity). What didn't wind up in those little black boxes under each gaming table would ultimately wind up with the hookers, of course.

And since this was a typical Batista fiesta, the sky was the limit for the more than a thousand invited guests who would feast on pheasant, drink the finest bubbly water, and nibble as often as they wanted on the sundry kinds of passion fruit available.

At the height of all the revelry, as movie starlets pranced high atop the tables in their birthday suits in the private suites, the bearded rebel was making his secret move slowly down the Oriente Mountains toward the outskirts of Havana. Then and there, as Fidel marched, Cuba's billion-dollar tourism started disappearing. A few months later Fidel was in power, but not before Batista had fled his palace with almost $400 million dollars to keep him company.

But, getting back to the opening-night party at the Riviera Hotel: I waved at a couple of high-class hookers who had flown down specially for the opening. They insisted this was going to be a vacation and absolutely no business would be transacted by them. One of the gaming bosses at the Riviera dragged me over to a corner of the lobby and introduced me to a man he called "Mister Ell."

The gaming boss blinked constantly, like an overworked bookkeeper, then twitched nervously when the loud screaming of an agonized crapshooter sounded like a human led to slaughter. So, the nice little man known as "Mister Ell," squirmed through the mob with me to an isolated corner of the lobby and talked about Las Vegas. Obviously "Mister Ell" was far removed from gaming casinos, hookers, and booze.

I asked him what he did for a living and he quietly said, "I'm a speculator." I had guessed right: He probably dabbled in wheat and grain futures. I dropped the subject. How he ever got invited to such a wingding puzzled me, but not for long. As we talked, I noticed four muscular gents with broken ears and noses to match forming a cordon between the mauling mob and "Mister Ell" and myself.

It certainly was a nice public-relations gesture on the part of the Riviera Hotel management, protecting a couple of its invited guests from being trampled.

Even though "Mister Ell" was a pleasant little fellow, I wasn't in the mood to talk about the wonders of Las Vegas or listen to wheat speculation and market trends. So I excused myself as politely as I knew how and started back into the casino. Looking behind, I noticed the four muscular gents escorting poor "Mister Ell" through a door that opened almost mysteriously as they got to it. And that was the last time I ever spoke to him.

But as I walked into the casino I asked the pit boss who introduced me to "Mister Ell" if that little man made any money in wheat. Tommy, the gaming boss, looked confused. Then he broke up.

Giving me one of those Hollywood double takes, Tommy whispered hoarsely, "You mean you don't know who 'Mister Ell' really is?"

Annoyed by his obvious imbecility, I snapped, "If I knew who that little jerk really was, would I be asking?"

By now Tommy had turned slightly green, and his graying hair seemed to be whitening as we talked. Grabbing me by the arm, he whisked me out onto the patio overlooking the bay.

"You stupid bastard," and he was still whispering hoarsely for fear of being overheard in nearby Miami. "That little guy was Meyer Lansky, you schmuck!" Then Tommy left in a hurry, assuming, of course, that I would do the right thing and hurl myself over the edge of the patio and onto the rocks bordering the bay far below.

All I could do was stand there with a silly grin on my face, muttering over and over again, "That nice little guy with the pleasant brown eyes was Meyer Lansky, the brains of the Mafia? A wheat speculator, my ass!"

Oh, somewhere in this troubled land birds are singing and children are romping through the streets while some columnists dream of getting the ideal story before they write -30- to their careers. I had the notorious Meyer Lansky all by myself in a corner and what did I talk about? Las Vegas, Boulder Dam, and the odds on the Keno games.

Six months later, when I returned to Havana, Castro was in control. He and his ragged followers had taken over in the otherwise nearly empty Riviera Hotel. Tourism was at a standstill, and the Beard was sounding off every twenty minutes on the hour. And that night, before I returned to the States, I had dinner with Meyer Lansky's brother and right-hand man, Jake. Also in the party were a vacationing Congressman, Adam Clayton Powell, and a blonde companion.

We were among the last Americans to visit the hotel before it became a regal, magnificently adorned YMCA for Castro and his followers. The next time I run into Meyer Lansky— and it will probably be in Tel Aviv if he's still a resident there, I must remind the man about those days at the opening of the Riviera Hotel when he had me thinking he dabbled in wheat and grains.

PEARLIE WUZ A LADY

The lady, no newcomer to show business or the Las Vegas saloons, is probably the most complex, lovable soul I ever met in the City of "Lost Wages" (a title frowned on mightily by the Chamber of Commerce and the gaming bosses). I've been the recipient not only of her enormous friendship but her awesome venom.

In the time I've known her—more than a quarter of a century—this lady has always been a combination of Billy Graham, Ma Barker, the late Martin Luther King, Jr., and Aimee Semple MacPherson. A joyous soul, she would just as likely worry about a Las Vegas chorine with terrible problems or a waiter who had a skin rash and needed advice. Add a pixyish sense of humor to all her qualities, and you could have a blurred bird's-eye view of a remarkable performer named Pearlie Mae Bailey.

I spent many a night catching her openings here in Las Vegas. But one in particular stands out like a huge fried egg hanging from a handlebar mustache.

Pearlie Mae was always resurrecting, evangelizing, and making like a vice president in charge of staging comebacks for old stars no longer in the business. And, if you got her in a reminiscent mood, she'd gladly tell you of those wretched nights back East when she would sing, hustle drinks, and try conning the lowly beer drinker in third-rate clubs for that extra buck if she would sing a song for him and his party.

This particular time, Pearlie May came into Las Vegas to star at the Flamingo Hotel. With her on the bill was none other than Harry Richman, trying to stage a comeback. That was as likely as Tiny Tim's stepping into Frank Sinatra's shoes.

Richman had been a great star in his time. In his seventies when Pearl brought him into the Flamingo, he suffered from a chronic respiratory ailment.

I knew that asking him to sing on the Pearl Bailey Show had to be sheer disaster, because I had heard Harry try to sing at a benefit several weeks earlier in New York City. He couldn't have improved that speedily.

I tried reasoning with Pearl the afternoon before the opening-night show. But the Ma Barker in her prevailed. She was determined to help Harry Richman launch a comeback, and nothing was going to change her mind—not even Ralph Pearl.

Naturally, the show was an embarrassing debacle. Harry tried to sing, but harsh, raspy sounds came out instead. The café-goers in the room fidgeted and got involved with their lamb chops. Harry refused to quit. He kept right on singing.

The following day I lambasted Pearl in my column for submitting poor Harry Richman to such torturous, undignified moments. Sure, he needed the money. But Pearl could easily have used Harry in the act to highlight several Richman tunes from the past, the way she would sing them. All Harry had to do was sit at the side of the stage and reminisce.

Pearl Bailey didn't forget that column. She didn't talk to me for a full year. Then, one night, she came back to the Flamingo, saw me sitting at ringside and gave me a large, toothy smile of recognition. The feud was over. Or so I wanted to believe.

Toward the end of the show, her line of girls swirled everywhere onstage singing and dancing while Pearl started a closing "Won't You Come Home, Bill Bailey?" chorus.

Then she suddenly reached down at ringside, grabbed my hand, and yanked me up on the stage to join her in the closing routine. I accepted with much reluctance. I didn't relish the idea of making myself an idiot in front of all those people. However, the feud was over and I wanted to be cooperative. Pearl pushed me toward the girls, who surrounded me and began pushing and shoving at my robust little Jewish body.

I took it good-naturedly. After all, it was part of Pearlie Mae's closing number. Now the girls pushed me back toward Pearl. I should have seen that look of evil on her jovial countenance. Ma Barker was coming out in her again.

Standing about ten feet from me, Pearl loudly asked how

come my fly was open. Sure enough, not only was my fly open, but part of my shirttail was sticking out. The roars of laughter from the boozers, losers, and lovers out front—not to mention the hilarity enjoyed by those onstage—were painful moments that come back to haunt me several times a year.

Pearl and her cast vow to this day they had nothing to do with that spectacular rearrangement of my trousers. But she never fails to remind me of that fly opening whenever we meet, whether in Las Vegas, New York, Miami, or Hollywood.

As a matter of fact, after I dashed off the stage that night clutching my fly like a desperate mother grabbing a falling child, Pearl wanted to sign me then and there to travel with her and do that same bit on her show.

"It would be the greatest show-stopper I've ever seen," she said. As I ungratefully declined, I made a mental note never to accost Pearl Bailey again until I had carefully checked the region of my crotch.

SAMMY DAVIS, JR.

One summer, while I was guesting on the Mike Douglas TV talk show, that pleasant, affluent Hibernian asked me if I would care to give his viewers my choice of the five most popular entertainers ever to play Las Vegas. Without hesitation, I rattled off Judy Garland, Frank Sinatra, Tony Newley, Danny Thomas, and Sammy Davis, Jr. And just to put some icing on that cake, I threw in such fancy honorable mentions as Mitzi Gaynor, Tom Jones, Elvis Presley, and Dean Martin. To this day I don't know why I left out Barbra Streisand and didn't mention that Elvis Presley had broken all attendance records. Maybe subconsciously I thought mostly of the old-timers.

Mike then asked me to recall the most important show-business story I'd written in my twenty years in Las Vegas. I backed away by explaining it had to be an impossible task, especially with the director flashing a "one minute to go" to Douglas as a wrap-up.

However, if there had been a bit more air time, I could have told Mike's twenty million television viewers about a night back in 1954 when a young, Black, blockbusting dynamo, Sammy Davis, Jr., was getting ready to leave by automobile immediately after he and his father, Sammy, Sr., and Uncle Will Mastin finished their midnight show at the old Last Frontier Hotel.

It wasn't the most important story I ever wrote, but for sheer nostalgia I had to remember that one. Sammy had an auto and his chauffeur, Charlie, waiting in front of the hotel. The guy would drive him to Hollywood and get him there about eight o'clock in the morning—in time for Sammy to put in about six hours recording a couple of sides, then jump into the car and get back to Las Vegas in time to do the dinner show.

Sammy, of course, would sleep in the back of the car and be as fresh as possible for his recording chores. Sammy apologized to me for backing away from an interview that had already been set up. "I'll talk to you tomorrow night when I get back, Ralph."

Things were starting to move for the three of them. They'd played every miserable cellar and attic in the nation for more than twenty-five years. Now things were looking up. The bosses at the Last Frontier wanted them back a couple of times a year for "fancy money," which happened to be $7,500 a week.

Sammy patted me on the back, "See you." Then he got into the car behind the wheel while his buddy, Charlie, would sleep for a couple of hours before taking over the driving from Sammy. The big black Caddy pulled away from the curb and headed for the highway leading to Los Angeles.

And as the huge marquee in front of the Last Frontier Hotel flashed on and off, "Will Mastin Trio—Starring Sammy Davis, Jr.," Sammy stuck his little black head out of the car and waved back at me standing there in front of the hotel.

It was approximately 2:10 in the morning of that chilly November day. I cursed him out quietly because if he had alerted me in time I would have been home in bed by now.

"Oh well, I can always catch up with him tomorrow night after the dinner show," I consoled myself as the wind howled and the sand blew steadily against my unprotected sinuses.

I would like to be able to note that I had a fierce premonition of doom as I trudged homeward, and then slept badly all night worrying about Sammy and Charlie. The truth is, I slept like a dead horse.

It seemed like five minutes later I was being awakened forcibly by seven hands. It was a worried Roz who was shaking me, "The office is calling. Sammy Davis has been in an auto accident just outside San Bernardino and is on the critical list." I staggered out of bed. It was about seven in the morning. I called the hospital. Sammy had many lacerations and internal injuries, also one blind eye. Charlie, sleeping in the back seat of the car, had suffered lacerations and a busted jaw.

A week later I got a wire from Sammy. It read, "Sorry I had to miss that interview, Ralph. Make it up to you when I get back to Las Vegas." But many months went by before Sammy was able to get around again. When he did, he wore a black patch where once had been a gleaming, happy eye.

After his hospital siege, Sammy was transferred to his home in Los Angeles, and I went to visit him. I didn't wait too long to come up with dopey question number one: "Will this cause you to give up show business, Sammy?"

Terribly drawn and still showing bruises on his face, Sammy snapped, "How long did it take you to come up with such a brilliant question, you stupid bastard?"

78

He was right. I was a stupid bastard for asking such an inane question of a lad whose very life and soul were made up of greasepaint, footlights, and spotlights.

"I'll bow out of this business only when the old guy in whiskers with the scythe comes after me. You know that."

Two months later Sammy and his papa and uncle were back playing Las Vegas. He didn't hesitate to poke fun at himself and that black patch over his left eye. He was greater than ever.

Sammy would bounce out onstage, gingerly point at the eye patch, then say, "I'm the only three-handicap golfer in all of show business. I have one eye, I'm Black, and I'm also Jewish. And you're gonna have to go a long way, baby, to find a golfer with more handicaps."

Now he was a member of the regal show-biz family of Sinatra, Dean Martin, Danny Thomas, Joey Bishop, and Lena Horne.

Suddenly Sammy Davis, Jr., began blossoming out as a swinger. He was being seen in the West and East Coast niteries with blonde, blue-eyed girls. And the world wondered, because Sammy Davis, Jr., wasn't exactly a Cary Grant or a Harry Belafonte in the looks department. But then again, Cary and Harry didn't have Sammy's personality and charisma. The white girls loved him. And, of course, it made things worse when Sammy converted to Judaism. His Black brethren accused him of "showboating."

But Sammy wasn't listening. It seemed as if he was deadly suspicious of Dame Fortune and wasn't taking any more chances of wasting away his young life when there was so much out there just for the taking. He carried on like he was living on a twenty-four-hour pass.

On that historic three-weeker I wrote of earlier when Frank Sinatra and the "Clan" opened at the Sands Hotel, one of the prettier, sexier Hollywood starlets in town with Frank was Kim Novak. A merry time was had by all that weekend. But the eventual upshot of it all was that Frank had lost a girl friend, because she was now hopelessly in love with Samala, the three-handicap "golfer."

So began a love affair that was international in impact. The Hollywood busybodies began whispering and giggling. The gossip columnists had a field day dropping items about "Beauty and the Beast."

Kim Novak, under contract to Columbia Pictures, had already made a couple of high-budget movies for Harry Cohn, which hadn't been released yet. Cohn was screaming in typical Cohn fashion about "that little Black bastard who'll cost me five million dollars if he marries Novak, the dumb Polack broad." And he wasn't just making with his mouth, because many movie exhibitors in the South and Southwest, aware that a marriage was imminent between Kim and Sammy, didn't want to book any of her pictures in their houses.

But Sammy and Kim didn't give a damn about all the confusion they were causing. All they knew was they were in love and "fuck everybody and his grandmother if they don't approve."

The more opposition, the more they were determined to get married. But Harry Cohn of Columbia Pictures was the kind of man who never heard of Cupid. He called the late Jack Entratter at the Sands one morning and screamed all sorts of dire threats on Sammy's head if he didn't stay away from Novak. It wasn't a good time for Cohn, who was then suffering from a bad heart—medically, that is.

"Jesus Christ, Jack," Harry screamed, "I wouldn't mind if she fell in love with Harry Belafonte, but with an ugly little momser like Davis, I can't believe it."

Now the pressure was being put on Sammy's Chicago backers, some being legit, the others not so legit. They descended on Sammy in force. And when the conference was over, Cupid ran for his life. Some of the niteries as well as TV and movie people had quietly threatened to keep not only Kim but also Sammy out of work.

One morning I got a wire from Sammy Davis, Jr., inviting me to a wedding—his wedding to a Black dancer, Loray White—who was then working at the Silver Slipper. The quickie marriage at the Sands Hotel fooled nobody. Not only had Sammy and Kim made sacrifices but Harry Cohn, who had almost burst a blood vessel in his attempts to break up Kim and Sammy, finally had to pay the extreme penalty. He suffered a fatal heart attack exactly thirteen months after Sammy and Loray married—a marriage that was annulled by Sammy within four months.

It didn't take Sammy too long to put out the torch he supposedly carried for the blonde, blue-eyed love goddess, Kim Novak, because less than a year later he was "terribly in love" with another blue-eyed, blonde love goddess, movie actress Mai Britt.

Davis was now flying high as one of the top performers in all of show business. At about the time he had completely stolen the Royal Command Performance and was personally thanked by Queen Elizabeth, the news got out that Sammy and Mai were a hot twosome. Sammy's romp with Kim Novak had been child's play compared to what he faced when it was announced that he and Mai would have an October wedding in Beverly Hills.

Starring at the Pigalle in London, Sammy had to fight his way through a band of pickets wearing swastika armbands and carrying signs: "Go Home Nigger . . . Sammy, Go Back to the Trees!" The pickets were members of Nazi Sir Oswald Moseley's band of degenerates.

Sammy and Mai couldn't wait to get out of London. They landed in Los Angeles and were driven almost immediately to the Democratic National Convention, where Frank Sinatra and a gang of performers were turning out for John F. Kennedy's drive for the nomination.

Sammy and Mai started mixing with their own, and then Sammy was introduced. Despite a strong round of applause, a sizable group in the hall began booing Sammy loudly and clearly. First London, now here at home among his own people! The mere fact that Sammy had converted to Judaism and now announced that his intended wife, Mai Britt, would also convert, had brought out the bigots, full force.

The poison began spreading around the nation. The Nazi storm troopers turned out to meet Sammy when he arrived in Washington to appear at the Lotus Club. Again the pickets and the signs were there, vilifying Sammy and Mai. Their next stop was the Sands Hotel in Las Vegas, and they were more determined than ever to go through with their October wedding in a Beverly Hills synagogue.

Sammy and Mai, of course, vowed this would be a marriage for life. They did get married, did suffer at the hands of bigots, but carved out a domestic life against heavy odds.

Less than a year after the marriage, Sammy sat in the lobby of a Beverly Hills hospital, tears streaming down his face after Mai had given birth to a five-pound, six-ounce girl, their first.

Emotionally strung out, Sammy vowed then and there his enormous love for Mai, vowed his eternal loyalty, and pledged himself to the good life. But less than four years and another child later, he and Mai Britt were divorced.

Now Sammy is married to a dancer who worked in some of his café shows. She's not blonde and blue-eyed or a temperamental movie actress. She's just Altovise, a nice Black lady who wants to make a good life for her little Black genius, Sammy Davis, Jr.

As Sammy has said many times onstage in a café, "What the future holds, baby, only da Shadow knows!"

MARIO LANZA

Several months before the fabulous Mario Lanza died, he sent me a note which read, "Dear Ralph: Thank you so much for the most flattering review in your Las Vegas *Sun*'s 'Vegas Daze and Nites,' your widely read column. I shall treasure it always as something that could have been but never was. The next time you're in Los Angeles, please drop over to the house so we can have dinner and re-hash that horrible night at the New Frontier. Regards, Mario."

"Could have been but never was?" "Horrible night?" To the reader those words must sound confusing from a star who had just gotten a flattering review on his nitery debut in Las Vegas. If only it was that simple to explain!

But let me take you back to that night in the summer of 1958 when the great movie and opera star, Mario Lanza, was getting ready to open at the New Frontier Hotel.* It hadn't been a simple decision on Lanza's part. After all, Las Vegas was a gaming spa with booze and broads and blackjack. Maybe it would be too tempting for him. But the bosses at the New Frontier came up with such a fancy salary Lanza couldn't turn it down. He would get $50,000 a week for four weeks.

So, here he was in a fancy suite at the hotel. More than a hundred newsmen from all over America and some from England had checked in for Lanza's debut. The reservations for Lanza's four weeks of shows were all gone. It looked promising. And the $50,000-a-week salary wouldn't be too hard to take either. Lanza's assets were in a jumbled state. A couple of Hollywood pals, up for the show, told me he was at the point of bankruptcy.

---

* Since 1945, when the Last Frontier Hotel opened its doors for business, the hotel has undergone a couple of name changes. It was the "New Frontier" from 1956 until Howard Hughes bought the hotel and changed it again, this time to just plain "Frontier," which it is now as we go to press in the summer of 1972.

So, the New Frontier debut was Mario Lanza's point of no return. This had to be it. And though he had alienated not only all of his movie bosses but many in the movie trade by his outrageous behavior, a goodly portion of stars came up for the Lanza show. Maybe some even were there to gloat if he fell on his whiskey-soaked ass, in front of eight hundred people.

Tense and deadly serious for the first time in years, Lanza prepared for his Vegas debut by going on a rigid diet for almost three weeks before coming to Las Vegas. Now, hours before his show he was petrified and he had to unwind. "I'm going out for an hour. Be right back," he told his wife Betty and his anxious manager.

That night I sat greatly depressed in my regular pew off ringside trying to eat my dinner. But it was no use. The lamb chops tasted stringy. "Maybe you should first take off the paper panties on the chops," suggested my wife Roz.

Good idea. They really did taste better without the paper doilies. But I was still as nervous as a cat in a dog pound. Will he be ready? Won't he be ready? I looked in the direction of the New Frontier bosses sitting in an adjoining booth. I felt slightly comforted. They, too, were swallowing their lamb chops, paper panties and all.

There was an electric excitement in that opening-night throng. The mere thought that Mario Lanza would soon be singing in a café had really tensed up those first-nighters.

Already suspended by MGM, Mario had practically thrown his enormous career into the toilet. His drunken sprees were now being hinted at in the newspaper columns around the country. Female stars begged off working with him because of his tantrums.

So, I sat with one of the New Frontier bosses, who was utterly unaware of Lanza's psychopathic behavior. All he knew was what many millions of Lanza fans knew around the world: that with a talent like Lanza going to make his debut

84

here, soon every newspaper in the nation—also around the world—would be carrying the story of the Mario Lanza triumph. Such publicity for a brand-new group of Frontier bosses who wanted to get off on the right foot!

"Irving," I noted dolefully, "I'm afraid of Lanza. He hasn't been acting well these past couple of years." Irving laughed at my old-maidish fears.

If ever I had been right in predictions, that was the day. Mario Lanza, who skyrocketed to fame and fortune and international stardom, fizzled out like an imitation firecracker at thirty-eight, twelve years after coming to Hollywood. If ever I wanted to see a man succeed gloriously in his Las Vegas debut, it was Alfred Cocozza, a simple soul with the voice that would never be forgotten by a grieving world.

Unfortunately, his New Frontier booking came a couple of years too late. His addiction for booze and food had reached tragic proportions. And no matter how he suffered to abstain, it was just a matter of days before he would break out in a roaring, drunken orgy. Already alerted by Mario's manager, the Frontier bosses told all the employees at the hotel to see that Lanza didn't get a drop of whiskey. That had never stopped him before. But now he was determined to stick with it. This four-weeker could do more to launch his movie comeback than any other project.

A small gathering of hard-eyed agents in the room started making book on Lanza. One guy went so far as to offer three to one Lanza would never finish out the night's opening show. Then I began remembering the horrible stories about Lanza during the past year. How he had gone on a rampage like a wild bull in a fancy meat market just the month before. How he despised one movie mogul at MGM so violently that he had gone to the man's swanky home in Bel Air during a party, peed on the front doorstep, then rang the bell before dashing off into the night utterly bereft of his senses.

Well, it wouldn't be long now.

Now it was 8:15 and a restless, keyed up throng of opening-nighters waited for the show to start. But there seemed to be a delay, as there usually is on opening nights. Now it was 8:30 and still no Mario Lanza. Then one of the bosses of the New Frontier came onstage to tell the people, "There'll be another slight delay before the show starts." Every ten minutes after that came an explanation until finally at 9:30 the beaming boss made another appearance and said, "Mario Lanza will be here in fifteen minutes."

With a 9:45 deadline staring me coldly in the face, that announcement reassured me that a show with the super-star, Lanza, was about to begin. But I couldn't wait for Lanza—otherwise I'd blow my deadline. So I rushed to a house phone, called the *Sun*, and dictated a glowing account of Mario Lanza's debut at the New Frontier. "Seldom in the history of this town has a star done a greater show or received such a standing ovation." I only dictated a three-paragraph story, but it would suffice until I really caught the show and did a follow-up for the following day.

Then I returned to my table, put some sugar cubes in my coffee, and took a couple of sips before realizing that I had just sweetened a cup of cold soup, which the waiter had failed to remove in all the excitement. But a few minutes of discomfort meant nothing. My Mario Lanza story was finished and my review would be out on the street about the same time this show was over.

Just then the owner came onstage again. He had the look of a mortician filing a bankruptcy petition. All the more ominous, he tried clearing his throat several times unsuccessfully, then said, "I regret to inform you that Mario Lanza will not appear tonight because of a severe throat condition."

I was already on the run for the phones before the last syllable was uttered. Maybe I could still stop that Mario Lanza review. I jiggled the hook nervously and finally got the operator, who said, "Mr. Pearl, there is a power shortage on the Strip right now and we can't get any calls through."

More running. By now I was frothing at the mouth while large tears streamed down my face. I jumped into a cab and headed for the *Sun* downtown. I got there just in time to see the *Sun* trucks pulling away with the first edition of the paper, so I headed back to the Strip and made instant plans to head for Mexico or Tahiti, whichever cost less by Greyhound bus.

What had happened to Mario Lanza? Simple. Utterly petrified at the thought of facing a sellout throng in a gaming-town hotel, he had taken many pills and enough booze in a nearby bar to launch a dreadnought. Came time to do the show and Lanza was out. He was so bombed he would have had a problem standing—no less singing.

Twelve hours later, much chagrined and sporting a huge hangover, Lanza decided that night clubs weren't for him. He took off for Los Angeles and left behind him at the New Frontier Hotel enough tranquillizer pills for a thousand breakdowns. A couple of weeks later, now back on his feet, Lanza saw the irony of that nightmare in Las Vegas, also my column about his sensational opening at the Frontier.

But that didn't end the Mario Lanza fiasco for me. In the room that night for the Lanza show that never showed was an author from New York City. He was writing a book about the strange happenings in show business.

When his book came out, there was a chapter devoted to the Mario Lanza "no show" episode, and a word-for-word reprint of my review on Lanza. Lanza never read that book because he died a couple of weeks before.

After that unfortunate Lanza review in my column, the whole town and many of the stars on the Strip made sure they wouldn't let me forget it. Jerry Lewis called one afternoon and said, "Hey, listen, I've got a bad cold. Would you

mind phoning in a good review on the show I won't do tonight?"

SOPHIE FELDMAN OF HARTFORD

Sophie Feldman stood behind the counter of Meyer Lemmelman's candy store in downtown Hartford dreaming of
the day she would be standing at the Copa in Manhattan or
the Sands Hotel in Las Vegas singing her songs and telling
stories in her inimitable way. And as she dreamed, she sold
candy to pimply-faced kids, elderly ladies, and careless old
men with high cholesterol counts.

Now there were no more customers in the store, so she
scooped up a handful of chocolate-covered almonds and
gobbled them down hungrily. Sophie Feldman needed chocolate-covered almonds like Jackie Gleason needs banana
cream pie in his daily diet. Only four feet ten, Sophie tipped
the scales at 195 and would never be picked as a look-alike
for Raquel Welch. But she couldn't help it. Candy made Sophie forget how she hated working behind a counter.

What made it all the more difficult to bear, many of her
friends and relatives—even many of her steady customers in
Lemmelman's candy store—who had heard Sophie tell stories and sing, swore she could make it big in show business.
True, Sophie Feldman wasn't kidding herself. A movie queen
she'd never be. But, though she was moonfaced and bloated,
her eyes were a beautiful purple. Like Elizabeth Taylor's.

All finished with the almonds, Sophie reached into the
showcase and came up with another handful, this time chocolate-covered pecans. She gobbled them just as hungrily and
rapidly as she had the batch of almonds. Then she took another handful.

Should she quit her job in the store, as her relatives and
friends wanted her to do, and try show business? Or should

she continue working for Lemmelman until she got diabetes or some other awful sickness? What to do? What to do?

Now she had the answer. She returned the uneaten pecans to the case and wiped the chocolate off her chins. She'd made the first of two momentous decisions: one, to stop eating those god-damned chocolates.

The second decision: Go into show business.

After all, hadn't one of the greatest ladies in all of show business, Sophie Tucker, also from Hartford, made it big? And Sophie Feldman, who worshiped "The Last of the Red Hot Mamas," always panicked her relatives and friends with a damned good imitation of Sophie Tucker singing that song.

Early Monday morning Sophie Feldman went down to the store and told Mister Lemmelman she was quitting. It wasn't an easy decision because Sophie had developed an enormous affection for much of Mister Lemmelman's chocolates, especially his chocolate-covered pecans. However, if and when she became a great success in show business, what the hell, she could buy herself a couple of Lemmelman candy stores.

Sophie Feldman had decided to take a stab at show business. Mister Lemmelman, untouched, told her in sarcastic Yiddish tones, "I'm sure you'll starve."

Now all Sophie Feldman had to do was get herself a singing job in a small club in Hartford. It was then she suffered her first setback. There were no small clubs in Hartford. There weren't even any big clubs in Hartford. However, she was told, there were many small clubs in Boston. It would be the ideal place for an embryonic singing comedienne.

During the ensuing three years, Sophie Feldman, who had long since changed her name to Totie Fields, had plenty of problems getting jobs. They were few and far between. But, as she worked a small club in South Boston, she met and married a comic on the same bill, George Johnson. Not only were they blissfully happy, but they really found it easier to get club dates.

Soon, however, Totie went back to working as a single.

And it was while she filled in one Saturday night at the famous Concord Hotel in upstate New York that I first caught Totie Fields in the showroom. She was an opening act for Steve Lawrence and Eydie Gorme, and was getting an unheard of (for her, at least) $300 for her night's work.

Out came a prancing Totie Fields. She was determined to be a big hit that night because her friends, Steve and Eydie, kidding her, had said, "Ralph Pearl, one of the owners of the Desert Inn in Las Vegas, is sitting out front. And if you make a good showing, you might get booked into the D-I."

Totie was so bad that I felt sorry for the kid. Her jokes were ancient and her delivery a bit too rugged even for that popular Borscht Belt resort hotel. However, still optimistic, she couldn't wait to finish her act before she was in the showroom hunting me out for my reaction.

"Totie, first let me explain that I'm not a Desert Inn owner but a columnist in Las Vegas. I'm afraid that any plans you may have had to play Las Vegas will have to be scuttled. You just don't have the talent."

I didn't see Totie for five years. Then one night in June of 1967 she opened in the lounge at the Riviera Hotel for $5,000 a week. It was impossible to believe that the Totie onstage and the one I'd seen back in New York were one and the same. What was even more phenomenal, three years after her opening in the lounge at the Riviera, she went into the hotel's showroom for $35,000 a week, and is today considered by this columnist to be one of the funniest performers (male or female) in the whole café business.

The Sophie Feldman of the late Fifties, who ate more chocolate candies than she sold in Mister Lemmelman's store, had finally made all her relatives, friends, and customers look good because they had predicted greatness for Sophie Feldman despite Meyer Lemmelman and Ralph Pearl's caustic comments.

WILBUR CLARK

Several weeks after coming to Las Vegas in 1953, I felt like many others who were settling here—this was the place for instant wealth. I hadn't been a native Las Vegan long before I got the urge to try my luck in the gaming casino—specifically at the Desert Inn blackjack tables. I wasn't looking for instant wealth. Hell, I was more than willing to take several days, maybe even a week, to accumulate $10,000 or so. And when I had it, that would be the time to gather up my typewriter, my wife Roz, an autographed picture of the greatest fourth estater in the history of journalism, Damon Runyon, who had gotten me that first job as a New York sports writer back in 1939, and head for the Island of St. Lucia in the Windward Passage.

Sitting at a comfortable Desert Inn "21" table, I started out playing a dollar at a time. As I played, I noticed that a distinguished, white-haired gent, Wilbur Clark, entered the gaming pit and stood behind the dealer watching me play. An elegant gent in his cashmere jacket and silk shirt, Clark looked on with a slightly amused smile on his face.

Well, he wouldn't be smiling much longer, especially when I started on a lengthy winning streak. We chatted briefly about the weather and the fact that Patti Page was the current attraction at the Desert Inn.

And as I gambled, I thought about the fabulous Wilbur Clark, whom I had met only briefly once before when I had started my column on the *Sun* ten days before. This Clark was a national figure in more ways than one.

In 1947 he had started building the Desert Inn with his two brothers and several small investors who raised $300,000. It didn't last too long and construction came to a halt. And that's the way it was for the next twenty months, the bare wooden structures bleaching under summer suns and discoloring under howling winter sands.

Now it was 1949 and a gent by the name of Moe Dalitz came all the way from Cleveland to chat with Clark, maybe even "invest a couple of dollars" in his still-to-be-completed hotel on the Strip just across the street from the prospering Last Frontier Hotel. When the chatting was all over, Clark had gotten himself a new partner. As a matter of fact, he had gotten himself *five* new partners, because Dalitz brought the members of his "Corporation," The Mayfielders from Cleveland, also along.

When the papers were all signed nice and neatly, Dalitz and Company owned seventy-four percent of the Desert Inn. It was they who saw to it that the D-I was completed with neatness and dispatch. Actually, poor Wilbur, who had suffered for several years in getting his project off the ground, could now relax with his six percent and a tidy weekly sum for as long as the arrangement lasted. The other twenty percent? That went to several more experienced gaming gents Dalitz brought in from Miami, New Orleans, and Arkansas.

Wilbur was strictly showcase dressing for the Dalitz group. He had absolutely no voice in the operation of the Desert Inn—even though the huge neon sign, the menus, the bedding, the gaming chips, and the promotional matter all advertised it as "Wilbur Clark's Desert Inn."

He was, of course, one of the greatest "handshakers" in all of Las Vegas, knew all the top athletes, U.S. senators, and big gamblers. And he didn't hesitate to tell his "life story," a most absorbing one, if he could get the syndicated columnists and feature writers in a corner. Not only was he a remarkably good public-relations man for the Desert Inn, he didn't do the city of Las Vegas any harm either.

Clark would gladly tell you he had been a bellhop at the old Knickerbocker Hotel in San Diego, not to mention many other sundry kinds of menial labor he did before he drifted to Reno, where gaming had suddenly become a legalized pastime. However, Wilbur didn't stay long in Reno. Another bellhop at that Reno hotel had told Clark he was going to work on a gambling ship outside Long Beach, California. Clark went along.

That job lasted as long as the one at the Knickerbocker Hotel in San Diego and the other one in Reno. However, when Wilbur got the hell out of Long Beach, he had become saturated with the gaming fever. Where else to go? Las Vegas, of course. That's where the gaming and the opportunities were positively big league.

After almost eight months of sucking in sand and slowly getting a complex from the clinging creosote bushes that grew outside his room just off the Strip, which then consisted of the El Rancho Vegas and Last Frontier, Clark managed to get himself a small working interest in the El Rancho Vegas Hotel. That proved to be the nucleus he would need in 1947 to start plotting his brainchild, the Desert Inn.

Though Wilbur was well off financially after Dalitz & Company opened the Desert Inn for him, he was still a frustrated man who tried to rid himself of those aches and pains by playing the horses and betting huge sums of money on football games, fights, and which way the sand would be blowing at the airport in exactly one hour.

Clark was really a paper prince in a false kingdom. He welcomed the VIP's, posed for pictures with royalty and the nation's leading statesmen, but couldn't get his favorite nephew a job at the Desert Inn even as a busboy unless he asked the personnel manager himself.

But it didn't matter to the outside gaming world, who didn't really know and cared less. To them Wilbur Clark was a well-dressed man whose picture they'd seen in *Life* Magazine posing with his wife after being presented to the Pope at the Vatican. During the last few years of his life, Wilbur Clark began investing his and his friends' money in business ventures in and outside Las Vegas. Many failed.

That's when he would quietly retire to his million-dollar

home on the Desert Inn golf course and try rebuilding his ego as well as his depleted bankroll. The "Wilbur Clark House" was, of course, a sightseer's delight as it rested just off the eighteenth hole of that golf course shining like one of Cartier's special rubies in his Fifth Avenue front window. Clark was so proud of his house, he talked about it to anyone who would listen.

It was Clark's greatest asset. As a matter of fact, it would become a landmark after he was gone. But as long as he was alive and kicking, that was his only "baby." That and his wife, Toni, who had once been a D-I cocktail waitress.

Built on four acres of plush green landscaping, the house had been carefully constructed along the lines of a small Roman palace, with marble pillars all around the swimming pool and the finest of everything, from silk and satin bedding to thick rugs, mahogany furniture, stereophonic music in every room, and a specially built electric eye at the front door. You pressed the bell and your image flashed on several screens in the house—even in the toilet.

Clark's health began to fail, maybe because he had to testify at the Kefauver Hearings in the early Fifties, along with Dalitz and his associates, about a crime syndicate tie-in. Having suffered a coronary before, Clark had another one several months after the investigations. Hence, it was comforting to be able to stray through the many rooms of his palatial "Roman Palace," completely shut off from crime investigations and aggravating daily confrontations with his "partners" at the Desert Inn.

"Wilbur Clark's Desert Inn" was one of the most prosperous gaming hotels in Las Vegas, but the man whose name glittered brilliantly from the huge marquee over the hotel was really a wealthy patsy who could only brag about his Inn to those who were oblivious to the behind-the-scenes power control there.

Early in the summer of 1965 he had another coronary and

a stroke. But just when it looked as if he would recover again, Wilbur Clark, the good-will ambassador of Las Vegas, up and died in August of that year. The man who had hustled almost all his life was fifty-eight years old. On his pinkie finger was a ring with many diamonds forming the numbers, "'07," which was the year he was born.

For several hours before he died, Wilbur Clark was doing what he liked best: betting on the horses at Santa Anita Park via the phone from his hospital bed. He had phoned in a bet on "Roustabout," his own horse, which was running later that day at Santa Anita. But he never got a chance to learn that the horse came in first and paid $39. He had succumbed an hour earlier.

Naturally, at the funeral, his "loving partners" stood bareheaded and solemn as many kind things were said about him at graveside. Some of the "boys" even had tears in their eyes. But what would have pleased Wilbur most, his obituary in newspapers around the nation glowed with adjectives about his many worthwhile deeds in this Show Capital of the World.

And though his name no longer sparkled in bright neon just over the name "Desert Inn" the way it did for many years (it was taken down when Howard Hughes bought the Desert Inn in 1966), many people around the nation still refer to the D-I as "Wilbur Clark's Desert Inn" when talking about Las Vegas. And that's exactly the way it should be.

Now, having digressed thirteen years in the twinkle of several pages, let me go back to that afternoon as I sat at the Desert Inn blackjack table playing dollar for dollar while Wilbur Clark stood behind the dealer smirking good-naturedly.

I was now a $15 winner and going full steam ahead. Clark came over. "Ralph, can the house get you a drink?" I politely thanked him, then refused the free libation. I was wise to his generosity. He wanted to get me drunk so I'd start gambling recklessly and probably blow all my winnings, that's what.

Clark walked away and I continued my streak. Twenty minutes later I was $32 ahead, and I hadn't made a bet larger than $3. I had to admit it was going to be painfully slow accumulating that $10,000 at this rate. Christ, it might be months before I reached that figure. But I wasn't going anywhere. Then I saw Wilbur Clark again.

He looked down, counted quickly, and said, "You're about $30 ahead. Why don't you quit?" Then he walked away, but not before he whispered something in my ear.

This time, after he strolled away, my luck vanished. I began losing steadily. In a matter of ten minutes I not only dropped back all my winnings, but also my original double sawbuck. I was crushed—momentarily. But I'd be back. Luckily for the gaming houses, that has been the rallying cry of many a gambler, "I'll be back."

I still piddle away at "21" with a sawbuck, maybe two if I'm in the dough that particular week, but always with the same results. I get ground out by the house. If I can win a few bucks, great. When I lose, I take to my bed and enjoy a good cry. I also remember that white-haired, elegant gent who could wear a different sweater, sport coat, shoes, shirt, or suit for three solid months without duplicating his attire.

"Ralph, the way you bet, the Desert Inn will never have to worry about your breaking the house," he had whispered so kindly in my ear that afternoon.

He had been so right. He had also been so right for this Show Capital of the World.

DON RICKLES, "MERCHANT OF VENOM"

Little Willie Weber, a man who had spent almost all of his adult life peddling second-rate acts to night clubs and theaters in the East, was here in Las Vegas to tell me about his latest find, "a comic who'll be the talk of the nation within three years." Sixty-five-year-old Weber had never had a client who was better than a second-rater. So I was overjoyed for his sake, because Willie was a salt-of-the-earth kind of a guy.

After he had come all the way out to Las Vegas to tell me about his "coming star," the least I could do was listen. Willie had been able to sell the Sahara on his client, and he was opening in the lounge of that hotel in two weeks.

But right now we sat in the hotel's coffee shop while Weber told me all about his new star. Then he pointed him out to me. The "star" was sitting at an adjoining table. Willie Weber had to be kidding me! That bald, sweating, pallid-looking guy was going to be Willie Weber's new star? I looked again, only this time I forced myself to stare.

True, I didn't expect to see a combination of Robert Goulet and Jerry Lewis, but that little fat guy sitting at the next table wolfing his scrambled eggs and setting off a strong glare as the light hit his bald pate had to be the wrong guy.

"Willie, you can't mean that fat little bald guy sitting over there with the sick-looking complexion! That's your big star? That's Don Rickles?"

Almost apologetically, Weber explained that I would forget what he looked like as soon as I saw his act. "He insults everybody in his audience, calls the women 'dogs' and the guys 'fags.' "

Now I was really confused. "And this guy Rickles is gonna be a big star within three years insulting people and calling guys fags?"

I must have spoken too loudly because the "star" stopped eating and gave me a nasty look, muttering something that sounded like, "Willie, who's the fat little fag you're sitting with?" Then he went back to his eggs.

The next afternoon Weber auditioned his "star" for some of the Sahara bosses, and I made it a point to sit in on that closed audition. Willie Weber wasn't kidding me when he said Rickles would be different from any act they had ever seen in Las Vegas. That he was.

Displaying a savage wit while constantly pacing up and down the stage, Rickles insulted everyone from the Sahara boss, Del Webb, down to the lad who guarded the door. And as he raved and ranted, never once letting up on his rapid-fire barrage of invectives, I looked over toward Willie once or twice and wondered if the veteran talent manager had lost his mind.

But the way it turned out after that spring afternoon in 1960, Willie was right and we were all wrong. Rickles was an oddity. People broke the doors down to get into the lounge to see that fat, sweaty, bald man berate everybody and everything. And even though many in the room walked away vowing they'd never submit to such embarrassment again, they were back again the next night to see Don Rickles.

That's what convinced me about Rickles' future. Deep down, people who came to see Rickles time and again really enjoyed being insulted by him. It inflated their egos in a left-handed manner. He made them feel important, believe it or not.

Leading all the laughter would be the Sahara president himself, Del Webb, Rickles' boss, who would take a tongue-lashing from the nervy gent who suddenly struck it rich after playing second- and third-rate clubs in Miami, Hollywood, and New York for almost ten years.

"That's my boss, Del Webb, sitting over there in the corner," Rickles would snarl while his eyes almost popped out of his pallid countenance. "Isn't this way past your bedtime, Mister Webb?" taunted Rickles. "Or have you gotten tired playing with your rubber ducks in the bathtub?" The losers, boozers, and lovers in the lounge roared, so Rickles would continue berating his boss until his beady, bloodshot eyes fell on another victim at ringside.

Grabbing the drink right out of the hand of his next "victim," Don would hold it up to the light and study it for a moment or two, give it back to the guy, then tell him, "I don't know how to tell you this, chum, but you've got sugar and should be dead before the end of the week."

Rickles has had an enormously successful career over the past dozen years. Recently, while I was talking with him in New York, he revealed that he had not only just signed a three-year contract with the Riviera Hotel in Las Vegas that would bring him $70,000 a week for ten weeks a year, but also a new TV show and a starring movie. I had to remember that afternoon back in 1960 when a little guy by the name of Willie Weber tried to convince me "that Don Rickles would be a big star within three years."

Willie Weber never got a chance to revel in the glory of Rickles' enormous successes because he was replaced as Don's manager three years after Don started playing Las Vegas. He died a year later, heartbroken and disillusioned.

ELVIS, "THE PELVIS"

Back in April of 1956, a bright young lad, who played a guitar and sang while gyrating as if his whole body was being racked by a fit, opened at the Last Frontier Hotel for two weeks. A big recording favorite in Nashville, Elvis Presley was now making his move for wider fields. And the gent behind Elvis was a dynamo by the name of Tom Parker, who had decided to give himself the imposing army rank of Colonel.

Presley had already made it in the recording field with his three hits, "Heartbreak Hotel," "Hound Dog," and "Blue Suede Shoes." The kids all over the nation were screaming his praises.

The bosses at the Last Frontier had decided to take a chance with this newcomer, even though some of the wiser ones rebelled. "What's a snot-nosed kid from Nashville

99

gonna do on a Las Vegas stage? Will he bring in craps shooters and blackjack players?"

The discussion went on for three hours before it was finally decided to sign Elvis Presley for two weeks at $8,500 a week. The way it turned out, the wiser heads had been right. Elvis was a flop. He played to more empty tables than customers. At the end of the first week, it was decided to let him go. Colonel Tom Parker, a brainy gent who had been in carnivals as a pitchman for years before taking on the late Gene "My Blue Heaven" Austin and Eddy Arnold, then finally Presley, screamed, "You bastards'll be sorry. The next time he plays Las Vegas you'll have to pay ten times more. Wait and see!"

Thirteen years later he was signed to open at the International Hotel, then owned by Kirk Kerkorian, for more than $100,000 a week.

During those thirteen years, Presley became an enormous record, television, and movie star. He came back to Las Vegas several times during that period to make a movie or two, also to catch some shows. And whenever Parker was approached by a Strip hotel owner to bring his lad into the showroom, Parker would gloat, then ask for (at that time) impossible sums of money.

Parker, the carny man who used to snag sparrows by the dozen, paint them yellow, and then sell them as canaries, held the upper hand. Presley was now being chased by every entertainment talent buyer in the business. The kid with the oscillating pelvis and colorful garb had finally made it big.

But back in 1956 when I first caught Elvis Presley on the Last Frontier stage, I told the bosses, "Fellers, you overpaid Presley $5,000 a week." Wisely, I had reported earlier, "Presley belongs in a Nashville theater where his young followers would come eagerly and in large crowds. Las Vegas showrooms are out of his league."

100

Years later, in the summer of 1969 when he opened at the International, I sat among two thousand others. Though many of the top café critics in the nation came in to catch Presley and raved about the lad from Tupelo, Mississippi, I still sourly noted, "Presley is a fine showman with an equally fine showcase, but his style of singing doesn't compel this columnist in the least."

But that sour notice didn't deter Presley, who has played the Hilton International Hotel many times since 1969. He has caused all sorts of jam-ups at the hotel as people from everywhere in the nation try every which way to get in to see him. To date he holds every record for attendance in a Las Vegas showroom.

Unquestionably the kid from Tupelo, whose papa had been a sharecropper, came a long way after those hectic days back in '56 when some of the Last Frontier bosses canceled out Presley after his first week.

Sitting with Elvis in his dressing room backstage at the New Frontier the night he had been canceled, I had tried to soothe the lad's rumpled feelings. But there was no need for it. Elvis didn't like Vegas then and still doesn't like Vegas. He would rather play theaters, and make movies and television spectaculars.

Looking even prettier than a girl, Presley fingered the cancellation memo sent down by the Last Frontier bosses. Then he grinned sheepishly, as if caught in his papa's barn back in Tupelo smoking a cigarette, and said, "I always wanted to play Las Vegas. So I did. Now I'll go on from here."

That he did, and with a vengeance. Six months later he starred in a 20th Century-Fox movie, *Love Me Tender*, then did fourteen more big-budget pictures before returning to Las Vegas as the conquering hero in a sleep provoker titled, *Viva Las Vegas*, made by Metro-Goldwyn-Mayer Studios in 1964.

During the shooting of that picture, I visited Elvis on the set. We hadn't seen each other since that night in his dressing room a few minutes after he had been fired.

Grinning from ear to ear, Presley cracked, "Hey, haven't I seen you somewhere before?" Then he thought for a few seconds while I stood there with a silly grin on my face. Finally he brightened, "Oh yeah, you're the columnist who told me eight years ago I didn't belong here. Right?"

LIBERACE, THE KID FROM MILWAUKEE

I first met him in 1945 when I was here to do a story for a Los Angeles newspaper about the progress being made by Benjamin "Bugsy" Siegel on his Flamingo Hotel. Playing in one of the only two Strip hotels in existence then, Liberace worked in the lounge at the Last Frontier Hotel by playing a lot of commercial piano. By "commercial" I mean the kind of songs you'd heard Jeanette MacDonald and Nelson Eddy sing on the screen.

He left Bach, Beethoven, and Debussy to concert pianists who weren't about to prostitute their art, or ever earn more than miserly sums of money annually. Liberace, though he only got $400 a week at that time from the bosses at the Last Frontier, had grandiose plans about one day earning "thousands of dollars weekly." The kid with wavy hair and feminine complexion had a scheme, but it didn't take shape until early in the Fifties when he began wearing garish costumes. Or is "garish" the proper word to describe costumes of lace, satin, silk, and furs heavily embellished with rhinestones and maybe even an occasional diamond?

It stood to reason Liberace had to be a courageous man to wear those kinds of costumes in a town that nurtured gamblers, boozers, and lowlifes from all over the nation. Sure enough, those early days were agonizing for Liberace. He rarely did a show in the lounge at the Last Frontier without coming in for jeering insults from the boozers, losers, and lovers.

One toothless old crone, with huge breasts that threatened to pop out of her dress at any moment, sat with her brawny-armed, tattooed goon, who strangely enough said very little. Both were fascinated (but briefly) by the piano player with the gorgeous hairdo and satiny attire.

Finally she found her voice, which was a combination death rattle and grinding of brakes. "Hey kid, didn't I seen you play the piano at Elizabeth Arden's on Fifth Avenooo the other afternoon?" Then she yelled, "Listen, after you finish playing on that fucking piano, leave us go to my room and I'll show you how babies are born."

Liberace grinned weakly, but he never missed a note on his piano. Add the old, insulting crone to hundreds of others who had heckled him over the years, and you can get an idea that it wasn't all wine, roses, and red carpeting along the road to fame and fortune for the Kid from Milwaukee. His toothy grin, which almost blinded me that night, was to flash on and off like those elegant million-dollar neon signs.

Feeling only sympathy for the man, I waited until he finished his act, then went backstage to chat with him. "Christ, Liberace, you were great," I said, lying a wee bit, because great he wasn't. More flashing of the teeth and a warm handshake, then Liberace said apologetically in his famous drawl, "It's pronounced *Liber-atchee*, not *Liber-ace*."

When I walked away from him that night, I was certain I'd never see the guy again, unless I happened to wander into a small-city café featuring a piano.

Eleven years later I broke an exclusive item in my column that ". . . Liberace has just signed a three-year contract with the Riviera Hotel for the all-time record salary of $50,000 a week."

And though he still has had many aggravating moments both with press and public who question his virility and scoff at the outlandish outfits that he wears on TV, in cafés, and in movies, the gent from Milwaukee is now one of the more affluent residents of Palm Springs and the Hollywood Hills.

He still scoffs at the patrons flocking to his café shows in Las Vegas. "Remember how I always told you I cried all the way to the bank? Well, I don't have to cry any more, because I own several banks now."

And he couldn't have been more deadly serious—and right. His gay manners at and away from the piano have been a solid-gold mine for him. And as he cavorts about the stages in Las Vegas displaying his diamond and ruby rings, his satin-and-rhinestone-draped suits, he says, "Sure, go ahead and laugh all you want. You paid for all of this."

But don't be misled that Liberace is a freak flouncing about café stages like a male mannequin. He is one of the more masterful performers in Las Vegas and can compare in drawing power with Frank Sinatra, Tom Jones, and Elvis Presley. Liberace may look anti-Establishment, but his delightful quipping and piano playing are tried and true and of the Irving Berlin vintage.

I caught Liberace's show many times in Las Vegas, but never did he slam back at one of his critics except this one time. A columnist for a London newspaper had written a wicked piece labeling Liberace a "freak act cashing in on his homosexuality." This particular night he was sitting ringside at the Riviera Hotel watching Liberace with a "show me what you can do, you bastard" leer on his Limey countenance.

Liberace fooled him.

The audience had enjoyed Liberace to the point of giving him a standing ovation at the end of the show. Liberace, looking squarely at the London columnist, then gave the Londoner a flowery introduction, and topped off with a toast to him. Holding his drink high over the columnist's head

Liberace poured the contents of his gooey liquor on the utterly astounded gent's bald dome.

The patrons, aware of the feud, gave Liberace another standing ovation. The Londoner fled in a screaming rage.

THE SCHNOZ

The first-nighters at the Desert Inn had been roaring at the antics of the seventy-nine-year-old entertainer, who had been cutting up hilarious touches with his sidemen, Eddie Jackson and Sonny King. Now the two, after taking their bows, left the stage, and the absolute star of Vegas niteries for more than a quarter of a century, Jimmy Durante, took the hand mike, strolled over to a small stairway at the edge of the stage, and sat down.

The band went into the opening chorus of a song, and the crowd hushed almost instantly. This was a side of the fabulous "Schnoz" rarely seen in cafés. In his internationally famous manner, Jimmy cocked his head, touched the battered old gray felt hat, then went into the opening verses of "Young at Heart."

The single spot on him emphasized the otherwise darkened room. In the familiar raspy tone, Jimmy acted like an instant Bloody Mary on many of the boozers in the room. He brought tears of nostalgia to the eyes of the others. It was a familiar sight to me. I have been watching Jimmy in Vegas cafés ever since the lovable gargoyle opened Bugsy Siegel's Flamingo back in 1946.

Remarkably agile and "stage-wise" for a veteran of more than fifty years in show business, Jimmy didn't linger too long on the sober side of the act. Now his partners came prancing out to rejoin "The Schnoz," and the familiar pattern of Durante hysteria returned to further mesmerize the café customers.

105

Sure, Jimmy might blow a line or miss a song cue from time to time, but those missed cues seemed to enhance his routines rather than impair their effectiveness. In short, the public has always adored Jimmy. He could do no wrong in their eyes.

And that goes for me. He can never do anything wrong as far as I am concerned. But there was a time back in the late Fifties when we did have a slight difference of opinion.

Always an inveterate craps shooter, Jimmy loved nothing better between and after his shows in Las Vegas than to get out in the gaming casino and raise hell as he would whoop and holler while playing silver dollars at the table. Those not recognizing Jimmy would have imagined, watching and listening to him, that every roll of the dice was a matter of life or death to him, his family, and his friends.

Jimmy would put eight silver dollars on the line and then carry on like his whole bank account was in jeopardy. But that's the way he played, with every ounce of spirit and gusto. That's the way he used to play craps when he was a Coney Island piano player getting $5 a night back in 1919.

Naturally, his fierce Vegas casino action never cost him more than $100 a night. Jimmy could never be classified as a high roller in any stretch of even a press agent's imagination.

One morning a New York syndicated columnist itemed that Jimmy "was a heavy loser in Las Vegas casinos. His losses stretch into six figures. . . ." The gaming boys here in Vegas fell down laughing. Six figures, my foot! So, in my column several days later I corrected that columnist by noting, "Jimmy's losses in the gambling casinos here are infinitesimal. If his losses are in six figures, they have to be $50, $40, and $65, which Jimmy lost the last three nights in the Desert Inn."

That night I got a message from Durante to drop by and see him in his Desert Inn dressing room after the dinner show. I was sure that Jimmy was going to laud my honest stand in correcting the erroneous item in that New York column.

Instead (and it was a rare moment), Jimmy was fuming when I walked into his room. "Whaddya tryin' ta do wit dat kind of a story, kid, hoomilerate me? Jeez, all my friends are kiddin' me since ya wrote dat story."

Calming Jimmy down, I said, "Supposing I had let that story run as it did, don't you realize that you would have gotten a visit from a member of Uncle Sam's Bureau of Internal Revenue wanting to know more about your losses and maybe some winnings in six figures?"

The thought struck Jimmy squarely between the eyes. He quickly took off his ever-present gray felt hat, rubbed a nervous hand over a perspiring brow, then said, "I never tawt about dat, kid. Jeez, you're right."

That was the first and last time Jimmy and I ever had a difference of opinion. He still gambles in the casinos, he still acts like his entire future hangs on each roll of the dice, and he still is one of the wealthier men in show business today.

RICHARD RED SKELTON

Though the blazing red has vanished from Red Skelton's once fiery head of hair leaving wispy, unmanageable strands of a faded orange hue which stand out in all directions, he has managed to retain the erratic imbalance generally credited to all redheads. A fixture in Las Vegas show palaces for almost a quarter of a century, Red is along in years and can't play Vegas more than four weeks a year now. The rest of the time, I hear rumored, he devotes to counting his money. In Red's case it can be an all-day job.

The average run-of-the-mine comic is just as funny as he has to be, no funnier. When those TV cameras turn off, so does he. The same holds for comics in cafés, theaters, and on the screen. They make with the laughs as long as they're getting paid. After that, it's strictly "showboating" to try to continue with an image of joviality and humor.

Not Skelton! He has never stopped being funny from the moment he opened his scarlet and purple eyes until he went beddy bye two or three days later. Talk about being the practical joker, that was Red. His favorite practice when playing Las Vegas is to go out among the slot machines amply supplied with pocketsful of coins.

Clutching a handful of quarters in his left hand, Red drops a quarter in the slot with his right hand, then pulls the lever with his right. As soon as the cherries, lemons, and pineapples stop rotating unfavorably for him, Red hurls his handful of quarters into the payoff slot at the bottom of the machine. He already has gotten himself an audience by merely walking over to a machine, and they scream appreciatively. So Red pulls the same trick every time he drops a quarter in the machine, and does it so skillfully that nobody catches on to his deceptive left hand loaded with quarters.

However, this is all child's play compared to an evening early in 1965 when Red was starring at the Sands Hotel. It had been a rather hectic evening for him. His dinner show was a most energetic one, which got him a couple of standing ovations. So Red showed his appreciation by doing more and more of his routines.

By the time that audience let him off, he was thoroughly exhausted. Staggering to his dressing room backstage, Red fell on the couch and was all set to doze off for an hour when he found one of his show-biz pals, Sonny King, already in the room.

"Sonny, order me a Chinese dinner, will ya. I'm gonna take a nap and eat when I get up." And Red immediately dozed off.

King, almost as talented a practical joker as Red, ordered the Chinese dinner, waited until it was brought in, then neatly finished it off while Skelton snored peacefully nearby.

Soon all that remained of that ample Oriental feast was a tableful of dirty dishes. Sonny King in a corner chair burped blissfully.

Now Red woke up, and with the customary stretching and groaning. The first sight to meet his rheumy eyes was a table full of soiled, empty dishes and Sonny King sitting in the corner reading a magazine and looking as innocent as a boiled potato. "How'd you like the Chinese dinner, Red?" asked King. Skelton, notoriously absent-minded, looked back at the empty dishes and tried returning to reality. Finally he let out a resounding burp and gave Sonny a reproachful look. "You shouldn't have let me eat that food. I've got a heartburn now that won't quit. You know pepper steak always kills me. Order me an Alka-Seltzer or I won't be able to do the midnight show."

Skelton never did find out the truth about that six-course Chinese dinner.

3. Feuds, Feuds, and More Feuds

The high-priced star opens his baby-blue eyes, now a violent pink, at high noon and hears from his secretary that Ralph Pearl has a nasty item in his column in the Las Vegas *Sun.*

The star had given a rotten performance that night before. Not only had he been terribly drunk, but he was abusive to the ringsiders in the showroom. And to add insult to injury, the gent's show had been boring, which fact I had noted in my column along with his nasty antics.

Now the star is reading my column and screaming wildly, "That little bastard! Imagine him writing that I was abusive to the customers last night! What the fuck did he want me to do, kiss their asses?"

Frankly, if I had been in his bedroom at that moment, I would have endorsed that suggestion—that he kiss each and every ass in the room that night, considering that the star was being paid $65,000 a week for his cheesy act.

Naturally, a feud started between us. The star insists on making Las Vegas his own personal playground, away from my prying, overly critical eyes. "Mind you," he says, "I'm a firm believer in free press, but Pearl overdoes it."

Over the past twenty years I've tangled with many stars who resented criticism in one form or another. It was all right for me to write favorably and many times too generously of their abilities behind the footlights, but watch those words, Charley, when the act stinks.

Not only have I tangled with the biggie male and female performers, but also with the hotel owners, who seem to want to be guardian angels for their acts. On a half-dozen occasions over the years I've been barred from hotels. However, at this writing, I'm only "persona non grata" in one big hotel because the boss there resented my critical analysis of several stinkers he had brought in, then watched bomb.

And though I've clashed with maybe thirty stars over the years, I made up with all of them except two: Dean Martin and Buddy Hackett, who continue to stick pins in their "Ralph Pearl Voodoo Dolls" hidden away in the privacy of their dens.

How I wish all those I criticized would have been as fair-minded as the one and only Mitzi Gaynor, who is not only a dear friend but a superb entertainer.

After complaining in my column about one of Mitzi's routines, I noted, ". . . she should pencil that 'tomboy' skit. It's not only terribly contrived but just as unfunny."

The next night, after Mitzi read the column, she had a long conference with her producer about that questionable routine. The next night it was out of the show, and, what was more important to me, she personally thanked me from the stage every show for the rest of her engagement. "Ralph Pearl's criticism is always eagerly accepted by me. If he doesn't know what's good for a Las Vegas stage, then nobody knows. He's a doll, and many of us performers love him for his fearlessness and utter honesty. Thank you, Ralph."

You won't find too many stars like Mitzi.

THE CREW CUT AND THE "DRUNK"

Jerry Lewis sat with me in the Sands Hotel lobby one night late in May of 1955. He was strangely pensive, which had to be a rare image indeed for the world-famous lad. He and his partner, Dean Martin, were the number one comedy team in the nation.

"I don't want you to say anything, you hear?" said Jerry. Then he stayed silent for several moments while I wondered if the poor kid was undergoing a nervous breakdown. It wouldn't be too strange in Jerry's case, because he had been one of the all-time great screwballs in show business for the past seven years.

"So what don't you want me to say, Jerry?" I asked. At that moment I would have testified under oath he was up to one of his harebrained practical jokes. That deadly serious attitude had to be just another Jerry Lewis put-on. I braced myself because Jerry could either hit me with a pie he had concealed; suddenly rip off the lapels on my very expensive $65 suit, which had come with two pair of pants; or, worse yet, he might just jump out of his chair and stomp on my toes. I would then learn in most agonizing fashion that he was wearing spiked golf shoes.

Speaking in little more than a whisper, Jerry said, "I'm gonna break up the act and go as a single." I giggled. "Yeah, and Willie Mays is gonna quit baseball and go on a lecture tour of the deep South speaking about 'Black Supremacy,' right?"

Jerry wasn't spoofing.

"I'm getting tired working with Dean. I think I'd feel better working alone for a change," he elaborated.

My only concern at that moment was how fast I could get to a phone so I could get that story into print. Then I heard him talking again.

"Listen, you little bastard, this is strictly off the record.

112

You're my friend, and I thought I'd tell you how I felt. I may not go through with it, but right now I'm thinking about it. So cool it please."

Then we separated, and the team of Martin and Lewis, a smash success in cafés, TV, and on the screen, closed out another highly successful Sands engagement, then went off to keep a TV date in New York City.

I stayed behind in Las Vegas, and made a note on my calendar, "Talk with Jerry about splitting with Dean Martin when the act plays the Sands this fall."

In those days the mere thought of a split-up of the act could be sheer disaster to Dean, who was a glamorous, virile straight man for Jerry. Dean sang a couple of songs and was the George Burns to Jerry's Gracie Allen. It was being rumored around the nation that Jerry and Dean might break up an act that was earning each of them a million dollars a year!

There was no doubt in anybody's mind in the café and movie industry that such a split-up had to ruin Dean Martin, who was the highest paid "shill" in show business at that time.

Three weeks later, in mid-June, while I was trying to get Jerry Lewis on the phone in Chicago, where he and Dean were appearing, the story broke that he and Dean had officially decided to part company once and for all time.

The records, of course, will show that Dean became a powerhouse in TV and in cafés as a single, while Jerry Lewis went his own way as a motion-picture producer and star on the screen, in cafés, and TV.

Early in 1960 Jerry Lewis, while playing at the Sands, made one of his frequent visits to my TV show. Then he proceeded to break up not only the show, but also its moderator. The first thing he did upon sitting down next to me behind the microphone was to tear up all my notes, then fling them in a spray at the camera.

113

That wasn't too bad for Jerry Lewis on TV. He had been rambunctious before when guesting on my show. So I ignored that move and proceeded to talk with Jerry—only to find he had gone to sleep, head down, on the desk in front of him.

I promptly picked up a glass of ice water, the cubes still in the water, and poured the contents, cubes and all, on Jerry's classic crew-cut head. Not only did he awaken, but he did so with a roar that shook the studio. Then he jumped to his feet and began shaking himself like a shaggy dog, sending a spray of ice water all over me.

Practical jokes are never, or at least hardly ever, played on Jerry Lewis. Usually it's the other way around.

Instead of returning to his place next to me, he took off and began roaming the studio. I sat there like a schmuck, with a live mike and a galloping Lewis. So, came a one-way commentary for the next fifteen minutes as I pleaded, threatened, and silently cursed him. I still had approximately eleven minutes remaining on my show. I had all but run out of conversation. And just when I was contemplating reciting the "Gettysburg Address," Jerry stopped in a corner of the studio, reached down, and pulled a plug out of the wall. TV viewers now saw Ralph Pearl, but there was no voice. Lewis had pulled the audio plug.

I began calling Lewis all sorts of names, the kind you would hear during a heated contest in a Brooklyn poolroom. "You dirty, rotten sonofabitch, put that plug back in the wall," I screamed. Jerry obliged instantly, but not fast enough to catch that salty description of him. If he had been quick on the plug, Ralph Pearl would be out of television, unless he would be selling TV sets from door to door.

So now Jerry had a new game. He would pull the plug as I talked, then put it back in the socket. My ensuing dialogue sounded like Bugs Bunny having a sneezing attack. Strangely enough, viewers began calling the station objecting to Jerry's actions. They felt he was psychopathic rather than funny.

About thirty seconds before the show ended, Jerry returned to his seat beside me, then asked innocently, "Now, what were you asking me?"

As far as Mister Practical Joker was concerned, it had been a riotously funny thirty-minute show. He wasn't even vaguely aware of the tremendous pressure I'd been under during almost twenty-seven minutes of that thirty-minute show. He assumed I always did a television show frothing at the mouth and looking purplish and apoplectic. He even thanked me warmly for having him on the show. "Invite me over again," he said.

As I ran out of the studio, spluttering and grinding my teeth, I vowed never to talk to Jerry again. There was such a thing as being overly cute on a show. But, after all, hadn't he been a willing, cooperative guest of mine for several years?

Yeah, I'd invite him over again, when Golda Meier was appointed ruler of Egypt and when Strip hotel gaming bosses began hiring their pit bosses out of Harvard Business School.

I voiced my indignation in the column the next day, and so started a feud with one of my closest friends in all of show business. He retaliated by denouncing me in a two-thousand-word letter to "Letters to the Editor" in my own newspaper.

And that's how matters stood. The following week he closed at the Sands, and Sammy Davis, Jr., opened for three weeks. By now my original flow of sour juices had stopped, and I was genuinely sorry about the break with Jerry. Sure, he had broken with Dean several years earlier, but that was different. They were merely partners, not friends.

The second week of Sammy's show, the wee one came down with a bad case of laryngitis. So who would the Sands boss get to pinch-hit for Sam? Certainly not Moshe Dayan. It was Jerry Lewis, who was between engagements in his Bel Air, California, home.

The night Jerry opened for the ailing Sammy, I sat at ringside dreading every moment, yet curious enough to want to call Jerry's hand. What would he do when he spotted me sitting right at ringside, a mere five feet away from him? Would he drop the mike on my head? Would he completely ignore me? He was capable of executing any act, violent or otherwise.

During most of Jerry's show, he kept glaring down at me but forebore any act of violence upon my person. His restraint didn't give my wife, Roz, too much peace of mind, and she kept on whispering, "Whadd'ya think he's gonna do?"

Now the show was almost over. Jerry had been his usually funny self, but it was noticeable only to me that he was most affected by my presence and our feud. Now he took several bows, then gave a humble thank-you speech.

"Incidentally, there's a man in this room I want to talk about." My heart sank into my Tom McAn sneakers. "Here it comes," I moaned. "He's gonna vilify me."

Instead of vilifying, however, Jerry was most humble about "this Las Vegas columnist who is truly Mister Las Vegas, and has been for many years."

I began breathing easier, until I saw through his crafty plan. He would praise another Las Vegas columnist, thus making me look bad by the obvious comparison he set up.

"He has done much for me during the many times I played here both as a single and with 'you-know-who' as a team. He's bold, fearless, and calls the shots exactly as he sees them."

Christ, the other columnist on the afternoon newspaper was none of those things. He was just a nice guy who always wrote pleasantly about performers whether they rated it or not. However, in getting back at me, Jerry would exaggerate. Anything to rile me. Roz and I wriggled uncomfortably in our seats, which suddenly became infernally hot.

116

". . . so, please give him a big hand. Ralph Pearl, get up and take a bow."

I was thunderstruck. Could he have accidentally used the wrong name? No chance, because Jerry, his face wreathed in a warm smile, was leaning down to ringside and extending his hand to me.

Utterly confused, I took a quick bow, then slumped back. The whole evening had been too much. But there was more to come. Naturally, Roz and I now had to go back to Jerry's dressing room, where else?

Waiting until all the backslappers and agents had left his room, Jerry and I were now alone. Both of us had tears in our eyes as we embraced. Words couldn't be spoken. We just stood there in the center of Jerry's dressing room in close embrace. And like a couple of lovebirds who'd just had their first serious quarrel, we finally stood apart and sheepishly grinned at each other.

"Here's the way I see it, Ralph." I'd never seen Jerry's other side. "We've been friends too long to break up over such a silly fight. If our friendship wasn't worth saving, I'd never have made the move to apologize. Now get the fuck out of here before I call in a justice of the peace and marry you!"

I grinned foolishly, tearfully. What do you say in such an instance? That's exactly right, nothing. So, I nodded most intellectually and, with lots of feeling, patted Jerry fondly on the face, then walked out. Our friendship has been one of the nicer things that I remember after almost twenty years in Las Vegas.

What has that got to do with Dean Martin, you're asking?

So, I'll tell you. Four years later Dean and I had a battle royal. We haven't talked since and never expect to.

By 1965 Dean Martin was a top-rated café star, though not as famous or as affluent as he is these days. But he could be mean, especially where his pal, Frank Sinatra, and his own kids are concerned.

Since I was already feuding with Sinatra and permanently barred from the Sands, it didn't take me too long to provoke Dean to go over to Frank's side. All I did was write critically about Dean one night when he goofed off during one of his dinner shows at the Sands. To add further rage to his already charged up Sicilian spleen, I noted one night that his daughters Claudia and Gail were "now going into show business by cashing in on the old man's reputation."

That did it. He made it graphically clear that he and I were now "unfriendly," so he went on a local TV show and for more than twenty minutes explained what a "louse" was one Ralph Pearl. His only frustration was that he couldn't bar me from the hotel I was already barred from by Sinatra.

I look upon the Dean Martin feud philosophically. As long as Jerry Lewis is my lifelong friend, who needs a reformed Steubenville, Ohio, blackjack dealer, even though he is the toast of the nation right now?

GUS GREENBAUM . . .
"WHO HAD INNER WARMTH"

When I started covering the show beat early in 1953, I was wet behind the ears about the backgrounds of the "boys" who ran the Strip hotels. True I'd heard weird stories—some confirmed, others rumors—about many of them. But I'd never heard anything about the boss of the Flamingo Hotel, Gus Greenbaum.

One night I walked into the Flamingo Hotel to attend the Tony Martin opening-night show. Standing off to one side of the showroom was Greenbaum himself. Looking at that cold-eyed expression, I instantly surmised that Greenbaum had to be a most disagreeable sonofabitch. I further surmised that he must have gotten into the gaming and hotel business right from a successful career as a cloak-and-suit operator on busy Seventh Avenue in Manhattan. What else?

He was not only a grumpy, disagreeable man given to violent fits of anger which discolored his complexion, but he always sounded as if he had just swallowed a handful of nails. Worse than that, every time I caught his eye he acted as if he was smelling something terribly . . . shitty . . . and I was it.

It preyed on my mind all night as I watched the Tony Martin show, while casting occasional, hurried glances at Greenbaum, who sat comfortably in a booth with several of his executives. I began brooding. Why should he be so comfortable and relaxed while I sat at a table no bigger than an outfielder's glove? As if that wasn't bad enough, the overzealous maitre dee, enriched by a double sawbuck, put a party of huge bodies directly between me and the stage.

My bitter juices started flowing and never stopped until I'd left the hotel, gone down to the *Sun*, and written my column, which contained my story about the Tony Martin opening. In part, I observed, "Talk about catching a bird's-eye view of the great Tony Martin, this columnist was treated to a side view of him because of our seat almost in the kitchen last night at the Flamingo. . . . And what made the evening a total disaster, the steak I consumed was colder than a gaming credit manager's heart. . . ."

The next morning, Gus read that appraisal and almost tore the phone off his wall getting all his executives together to discuss such an unfriendly act by a Las Vegas columnist. Later that morning I was told by one of Greenbaum's lieutenants to "stay the fuck out of this hotel, d'ya hear." This had to be one of the more humiliating incidents of my life in Las Vegas. Barred from the Flamingo Hotel by a former cloak-and-suit merchant!

Naturally, I rushed out to the Flamingo and began a relentless search for Greenbaum so he could tell me to my face that I was *persona non grata*. And there, leaning against an empty blackjack table, was Gus himself. Dashing over, I poked my finger almost under his nose, then screamed frantically, "Why, Mister Greenbaum, am I *persona non grata* in this hotel?"

"I'm not too sure what means *persona non grata,*" said Gus, "but if it means that you can no longer come into this hotel, then you're right. And don't point your goddamned finger at me."

Then I really started to scream and yell about my constitutional rights of free speech and free press. Gus just looked at me with a slight smirk on his craggy countenance.

Standing firmly, nose to chest (my nose to his chest), I continued to berate him. All Greenbaum did was look at me with contempt, also amazement, and finally respect. Now a strange gurgling sound came out of him. Later I was to learn that he was asthmatic. Anyway, he started roaring with laughter. Also gurgling. Finally, he turned to one of his associates.

"Did you hear this little bastard tell me off just now? I wish some of you guys had that kind of guts."

Turning to me, he said, "Hey, Pearl, you're okay even if you're a little bit crazy. Forget about what happened and come back tonight and see Tony Martin again, this time from a ringside table. Okay?"

Still playing the fearless, crusading columnist who never backed up a step for anyone, not even a tough ex-cloak-and-suiter, I thanked Gus, turned sharply on my heels, and walked right into a potted palm plant! I went sprawling on all fours while Gus and his associates stooped to help me to my feet. I slunk away terribly embarrassed, maybe more so because Gus and his boys were roaring with laughter.

Okay, I thought, let those bastards laugh. I really had the last laugh by standing up to them. Later that night, I was approached at the Sands Hotel by one of the owners of that hotel. Evidently news of my encounter with Greenbaum had reached his ears.

"I hear you really stood up to Gus Greenbaum this morning. That's one way of committing suicide, kid. Why?"

And though a cold, clammy feeling of terror hit me right in the belly, I started explaining to him that I didn't intend to get barred from the Flamingo Hotel by an ex-merchant prince from Manhattan no matter how ferocious he got.

Then and there, in a most patient manner, my friend from the Sands Hotel led me to a corner office, sat me down, and proceeded to tell me about Gus Greenbaum, who was an ex-merchant prince like Bugsy Siegel was a ballet master with the Pasadena Performing Arts League.

And as he continued detailing Greenbaum's long track record in vice and gaming, I got weaker and weaker. He ended his discourse by saying, "I can think of only one man who talked to Gus that way and walked away in one whole piece—Bugsy Siegel himself." I determined to give Greenbaum a wide birth from then on.

Several months later, in addition to his asthma, he began suffering from stomach ulcers. A constant diet of booze, bad food, and irregular hours had finally floored the "Iron Monster."

He had part of his stomach removed, and that was reason enough for his wife, Bess, to force him to quit the Flamingo. He returned to his home in Phoenix and tried living the peaceful life of a country squire and attending dinner parties at the Phoenix country clubs with his lifelong pal, Senator Barry Goldwater, as well as many other important Phoenixites.

Unfortunately, his retirement was short-lived. In 1956, forces in Las Vegas and Miami began making plans to bring Gus back—whether he wanted to or not. A new hotel, the $10-million Riviera, had been opened in March and was already in bad financial shape. As a matter of fact, it was headed for receivership.

As much as Gus protested about having to leave his life of leisure in Phoenix, the word went out from Miami to "get Gus to take over the Riviera." Reluctantly Gus came back to the scene of his earlier "triumphs," and took over the tottering high-rise hotel, the first of its kind on the Las Vegas Strip.

Back in action at the Riviera Hotel, his attitude toward me was one of calculated indifference. He would pass me by in the hotel with a slight nod of recognition—nothing more. And that was perfectly all right with me, because I was most allergic to sudden lumps on the head or body.

However, my ego got a big charge when mutual friends told me that Gus never went to bed before buying the *Sun* and reading my column. Gus would tell them, "Lemme see what that little bastard is writing about today."

A confrontation of sorts with the "ogre" came sooner than I expected.

One night in 1958 as I sat in the lounge at the Riviera Hotel watching one of the more skillful saloon comics, Shecky Greene, do his act, Greene suddenly began jumping on his boss, Gus Greenbaum, with both feet. Since it was all done in a spirit of entertainment, many in the lounge assumed that Shecky was ribbing his boss—nothing more. After all, didn't Shecky do an equally destructive job on Ed Sullivan, Gregory Peck, Danny Thomas, and Elvis Presley?

There was a reason for Shecky's hammering Gus—and nightly yet. Gus had cut off his credit at the casino cage—also the tables—and Greene was furious. But he shouldn't have been. In the inebriated stage Shecky was generally in, he would have blown a fortune on the tables. But he refused to see it that way. It was an affront to his pride, and everybody in the hotel was aware of it.

Yet, if Shecky Greene ever had a guardian angel, Gus Greenbaum had to be it. Before opening at the Riviera, the powerhouse comic had already been boycotted by several other Strip hotels for his violent behavior, drunk or sober. He had worked other hotel lounges and been canceled out because he was impossible to get along with. It was not unusual for Shecky, while in the throes of demon rum, to turn over a blackjack table, maybe even tilt a craps table or two.

Once over his fits of depression and violence, he acted like a puppy dog, lovable and contrite. But only his enormous talents and drawing power kept him in Las Vegas as a performer.

Since Greenbaum was almost a nightly visitor to the lounge when Shecky was working, he knew about the blasts Greene was giving him. There was just enough of a "kidding" attitude in Shecky's attack on Gus to keep it from being an out-and-out vendetta. Greenbaum decided to pass it off. But he was far from happy about Shecky's numerous acts of "ingratitude."

Checking quietly, I learned that, if it hadn't been for Greenbaum's help, Shecky might have had to quit show business in those violent years. Without the huge yearly income from the Riviera, he would have had trouble existing on the meager dates in other parts of the country.

Plagued not only by the IRS, but by his personal manager, Shecky's days had seemed numbered. Greenbaum, hearing that Shecky owed Uncle Sam several thousand dollars, gave him the money to pay off that debt. Then, when Shecky's manager prepared to hit him with an injunction for nonpayment of long overdue commissions, Gus again jumped in and paid off the manager.

All of this without a word of publicity about Greene's plight. Hence, it seemed incomprehensible that he would now be belting Gus from the stage because of a petty matter involving gaming credit. It shaped up as a good column story. A couple of days later, I revealed Shecky's ingratitude to his boss in my column.

Shecky stopped pounding Gus and started pounding me. That night I ran into Greenbaum. His craggy features had softened and his gravelly voice had become subdued. He thanked me for the column, then walked away without another word.

Gus Greenbaum and Ralph Pearl were now friends. Four months later, I got a call from Gus wanting to know if my wife Roz and I would have dinner with him and his Bess later in the week.

I had to ask for a rain check. "Roz and I'll be out of town this weekend, Gus. Why don't you ask us again early next week?"

That seemed all right with Gus. Roz couldn't help noting sarcastically later that night, "You're really moving up in the world, big shot. Dinner next week with the Greenbaums, next month maybe with the Lansky's?" Despite her caustic cracks, I pondered about that dinner date, then went to sleep that night with Gus Greenbaum's picture under my pillow.

The following week, expecting a call any day from Gus about the delayed dinner date, I read where he and Bess had gone off to their home in Phoenix for several days. It was now December 1, 1958.

Two days later Phoenix police found Gus and his Bess sprawled over blood-soaked beds with their throats cut ear to ear and their skulls smashed in by a heavy wine decanter. Nary a dollar or a gem had been touched during that assassination. It was, of course, a deliberate act of murder.

Reasons for the killing were offered—each more illogical than the last. But one thing was vividly clear: Bugsy Siegel and Gus Greenbaum were liquidated for stepping out of line.

The most logical reason for Greenbaum's liquidation had to be his determination to expand the Riviera, now that he was boss man there. He had begun campaigning the boys back in New York and Miami to give him $2 million so he could carry out his plans. And he wouldn't take no for an answer—even threatened to bring in fresh, outside money if he couldn't get it from Lansky and Company.

Whether or not he knew the risks at the time, Gus had been following the pattern that resulted in his ex-partner, Bugsy Siegel's, extermination—stepping out of line while making extravagant demands for more money. What sealed Gus Greenbaum's fate was that the hotel was slightly in the red, and gaming had been off for the previous couple of months. Greenbaum, like Bugsy Siegel, had suddenly become expendable to the organization.

Thus, following the age-old principle of never spitting in the same basin where you wash, after the "boys" ruled thumbs down on Greenbaum, they waited until he left for his Phoenix retreat before killing him. Certainly they weren't about to kill Gus in Las Vegas where many of their geese were laying golden eggs. It just wouldn't look good—especially in the nation's press.

Immediately after the killing, a few kind friends of the Syndicate offered suggestions that possibly the Greenbaums were slain by a western mob resenting the idea that Gus wanted to quit and set up "shop" in Phoenix. Few, if any, accepted that trumped-up theory.

Greenbaum and his wife were buried, a few days after their murder, in a Phoenix cemetery. More than four hundred attended—probably his very assassins were there. A kindly rabbi delivered a touching eulogy, in which he concluded that Gus "had inner warmth."

That was one way of putting it.

FRANK SINATRA

"Dear Ralph: We may have had our differences, but that was a thousand years ago and time heals better than any salve. I am

a man who's not immune to kindness. In these days kindness is very rare. May I say thank you for the nice words, and maybe one night we'll have a drink. Best, Frank Sinatra."

Beautiful? I can hardly remember our first feud back in the late Fifties. Frank was very touchy in those days. I guess he grabbed more newspaper space because of his feuds with the press than Jackie Onassis does today.

In jest I had reported in my column that Frank had knocked an aggressive photographer down, and I quoted from the New York papers where the incident had occurred. I guess it wasn't funny to Frank, but six months later he forgave me and sent the above note and we were friends again.

But this happy state of affairs didn't last. It was in the latter part of 1961 that we had our longest and most bitter feud. And, strange as it may seem, I got into trouble by defending the late Dorothy Kilgallen, another fourth estater who had a syndicated column.

On that memorable opening night at the Sands Hotel, Frank came to Las Vegas with a violent dislike of Dorothy. He went into a diatribe about the lady that lasted for more than twenty minutes before a glamorous group of first-nighters, many from the Hollywood film factories.

Noted more for his singing talents than his oratory, Frank refused to get off the subject of Kilgallen that night, while the losers, boozers, lovers, and just plain tourists listened in bewilderment. It was costing them about $25 per person to witness the Sinatra vendetta against Kilgallen.

Sinatra finally got all the poison out of his system, and went back reluctantly to singing a few of his songs. But the night had really been ruined for the patrons, many of them fair-minded enough to feel that Frank had resorted to a gutter-style, vicious tirade harping on Kilgallen's facial shortcomings.

I reported it all in my column the next day, then criticized

126

Frank on my TV show that night. "By the way, Frank," I said on the air, "you were in gross error last night at the Sands when you devoted much of your show to Dorothy Kilgallen's alleged facial deformities. You should be the last guy in the world to attack the lady in such a lowly, unethical manner no matter what she said about you. After all, Frank, a Rock Hudson you ain't by any stretch of imagination."

Frank Sinatra, reclining in the Sands Hotel Health Club watching me on TV, let out a yelp that shook the penthouse and knocked a portrait of Nick the Greek off the wall. Hurling a pot of coffee at the TV set, Frank and the late Sands Hotel boss, Jack Entratter, got on the phone and proceeded to bar me from the Sands in pretty strong language.

I didn't go back to the Sands for more than four years, or until the famous incident between Frank and gaming boss Carl Cohen, who knocked out two of Frank's teeth following the singer's insistent, insulting demands for more gaming credit one night. In ordinary times, when the Sands was owned by Carl and his associates, that demand might have been met.

However, a gent by the name of Howard Hughes now owned the hotel, and he and his top brass weren't even slightly impressed with Sinatra's power in Las Vegas. They were determined to run the hotels like a corporation, cold and businesslike. As far as they were concerned, Sinatra was a well-paid entertainer at the Sands and wasn't going to get special privileges, regardless of the fact he was the biggest single draw Vegas ever had. When he was in town everyone benefited, even the rival hotels. He had a charisma that was unique. The well-heeled customers came in droves when he entertained.

The upshot of the whole mess, widely publicized in the world press, was that Frank quit the Sands and went over to Caesars Palace. And the big problem that now existed was the status of one Ralph Pearl at the Palace. Would Sinatra's ban apply there? I found out quickly enough when the Palace boss at that time, Jerry Zarowitz, brought me together with Frank the night before he opened in the Circus Maximus Room at the Palace.

It happened to be Frank's birthday, and the hotel bosses were throwing a party for Sinatra in one of the hotel's convention rooms. Only a choice gathering of Frank's friends were invited. Strangely enough, I got a special invitation to that party.

Walking into the room, I felt like a guy crashing into an all-girl Sweet Sixteen party without any clothes on! Frank's friends, aware of the feud between us, eyed me coldly, then walked away from me like I had a contagious disease.

Then Frank spotted me, and he came over instantly. It was as if we had never had cross words. He greeted me warmly, offered me a piece of birthday cake, and then posed for pictures with our arms around each other. In the twinkle of a Sinatra eye, a four-year feud had come to an end.

A year later Frank crossed swords with a Caesars Palace gaming boss—also the district attorney here in Las Vegas—and he vowed never to return either to Las Vegas or the Palace. He never deviated from that resolution for the rest of his professional career, which lasted until 1971, when he announced his complete retirement from show business.

Sinatra wasn't mincing words about never returning to Las Vegas. When his dear friend, Joe E. Lewis, was given a testimonial dinner shortly after Frank issued that edict, Frank stayed away even though he felt badly about not being there to honor Joe, whom he loved and admired. Then in the summer of 1971, when his kids, Nancy and Frank, Jr., opened at the International Hotel, Sinatra was again glaringly conspicuous by his absence.

The love affair between Las Vegas and Frank Sinatra had met a violent end, and nobody or nothing could bring them together again.

And though there were many owners in Las Vegas who talked down Sinatra because of his inflammable temperament while he was an attraction here, now that he's away, they are forced to admit that there'll never be another star who can come close to matching Frank's enormous drawing power. He was an instant "prosperity wave" all his own. Some of the biggest, most affluent people in the nation, betting or otherwise, came to Las Vegas only when Frank played here. They rarely visit Vegas now.

SHECKY GREENE

As for Shecky Greene, he has always been a story all by himself, and unlike any other performer I ever tangled with here in Las Vegas. Born in the Chicago ghetto as Shmoil Greenfield, he was determined to make a name for himself— and that name wasn't going to be Shmoil Greenfield too much longer. He aspired to loftier things than hand-me-down clothing from his cousins. "Especially when my cousins were fat, little-girl monsters," Shecky would say.

As soon as he got out of the service in 1945, Shmoil began working in third-rate clubs in and around the Chicago area. And since the name Shmoil Greenfield wasn't one you'd seen in Walter Winchell's column in a romance item with Ava Gardner or Lana Turner, the stocky one changed it to Shecky Greene. He had superb ad-lib qualities behind those footlights. His humor was rakish, explosive, and crowd-pleasing.

Soon he became a big favorite in Las Vegas. Unfortunately his conduct before and after he entertained was just as violent, but not as funny, when he tangled with the law or anybody who opposed him in those days—especially this columnist in Las Vegas. The Tropicana Hotel bosses were unable to cope with his tantrums and finally cut him adrift. He was immediately picked up by the Riviera, which was more than happy to put up with his shenanigans.

Shecky didn't wait long after joining the Riviera to start cutting up in the gaming casino in the wee hours of the morning after his nightly chores in the lounge had been completed. Generally it started after he got wiped out at the blackjack or dice table, especially if he had been drinking. I would note this behavior in my column, then step back for the blast that was sure to follow from Greene.

I never had to wait too long. Generally, there'd be threats and promises that he'd one day bash my head in until it looked like a rutabaga. But that's all they were—merely threats.

Now he was playing a small nitery in Manhattan. One late night a press agent pal called me from there. "Hey, a pal of yours, Shecky Greene, is here in night court for disorderly conduct. He ripped a phone off the wall in the club where he was working, so the owners had him arrested."

After getting more details, I devoted most of my column to Shecky Greene the next day. The mere fact that he had landed on page one of the New York City newspapers didn't bother Shecky Greene. What did matter was that I had devoted most of a Las Vegas column to his Manhattan high jinks. He was furious. Four days later he opened in the Riviera Hotel lounge, and danger signs were up all over the hotel. The human battering ram, Shecky Greene, was gunning for me!

He devoted a part of his show that night to Ralph Pearl, "the Louella Parsons of the Desert," by ripping away at everything from my questionable birth to his stark discovery that "Ralph Pearl is the only columnist in America with a mental harelip."

So far so good. Sticks and stones would break my bones, but Shecky wouldn't give me any fractures by blasting me orally. However, I did make a practice of staying the hell away from the immediate vicinity of the Riviera. Like five miles away. One night, however, I weakened because of overwhelming curiosity, and silently crept into the Riviera lounge through a side entrance. Too many reports had gotten back to me about Shecky's withering blast on Ralph Pearl, "the Louella Parsons of Las Vegas," which in itself was libelous.

There in the shadow of a back booth I watched the irrepressible Greene hack little Ralph Pearl into a sorry mess. Every time the losers and boozers in the room howled, which was constantly, I shrank lower in the booth.

One day a mutual friend, show producer Dave Victorson, came up with a pretty fair idea—to appoint himself a committee of one who would bring Shecky and me together to smoke the peace pipe. I agreed—provided, of course, Shecky liked the idea, too.

Later that week, on a sunny afternoon, Shecky and I sat in a Strip hotel coffee shop face to face and squirming with embarrassment. It proved to be a "confessional" to end all such confrontations. As soon as we faced each other, I saw that Greene had already imbibed freely before meeting me in the coffee shop. He started being abusive and far from cooperative. The smoke from the "peace pipe" turned into a killer smog.

Shecky began rehashing the many times I'd "maligned" him in my column, then followed that up with violent adjectives strongly implying that my mama and papa had merely been good friends, nothing more, when I was conceived. One harsh word led to a flock of others by Greene. But I wasn't taking it all meekly. I kept saying, "Oh yeah, wise guy?"

During all this verbal violence, I noticed that our mutual friend, Victorson, the arbiter who had suggested this peace talk, had quietly vanished from the scene. So there we were, two snarling Jews, chin to chin and ready for mortal combat at any moment.

But Shecky had done all the screaming he intended. Now

he jumped to his feet, slightly tilting the table, which immediately caused a pot of hot coffee to slide into my sensitive crotch. I jumped three feet into the air, screaming even louder.

Shecky had his tightly clenched fist inches under my trembling chin. Then he said coldly, "Stay the hell away from me, you rotten little columnist bastard, because the next time I run into you either here or anywhere I'm gonna bash in your head!"

Not to be outdone in such a violent exchange, I quickly repeated, "Oh yeah! You and who else! Any time you think you're big enough to do the job, you know where to find me. I'll be waiting for you in my apartment." I didn't have to specify it any further because he had visited me there many times in the past when we were on friendly terms.

Shecky then rushed away, while I sat quivering like a glob of lemon Jello. Though small in stature (five foot seven), Shecky is almost that wide. He could easily have passed for a large fire hydrant. And, when aroused, he could have ripped a phone book into small pieces with his bare hands with ease. Or a Ralph Pearl into just as many pieces.

At that moment Pete Witcher, who was then the security chief for that hotel and later the Las Vegas chief of police, came over with hand extended. "I heard it all, Ralph, from the table behind you. It took guts to tell him he knew where to find you."

My quivering jowls stopped rotating, and a sickly smile spread over my face. "I hate to disillusion you, Pete. But do you think I'd be stupid enough to tell that enraged bull where I really live? I moved from my old place three months ago!"

Ultimately there was a change. Shecky, who had earned about $500,000 for twenty-two weeks of work annually in the Riviera's lounge for more than eight years, really hit the jackpot late in 1971 when his salary was doubled and he began working as a star in the main showroom. Up until then he had been unmanageable but very necessary to the bosses of the Riviera. They overlooked his tantrums because he was one of a rare few entertainers who could fill the room every show, any night, rain or shine or sandstorm.

However, when he started moving up into the big show-room, the Shecky Greene personality underwent a dramatic transformation. He no longer ate columnists for breakfast. Now he is benign and understanding. And he watches his whiskey intake as carefully as Adelle Davis watches her carbohydrates.

These days we hardly recognize Shecky Greene. He sends personal letters of thanks to columnists who write well about his nitery skills. No longer does he indulge in vigorous exercises as in the old days when he would turn over a blackjack table or tilt a ponderous dice table without even raising a sweat.

Frankly, I miss the old Shecky.

BUDDY HACKETT, THE ORIGINAL "JEWISH BUDDHA"

In the mid-Fifties, that lovable "human blow torch," Swifty Morgan (whom Damon Runyon made famous as the original "Lemon Drop Kid") in town for his pal, Joe E. Lewis at the El Rancho Vegas Hotel, stopped me just as I was getting ready to slash my wrists with a rusty razor blade. Still young and impressionable, I had crossed swords with a popular café star, who promptly cut me to ribbons.

Not only was the lady a tremendous favorite here, but she always got favorable reviews from both the local and out-of-town critics whenever she played Vegas. But I felt she had goofed on that opening night, so I reported it that way. Since I never knew the lady had a poolroom vocabulary, I was terribly disturbed by her verbal attack.

That's when Swifty came to the rescue by tapping me

affectionately on the noggin with his cane as I was on the downswing with the razor blade. That lady star, who had been my idol for many years, had been the one to suggest self-destruction. And like the emotional schmuck I was, I was doing it.

Naturally, I was always grateful to Swifty, who also helped me build an immunity to other stars over the years who ranted over unfavorable notices in my column. Unfortunately I was never able to build up an immunity to one of the funniest men who ever played Las Vegas, Buddy Hackett, the "Jewish Buddha."

Looking like a composite of the world's greatest losers, Buddy had only to walk onstage, pat his huge tummy, and grin owlishly. I'd scream with laughter and almost choke on my Baked Alaska. Then he'd tell about his childhood, and I'd roll in the aisles. Evidently the patrons felt the same way. Opening night on a Buddy Hackett show you could hardly get a table. No matter how often he told his stories, they seemed to get funnier all the time.

It was in the late Sixties that Buddy subtly started changing his act. Slowly but surely he was injecting more and more blue material. Even though we live in a pornographic-oriented society and Las Vegas is no Pasadena, I felt his obscene gestures in the pubic area were entirely out of line—not to mention his pointedly heavy usage of four-letter words. One night during an engagement he asked a very dignified matron sitting ringside why she was afraid of the word "shit." Didn't everyone use it? he asked. And to buttress his position, he declared that the only dirty word in the English vocabulary was "kill." He might have had something there, but at that time I felt a brilliant comic like Buddy Hackett didn't have to stoop so low to get a laugh, because he was up there with the top entertainers.

Of course, my criticism didn't stop Buddy, and one day he

134

went to Minneapolis to attend the inauguration of a multi-million-dollar auditorium. Among the other invitees were the then vice president Hubert Humphrey, members of the clergy, both U.S. senators from Minnesota, congressmen, and many national educators. Buddy shared the dais with some of them.

Came time to do his bit of performing and Buddy told a series of violently distasteful stories embellished with every obscene three-, four-, and five-letter word in the Longshoreman's Manual. Needless to say, the prominent people on the dais as well as the audience were shocked by such an indiscriminate use of filth. After all, this was not Las Vegas.

Buddy was asked to leave the stage, the auditorium, and the state. One of the people in the audience, a Las Vegan who had been invited to that opening, called me that same night and told me all the gruesome details. The next day the morning newspaper in Minneapolis ran an eight-column banner headline about Buddy Hackett. The headline writer also used a four-letter word that started with an "S" and ended with a "B."

My column in Las Vegas the next day was more critical than usual. I really hoped to be helpful to Hackett about the whole sorry mess in Minneapolis. I reiterated that Buddy's frequent use of insensitive words, especially at dinner shows which were attended by teen-agers and their parents, was certainly not in the best of taste.

Three days later and still smarting from the storm he had raised in Minnesota, Buddy opened at the Sahara. And when he spotted me in the audience, he blew his cool and proceeded to cut me up piece by piece until I felt like wilted shredded lettuce. He then did his regular show without deleting one obscene word or gesture.

The feud was on. I continued to berate Buddy in my column and TV show, while explaining that he was my favorite comic without the filth. It didn't help. Buddy wouldn't give in, and continued using the objectionable material. And more.

Now, whenever Buddy Hackett plays the Sahara, Del Webb puts up a poster in front of the showroom, "Only Adults Admitted."

In the summer of 1970, Buddy tried to make up with me. He opened at the brand-new Kings Castle Hotel in Lake Tahoe, and I went up to that opening. Many notables from Nevada and Hollywood were there.

Always one of the more active nonconformists, Buddy decided to make a different entrance that night. He came onstage utterly in the *nude* with merely a large pendant hanging from his neck and over his pubic area! Talk about shock, the governor of Nevada, sitting in the balcony, almost toppled over the rail.

Barbara Stanwyck, who had made a TV movie with Buddy, almost followed the governor over the rail.

So that *would* be the night that Buddy decided to make up with me by referring to me flatteringly several times during his act. It didn't help. I griddled him to a crisp, well-done brown in my next column. Any ideas of peace between us went out the window.

One day that pendant might just wind up in cement in front of Grauman's Chinese Theatre in Hollywood, along with the footprints of the stars. Those sitting on either side of Buddy that night at Kings Castle Hotel soon found out, as Buddy's pendant jiggled, that he was definitely Jewish.

Last summer my sister and brother-in-law Grace and Ab Farrell, innocent souls visiting from New York, ran into Buddy at the Stardust Hotel. Up piped Grace, "Buddy, I'm Ralph Pearl's sister-in-law. I always wanted to meet you."

He snarled back, "That little bastard Ralph Pearl, tell him to drop dead!" I don't suppose my family will ever get over that. Roz had written such glowing letters about glamorous

136

Las Vegas and how well Ralph was doing, and how all the stars loved him.

Well, you can't win them all. But I'd appreciate a little favor. If you should be taking one of those guided tours through Beverly Hills and the movie colony, ask the guide to point out the Buddy Hackett house. Pay especial attention to his driveway. If I'm lying there with my ass pointing upward, run to the nearest friendly neighborhood police station and report it.

4. Howard Robard Hughes, the "vanishing American"

The gaunt, poorly attired gent with the flashing black eyes and nervous manner sat in a booth in the back of the showroom at the Flamingo Hotel one June night in 1954 with a bosomy blonde who had a ravenous appetite.

He seemed as out of place in those surroundings, with star Tony Martin entertaining onstage, as Zsa Zsa Gabor might have been at an outdoor rally of the Daughters of the American Revolution in Pasadena. He was unshaven and wore a creased, dark seersucker suit that had seen better days, and battered sneakers, which would become a symbol through the years to identify him to the world at large.

That man was Howard Robard Hughes, and the lady with him was another of his starlets, who had been kind enough to keep him company away from her acting chores on the Hughes movie lot in Hollywood.

A world-famous eccentric who specialized in aircraft and movie studios, Hughes (it was being rumored) was now interested in a highly secret venture known as Space Age Dynamics. A frequent visitor here in Las Vegas, Hughes could have worn burlap and still been eagerly accepted in far more desirable places in the world than Las Vegas gaming inns.

It was a known fact that Howard always brought a stack of crisp, brand-new hundred-dollar bills with him on his trips to the pleasure palaces in Las Vegas. And the employees kept a sharp eye peeled for him. H.H. handed out those "C" notes for the slightest courtesies extended him.

That night I sat watching Tony Martin from a booth next to Hughes. But even though I kept on nodding pleasantly and constantly, until I got a kink in the neck, he seemed to ignore me. I could just as well have been nodding to the wall or the ornate ceiling. But I didn't give up. After all, I wasn't a complete stranger to him. We had met on a couple occasions during the past year, and he had been most cordial.

So I nodded again. This time Hughes grudgingly nodded back, but so stiffly I was sure his neck would crack. Then he turned back to his lettuce-and-tomato triple-deck sandwich. I knew what I had to do as soon as the show was over—get an interview with Hughes for my column. It wouldn't matter what I asked as long as H.H. gave answers.

But I did have definite questions. I had heard from a pal in the eastern money markets that Howard Hughes was planning to move his vast aircraft facilities from the West Coast and set them all down in Nevada, possibly outside Las Vegas. This would give him many tax benefits. More important, he'd get isolation and desert dryness. I stopped watching Tony Martin onstage and kept an eye on Howard Hughes. He could be most elusive.

Sure enough, about ten minutes before Tony ended his show, I noticed Hughes starting to slide out from his booth. Leaving the lady with the lemon-blonde hair still sitting there up to her elbows in her filet mignon, he started taking giant steps toward the exit. But I was close behind him. It looked like Ichabod Crane and little David in a foot race.

Hughes, surrounded by three burly bodyguards, was heading for the parking lot. As he ran for his black limousine, he kept looking nervously over his shoulder like Liza crossing the ice floes ahead of the pursuing hounds.

In my finest falsetto voice, I yelled, "Hey, Mister Hughes, can I have a word or two with you?" But it seemed futile because the man who was worth about $700 million in that year of 1954 was making strides like a thin-assed flamingo in that Flamingo Hotel parking area.

I finally caught up to him as he tried getting into the back seat of his limousine. "Please, sir, just one question? You know who I am, I'm Ralph Pearl and I write a column for the Las Vegas *Sun.*"

We were at that moment about ten feet apart and Hughes hesitated, with one foot inside the car and hanging there like a human stork caught in the branches of a tree.

Hughes, visibly annoyed by such an intrusion on his privacy, was now facing me. "What is the question, Mister Pearl? And please make it fast."

"Well, sir, is there a possibility that you are at this time planning to move your aircraft business from the West Coast and settle here in Nevada—or maybe Las Vegas?" Grimacing slightly, Hughes didn't answer right away. He just pondered for a moment or two or three, choosing his words like a guy without much money trying to send a ten-word Western Union message.

"No, Ralph, there's absolutely no truth to such a rumor. I have no plans to move my aircraft plant to Las Vegas or Nevada." At that moment I remember trying to analyze his voice rather than the answer to my question. He spoke in a nasal, hesitating manner.

But miracle of miracles, he was still talking. "The gaming casinos and never-ending supply of free whiskey to the gamers would make it highly impractical. Especially if those gamers were employees of mine. I'm not about to compete with

140

blackjack, craps, and the slot machines at their easy disposal."

"So, Mister Hughes . . ." I had to grin as I spoke, because my falsetto voice wasn't too different-sounding from his high-pitched tones, "can you tell me . . . ?" I could have stopped then and there, because I was no longer talking to Howard Hughes but to a gaseous carbon monoxide spray let out by the black Cadillac limousine speeding off with Hughes and his three bodyguards.

However, a curious, beady-eyed gopher came out from behind a rock at that moment and blinked at me.

The next day I had half a column about my meeting with Howard Hughes in the Flamingo Hotel parking lot.

I know what you're probably asking, "How come, you schmuck, you didn't ask Hughes that night if he'd ever build or buy a Las Vegas hotel?" I would have probably scoffed at you for asking such a foolish question. Howard Hughes buying or building a hotel in Las Vegas! Stupid, man, stupid!

In the wee hours of morning, November 27, 1966, a large truck pulled over to the abandoned service elevator at the Desert Inn. The doors opened and a tall man, dressed in pajamas, walked out of the truck and into the elevator. Exactly twelve years and a few months had elapsed since my interview with Hughes back in 1954 under starlight in the Flamingo parking lot.

That was Howard Robard Hughes returning in his unorthodox fashion to Las Vegas. A trusted aide informed me, after it was revealed that Hughes was ensconced at the Desert Inn, that he would live here for the rest of his life.

Being money-conscious, I impulsively asked, "He's gonna live at the Desert Inn for the rest of his life? Do you know what a fancy suite at the Inn costs daily?"

Though the mysterious stranger had registered as "Robert Murphy," only a few people in Las Vegas didn't already know it was none other than Howard Hughes on that ninth floor. Las Vegas innkeepers have never been eager to rent their "precious rooms" to other than gamblers. And since H.H. was definitely not a gamer of any sort, it was most puzzling at that time, I remember. Why would the D-I boss, Moe Dalitz, give up a much-sought-after suite to a nongambler even if he was Howard Hughes?

Not too long after, the sensational news broke about Hughes' purchasing the Desert Inn from Moe Dalitz and Company. The historic ninth floor at the D-I soon became a fortress. It was equipped with a special elevator, operated only by a select group of male aides servicing Hughes. Also specially installed were phone systems, switchboards, closed circuit TV's, and ultra-special air purifiers in Hughes' suite, not to mention amplifying equipment for the slightly deaf tycoon.

However, some four years later, on November 25, 1970, Howard Hughes would pick up his gadgets and flee in the early dawning to the Britannia Beach Hotel outside Nassau in the Paradise Islands. Talk about the shit hitting the biggest fan in the whole universe, that news hit page one in newspapers all over the world. Even in Georgia and Mississippi.

A couple of days later, Hughes' number one man, Robert Maheu, who had been in absolute control of all Hughes operations in Nevada, was fired with a neatness and dispatch that was to make almost daily news from then on. Having been employed for more than four years by Hughes for the neat sum of $500,000 a year, Maheu wasn't about to fold his tent and steal away. He started a $50-million lawsuit against the Hughes Tool Company and Howard Hughes for an unlawful termination of his verbal contract.

Thinking back to those days in 1971 and 1972, Hughes must have wondered many a night—whether he was in his fortress at the Britannia Beach Hotel or later in Managua, Nicaragua—"Why didn't I build an aircraft factory as suggested by that plump little Las Vegas columnist that night in

1954 in the Flamingo Hotel parking lot? Certainly I know more about aircraft than the complex, brain-racking job of running gambling palaces."

In that four-year period from 1966 through 1970, Howard Hughes was on record in Nevada for having invested almost $300 million in acquiring the Desert Inn, Landmark, Sands, and Frontier Hotels. Also the Castaways, a TV station, Silver Slipper, a local airport in Las Vegas, and Harold's Club in Reno. Many of those ventures were heavily in the red when Hughes fled to Nassau.

The reason for Hughes' sudden flight was simple. He was now sure that his Nevada operation was backfiring on all cylinders and losing him millions of dollars. He had a staff who belonged in the driver's seat like Truman Capote belonged in the Green Bay Packers' backfield. And since Bob Maheu was his number one man and responsible for the operation, he put together a few simple facts, then fired Maheu pronto.

Bob's idea that the Hughes hotels could be run like General Motors, U.S. Steel, and R.C.A. had proved to be utterly disastrous. His idea of doing away with free booze, lodgings, junkets to the gamblers, and operating on the practical theory of profit and loss had fizzled.

Fine words and noble thoughts in a town like Los Angeles, New York, or Chicago. But to fight a tried and true system set down by an astute gang of hard-headed gamblers, who have made Las Vegas a billion-dollar industry, was downright foolish. Sure, gaming guys like Siegel, Dalitz, Katleman, Prell, Webb, Zarowitz, and Kerkorian gave away a lot in making Las Vegas what it is today. But it all came back tenfold.

Another asinine move by Hughes, or Maheu, or both was the hiring of topflight ex-FBI men to oversee the hotel gaming operations. As soon as it leaked out, many high rollers in the Sands, Desert Inn, Frontier, and Landmark gambled elsewhere. One thing they certainly didn't want was an ex-

FBI man looking over their shoulders when they were splurging with the big black chips in enormous quantity on that green felt table.

One heavy bettor from Chicago didn't give a damn whether or not an ex-FBI man in a Hughes hotel looked over his shoulder when he bet. And, Charley, that Chicagoan could really bet. He had an unlimited credit anywhere in Las Vegas. I'd seen him win or lose in the area of $50,000 many a night.

He won $46,000 one night at the Sands and, when he got back home to his desk at the factory, he got a visit from an agent at IRS wanting to know more about "46 big ones" and was he going to declare them? That's just one example of how ex-FBI guys in Vegas gaming parlors are about as necessary as a publicity man in a Nevada brothel.

There are a thousand and one ways to cheat the house, also a thousand and one cheaters drifting into casinos from all over the world. It's a wonder, during the time those ex-FBI men worked in Hughes gaming casinos, that the cheaters didn't walk away with their underwear or false teeth. Or did they?

H.H. preferred the young and bright "nothings" to the gnarled, hard-talking veterans of many years, who could spot a cheater just by watching the gent operate for a few minutes. But that didn't stop him from also watching the dealer, who might have some ideas of his own about going into business for himself.

Much was written in newspapers and magazines all over the world about Howard Hughes' coming to Las Vegas to invest many of his millions in that legalized gaming hotel industry. Locals were tremendously pleased. They felt it would enhance the economy—also create more jobs. As for some of the gaming owners who'd been taking a beating from the boys in Washington who were out to get them, they hoped Hughes would be the answer to their troubles.

144

Not only was the gaming industry in Nevada extremely happy to see Hughes and his millions investing in that economy, but the gaming commissioners and county officials also breathed peacefully for a change.

But their happiness became grief when Howard Hughes vanished from the Desert Inn on Thanksgiving of 1970. Suddenly the once grateful City Fathers began sniping away. They started spouting sickly half truths and assuming a holier-than-thou attitude trying to protect the "poor little gaming" and hotel industry here from that bad, bad Hughes person.

"If Howard Hughes thinks he can disappear without a word, then expect to return to Las Vegas and pick up where he left off, then he's got another guess coming," screamed some of the county commissioners, who were no longer as grateful as they had been in 1966 and 1967 when Hughes began pouring millions of dollars into this industry. In 1966, when it looked as if H.H. might become a part of the Vegas industrial scene those selfsame commissioners were palpitating with joy.

But now one of the politicos was screaming, "Is Howard Hughes a person or a ghost? Let him come forth, or let's revoke his license to operate his hotels here in Las Vegas." Big words. But they were now coming when H.H. had almost $300 million invested in Las Vegas and in Reno.

The "Screw Howard Hughes" campaign got bolder and bolder even though his hotels and clubs employed almost ten thousand local people.

The important townspeople suddenly forgot what had happened after he came to Las Vegas. After buying the Desert Inn and Sands, Hughes suddenly bought the Landmark Hotel, a white elephant which had been built, but unopened for several years, while scores of creditors fought for control of that structural fiasco. An absolute stalemate existed at the Landmark until Hughes bought it at the inflated price that was asked. Actually, he could have picked it up for thirty cents on the dollar.

Not only did he buy the hotel, he also settled all existing claims by many creditors, who had already written it off as a bad debt. Immediately a thousand people went to work at the Landmark Hotel. Joy to Vegas land!

Now, of course, those good deeds were all in the past, and the politicos looking for free space in the newspapers for their gaseous utterances were moralizing, "Let's protect this industry and its employees from Hughes." Horseshit!

Las Vegas was full of rumors following H.H.'s flight to Nassau. Everybody in the nation was making guesses where he was or wasn't. At three o'clock one morning I got a call from a guy who should have known better. "Get down to the Desert Inn right away. My girl tells me Hughes is sitting in the lobby. She swears it's him. He's wearing a beard and dark glasses."

Knowing it was an utter impossibility that THE MAN would dare sit in a Vegas hotel lobby with the whole world searching for him, I told my friend to drop dead, then went back to bed. But who could sleep? Maybe the Ichabod Crane of the twentieth century had really made a mysterious return to Las Vegas. It wasn't logical, but since when had the bashful billionaire ever been that?

I kept worrying that an unheard of second stringer for a paper in Jean, Nevada, would beat me to the punch by going over to the Desert Inn, discovering it was really H.H., then writing a world-syndicated, copyright-exclusive story I'd never get over. So, twenty minutes later, a coat over my pajamas, I trudged into the Desert Inn lobby, searching. About the only people around at that hour were a few stray slot players, a sleepy gent, a fat lady at the "21" table, and three hoarse losers at the dice tables.

However, there in the corner was the "MAN." Sure enough, he wore a beard and dark glasses and sat quietly reading a newspaper. As I approached him, he stood up and began striding rapidly out of the lobby toward the swimming pool. So far, so good. He seemed to be the same height as Hughes, but a bit fleshier. But then maybe H.H. had put on some weight? The chase was on. Finally I collared him.

"Sir, would you kindly identify yourself?"

"Gladly," said the man as he took off his dark glasses. "I'm Howard Hughes, but the people who work here," and he pointed back inside the lobby and the casino, "won't believe me." Then the forty-year-old man, who was of Mexican or Spanish origin, dashed off, his coattails flying in the breeze.

I went back to bed, and I didn't sleep for the rest of that ghastly early morning.

Several days later, while the hue and cry over H.H.'s sudden disappearance from Las Vegas was still being written about in papers all over the nation, County Commissioner James "Sailor" Ryan,* an explosively candid gent, commented about the shabby condition of the Hughes hotels, which were heavily in the red.

"It proves once again that the mob boys who have been running these hotel gaming casinos for the past thirty years are without equal when it comes to operating legalized gaming."

Today all of the Hughes gaming casinos have undergone drastic changes. The bright, apple-cheeked lads with army or FBI training are no longer in evidence in those gaming pits. And that's the way it should be. The cheaters of the world, who had beaten a hurried path to the doors of the H.H. gaming parlors, are now giving them a wide berth, because many of the veteran gaming executives—those who grew up in the business working in illicit craps parlors all over the nation— are back in the saddle and casting suspicious eyes at everyone.

*County Commissioner Ryan was indicted in the summer of 1972 for taking a $5,000 bribe, but the case was thrown out of court.

One more point that needs clearing up about Howard Hughes and his adventure into the land of the green felt tables: There has been a unanimous opinion among those in high places (Las Vegas, Washington, and New York) that Hughes would be doing an enormous favor for the legalized gaming tycoons in Las Vegas and other Nevada gaming parlors by coming here. "Howard Hughes will have nothing to do with the 'undesirable element' making up part of the gaming economy here," said one blue-nosed hypocrite in Carson City. "He'll whitewash our gaming industry."

But don't forget this: The first hotel Howard Hughes bought in Las Vegas was the Desert Inn. And though it was "Wilbur Clark's Desert Inn," you already know that poor Wilbur had no authority, because the D-I was owned and operated by Moe Dalitz and his associates. The only way Hughes was able to get his foot in the solid gold door that's Las Vegas was to be close enough to Dalitz to be able to negotiate with that gent for the Desert Inn.

Our Moe had had more than his share of national and international notoriety during his hectic years as a gaming (Desert Inn and Stardust Hotels) tycoon. Or didn't you know about the Kefauver Reports in the Fifties that got almost daily newspaper and TV coverage?

If Moe Dalitz and his associates were "undesirable elements making up part of Las Vegas' gaming economy," then Howard Hughes couldn't have given a damn. He was directly indebted to Dalitz and Co. for being able to get into Las Vegas. Of course, the way things turned out, Howard must have cursed Moe plenty in his troubled sleep for ever having let him buy in.

There is further evidence to suggest that there was more than a "buyer-seller" relationship between Howard Hughes and Moe Dalitz. In the summer of 1966, Dalitz was retained by Hughes as a "consultant for the Howard Hughes gaming casinos." Moe lived in a house on the grounds of the Desert

Inn until H.H. did his disappearing act that Thanksgiving night in 1970. But by then H.H. had already gone for $300 million.

In January, 1972, all hell broke loose once again. Howard broke his long public silence and spoke with seven newsmen and TV commentators by phone from his retreat at the Britannia Beach Hotel in Nassau. The main reason for his breaking his long silence was that a slick author by the name of Clifford Irving had "revealed" to the press that he had "an authorized autobiography of Howard Hughes." It had been given with H.H.'s blessings and complete support, he said.

Howard Hughes, speaking with the fourth estaters, denied having had anything to do with Irving, who was a complete stranger to him. Hughes' other reason for speaking out was that Las Vegas sources were stating that he was either a vegetable, unable to talk, or a captive held by plotting members of his empire.

Speaking for more than two and a half hours, H.H. even promised to make a public appearance in the future to disprove rumors that he had "hair away down his back and fingernails six inches long." His public statement came as a relief to me. I had said many times, on my local TV show, that Howard Hughes was well, "but not ready to play pro football or go mountain climbing."

The bashful billionaire spoke clearly and most intelligently during that long session on the phone, and newsmen who had spoken with him over the long years vouched for his authenticity. It made several warring anti-Hughes factions, both locally and nationally, backtrack hurriedly.

And it very likely helped send Edith and Clifford Irving to jail.

At this writing, Howard Hughes has not made that promised public appearance. Waiting for that event are the palpitating public, the Nevada banks, and his more than ten thousand Las Vegas employees and investors, who would like nothing better than for H.H. to continue keeping his $300 million working for them here.

But no matter where the bashful billionaire happens to be at this moment—the Bahamas, Nicaragua, maybe even right here among us on his Blue Diamond, Nevada, ranch, or possibly sitting in a hotel lobby wearing dark glasses, a beard, and dingy sneakers—he has done a lot to get a troubled world to momentarily forget its sicknesses.

As for me, I keep hoping I'll run into Hughes again, maybe in a showroom or a parking lot. And when I do, I hope to be fully prepared with the proper questions—and a Brownie camera.

5. Hookers, Hustlers, etc.

It happens almost every day in Las Vegas.

An eager young lady with stars in her eyes steps off a plane or a bus, stoutly determined to get a job as a dancer, singer, show girl, or what-have-you in one of the celebrated French shows playing on the Strip. In many cases she comes formidably equipped with a scrapbook and a dozen or more clippings from her town daily or weekly newspaper, reporting her triumphs in the annual high school or college musical revue.

Now all she has to do is get the impresario of one of the Vegas shows to look at her. That, generally, is as easy as scaling Mt. Everest in a kiddie car. It's safe to estimate that five thousand of these fresh, starry-eyed youngsters will come here for fame and fortune every year.

Less than half of one percent succeed; they're competing with singers, dancers, and show girls fresh from Broadway, Los Angeles, and Chicago shows. In the old days each showroom had a "girlie line" at the start of its regular show, which starred such well-known entertainers as Jimmy Durante, Danny Thomas, Sammy Davis, Jr., Frank Sinatra, the late

Joe E. Lewis, and a dozen other topflight café stars. A girl coming into town had a better chance for a job if she would "play ball" with the guy bringing her to the attention of the show producer.

Then, about ten years ago, the hotel producers found girlie lines impractical—a waste of money. They reasoned correctly that café-goers, who came to see a Danny Thomas or Mitzi Gaynor, couldn't care less about a line of high-kicking femmes who opened the show and only stayed on a few minutes.

There are numerous forms of "juice." It could be a high-rolling gambler at the Stardust Hotel, for instance. The high roller has taken a fancy to a pink-cheeked little tyke who sits opposite him in the coffee shop.

Down to her last double sawbuck and clutching her return bus ticket in one hand while stirring her coffee with the other, she blinks her eyelashes at the guy, who isn't at all bad-looking if you like the Ernie Borgnine type.

Soon the high roller is chatting with Suzie Pink Cheeks and hearing all about her frustrations with a lecherous bastard who promised to introduce her to a man who was a "friend" of the producer of the "Lido de Paris" show at the Stardust.

Our rugged hero, who's still smarting from the loss of $20,000 at the dice tables in the Stardust the night before, pats the youngster's hand and assures her she'll not only get an audition but a real chance for a job at "Lido de Paris."

You can bet your toenails that the boss at any hotel, including the Stardust, will listen eagerly to suggestions offered by a regular customer who gambles heavily and regularly in his casino.

How grateful Suzie Pink Cheeks must be is strictly up to the high roller, whose demands can be usurious in a physical sort of a way. Then, of course, it's strictly up to Suzie.

If she has a smattering of "hooker, hustler, whore" in her, she'll use her glamorous, unclad body behind those footlights to lure a high roller or anyone else who can supplement her meager salary of $250 or so a week.

That brings me to a nice lady by the name of Gloria. She's an out-and-out hustler, but will tell you indignantly that she mustn't be confused with the lower-grade hooker or whore.

"Whether you know it or not," she told me one afternoon as we loitered in the lobby of Caesars Palace, "I leave nothing to chance in my job. I know how to service my customers," which was exactly the word she used—"service," instead of the more familiar one used in poolrooms, gaming casinos, and ladies' beauty parlors.

"I hustle to make a living, but you won't find me soliciting from a hotel lobby or a back street. And I won't settle for a couple of free Scotches, a meal, and a $25 *shmata* [Yiddish for dress]."

Gloria then went into intimate detail while passing locals gave me the fish eye. She had been a typist in a huge utility company back in Kansas City. At least once a week she had to jump into the hay with her boss, and if she was lucky that week, he paid off with that *shmata* she mentioned.

One day she got pregnant. The boss denied any or all participation, but generously paid for the abortion. That's when Gloria kissed him off, packed her cheesy $5 Gladstone, and took off for Las Vegas.

"I've been here ten years. I mind my own business, and I try to stay the hell out of public places and away from those vice-squad bastards. No, I'm not coming from the room of a client right now. I like the beauty parlor in this hotel, that's why I'm here. But about my men: I own a ten-room house on the Desert Inn golf course and turn my tricks from the comfort of one of my four bedrooms."

Gloria, about twenty-five and a premeditated blonde, has always been taken for Tuesday Weld, the movie actress. She was dressed simply but elegantly in a Saks Fifth Avenue sort of way. Unlike the "hookers and whores" she had sneered at earlier, Gloria snared a job as a showgirl when she first got here. It paid $195 a week, but Gloria wasn't about to devote a good part of her youth prancing about a stage in a naked state while accumulating muscles in the wrong places.

"But that's the greatest place in the world—the stage of a French show—to start picking up a clientele from the big spenders drooling up at you from the ringside. The first six months in that job I always had a guy waiting for me as I came into the lobby. My income increased enormously. I made $80,000 those first six months. That's when I quit my show-girl job.

"No, I don't have a set fee for clients," continued Gloria. We had left the lobby of Caesars Palace and were roaming about the grounds on that sun-drenched August afternoon. "But you can bet your ass, even mine, that I won't take on a guy unless there's at least a 'C' [$100] note to start with."

Gloria then went into a discussion of "hookers and whores," who were ruining her business here in Las Vegas, she said.

"Those girls are emotionally screwed up. They'll hump for a meal, a fur piece, or a pair of shoes, if they can't get the guy to come across with money. They'll even try getting the guy to fall in love with them, which isn't a bad idea if you can get marriage from those hot-assed little monsters. But in nine cases out of ten, a whore or a hustler will wind up with her ass in the can.

"From then on she's a marked woman for the vice-squad guys prowling about. Me, I have a telephone answering service and I'll never take a guy who hasn't already come highly recommended from a satisfied customer. Shit, I'm not about to pick up a slob in a casino, then find out after I've been in the hay with the sonofabitch that he's a vice-squad guy or a hopped-up freak."

Gloria then explained her "business operation" at home. "I get about ten calls a day, but only take on three a day

154

from Wednesday through Saturday. The other three days my boy friend and I get away from Las Vegas. We're either on the boat (a thirty-foot job with two bedrooms) on Lake Mead or off to Hawaii in the winter."

Suggesting that her boy friend might be procuring in order to keep it all in the family, Gloria let out a howl. "Hell no. He operates his own business downtown. No, not a casino."

"One more point puzzles me, Gloria," I interjected. "You said you get about ten calls a day. If you work four days a week, that amounts to twelve clients. What happens to the other fifty-eight clients?"

"Oh, I forgot to mention," said Gloria. "I have three other girls working for me."

POOR, POOR MIKE

He was a fat, bald, wealthy Miami Beach realtor in his early fifties who was approaching a nervous breakdown from too much work and no play. It worried his wife and their two daughters (who were home from college for the summer). They didn't want papa to die.

"Why don't you go visit your friend, the hotel owner in Las Vegas?" his wife asked. "As a boss at the Dunes Hotel, he'll probably show you a time like you never had it before." She sounded like Myron Cohen doing one of his popular Yiddish jokes.

Mike balked at the idea of a vacation, but his everloving wife, Rachel, and his daughters finally persuaded him to call his friend, Harry Fineman, in Las Vegas. Harry, of course, was overjoyed at the idea of his pal, Mike, coming to visit him. Now Mike was at the Miami Airport, ready to depart for Las Vegas. He kissed Rachel and his daughters, then disappeared into the Las Vegas-bound plane.

Rachel and the girls went back to their ten-room house on the beach. Papa was going to have fun. If Rachel at that moment could have realized how much "fun" her "Mottel" was really going to have, she would have sprouted wings at that moment and intercepted the plane taking her husband to the "Fun City."

Back in Las Vegas at the Dunes Hotel, Harry was briefing one of the chorus cuties he had already assigned to be Mike's steady date when he got here. "Stay out of the show for the next ten days and move into the hotel. You'll be a recent widow getting over your loss. Romance the shit out of him, and, if you give him the idea you work here at the Dunes or once worked in a whorehouse, I'll flatten your skull. You hear?"

Julie didn't look like a former whore. She had a sensational figure from either side and wasn't too bad from the front or back either. Her blue eyes glowed innocently.

One thing you had to say in Julie's favor: When it came to big money she could take orders even if it meant shacking up with a Shetland pony. What made it all the better, sweet Julie didn't look the type.

So, along came our innocent, bone-weary Miami Beach hero to Las Vegas. He had it all figured out to the minute. "Get up about eight, sit in the sun a couple of hours, do some swimming and reading, then go back to the room for a nap." Later in the day, after lunch with his pal, Harry, he'd go back to the swimming pool area and do some swimming and reading again, and maybe even strike up a conversation with somebody.

At six he'd go back to the suite, shower, shave, then call his Rachel in Miami Beach and give her a rundown of the day's events before he went downstairs to see a show on the Strip. Back in the hotel by ten, Mike would watch some television before climbing into the sack alone for a good night's sleep.

And that's exactly what Mike did for the first two days. But on the third day Julie was at the pool. Even though she wore an abreviated swim suit, Julie looked like she was coming out, because no bikini was made that could cover her forty-two-inch bust.

As they sat at the pool ten feet apart, out came Mike's "guardian angel," Harry, who introduced Mike to Julie. Then he went back to his chores as boss of the Dunes, never to be seen for the rest of the day. Julie's hesitant, shy story about her misfortunes hit Mike with the impact of a bowling ball smashing his toes. He actually had tears in his eyes as he sympathized with this brave girl and her tale of woe.

They began seeing each other day and night. And during that first week Mike never dared get out of line. He would leave her at her door, after days in the sun and nights having dinner and seeing shows. For a while a kiss on the cheek sufficed. But something was bound to happen sooner or later as Julie kept rubbing against Mike "accidentally." He finally got the message.

So he took her to bed. Julie, the thirty-year-old ex-whore, chorus girl, and swinger, moaned and groaned most convincingly as our Mike "violated" her that first night. Julie actually screamed in "pain" when Mike entered her. This had to be sheer fantasy on her part, because she hadn't screamed in pain at intercourse since she was sixteen back in Kansas City. But Mike was gallant. Later that night he went out and bought Julie a $100 dress.

Now the romance really got into high gear. Mike's phone calls to his Rachel became infrequent. But his good wife back in Miami Beach was understanding. Harry was probably giving him such a great vacation that Mike didn't have time to call.

Mike had become a veteran in the hay. He and Julie no longer wasted time lounging by the swimming pool. Julie was moaning less and less every day. One evening, while dining by candlelight and soft music, Mike looked into Julie's blue eyes and said, "I'm very much in love with you. Sure, I know it's too soon to marry again after what you went through, but will you be my wife?"

Always a hustler but never a wife, that proposal almost caught Julie with her panties down. But she recovered quickly by blinking her false eyelashes several times, then shyly agreeing. After all, Mike was a millionaire realtor from Miami Beach. At that moment, Dunes Hotel boss Harry Fineman stepped into the picture. He called Julie in and slapped her around so persuasively as to convince her that marriage with Mike was definitely out.

Early the next day, her eyeballs and front teeth smarting from Harry's hand-to-face encounter, Julie went to Mike prepared to give an Academy Award performance that would gladden the hearts of Otto Preminger, Darryl Zanuck, or Mike Nichols. After all, she had a very affluent fish on her carefully baited hook. The idea was to let him off, but make him pay.

Mike took one look at Julie's puffy eyes and lacerated mouth and almost had that long-expected breakdown then and there. "My God, darling. What happened? Did you fall down?"

"Yes, sweetheart," purred Mike's Juliet. "You see, I didn't sleep too good last night worrying about our future. So, I got up in the middle of the night and began walking up and down in the dark. I didn't notice the closet door was open and walked right into it. But don't worry about my face. It will be all right. I've made up my mind that I can't marry you, dear, because I keep thinking of your wife and daughters in Miami Beach. I just can't take you away from them."

Then Julie threw herself violently on the bed, her skimpy skirt flying almost over her head and exposing the more important parts of her anatomy to a lovesick idiot from Miami Beach. She began crying as if her heart would break. It wasn't too hard for Julie to cry, because her eyes and mouth still ached from that bastard Harry's slapping.

Mike swarmed all over Julie on the bed. "Don't cry, darling. It's all my fault. I never should have let you fall in love with me." Then he proceeded to crawl into her while reflecting, "Why couldn't Rachel screw like this savage, Julie? She has more motions than a Joe Namath in the backfield."

As for Julie, "I wonder how much this little sonofabitch will give me before he goes back to Miami Beach." She didn't have to wait long to find out.

Before she walked out of his life forever, Mike sat down and wrote out a check for $25,000 for his "suffering" Julie. "I know this'll never take the place of what you and me had together," said Mike, "but it'll help you forget."

Mike went back to his normal routines at home and in his office while Julie, her glorious assignment at an end, returned to the chorus and her $175-a-week job. As for Harry Fineman, the matchmaker, he made a mental note never to invite any of his pals to Las Vegas again unless they were single, poor, and a bit on the queer side. But that wasn't the end of the Mike, Julie, Harry episode.

Back in Miami Beach, Mike carried on with a broken heart and slightly bent savings account. But it didn't matter. True love was worth every penny of the $25,000. Many times during his working day Mike was tempted to pick up a phone and talk to Julie. But he didn't. He just continued carrying the biggest torch on the beach.

Not long after he got back, while sitting in the john one day at the office, Mike was looking through the pages of a girlie magazine. His fingers froze on a page that featured several girls clad only in G-strings and girlish giggles. One of them was his Julie! She was posing with a couple of showgirls on the stage of Harry's hotel in Las Vegas. Mike's eyes popped as he read the caption: "Julie Beam, Dunes Hotel

159

showgirl, celebrates her eighth year as a Las Vegas lovely."

Mike was stunned. He stared at the photo on the page for fully a minute. This was his Julie Jorgensen, ex-schoolteacher and grieving widow! Without a doubt he had been duped not only by Julie but by his old friend, Harry Fineman. Still, there might be an explanation. Mike got on the long-distance phone and called a bellman at the hotel who had been most friendly.

In a matter of minutes, the bellman gave Mike the whole story about Julie. And a sordid one it was. Hurriedly he called the bank to learn sorrowfully that his $25,000 check to Julie had been cashed the same day he gave it to her. He hasn't talked to his friend Harry in Las Vegas since. Nor has he returned.

A DEDICATED HOOKER WAS JUNIE

She was a hash slinger in a Toronto drive-in restaurant and never failed to read the pulp magazines with the lurid tales about what movie actor was doing it to what movie actress and vice versa. Naturally, the one place she always wanted to take in was Las Vegas. Her name, let's say, was June Blackman, and she measured 39-27-37, stood five feet eight, and had been tossed into the hay by more Toronto musicians and third-rate comics than she could remember.

One morning she picked up a Toronto newspaper and read in a column where the Tropicana Hotel in Las Vegas was auditioning show girls for its new show. June Blackman went back to her one room, packed a bag, and was winging off for Las Vegas the next morning. Believe it or not, she was one of the sixteen girls picked for the new show. June was now on the first step to fame and fortune—mostly fortune.

One afternoon during rehearsals at the Tropicana, I sat and chatted with June during a coffee break. She was in a reflective mood and expressed her views about Las Vegas and why she was here. She spoke strongly and with much conviction.

"Since I started working here at the Tropicana, I've met a few interesting guys who were not only big spenders and high rollers, but they paid off nicely." Then she took out a small calendar from her handbag, also a pencil, and deliberately circled that day's date, "June 16, 1962." Then she admonished, "Remember that date, kid. One year from today I intend to have $150,000 stashed away, also whatever other goodies I can accumulate from these high-rolling finks. They'll pay and pay and pay, or my name ain't June Blackman.

"They come here to gamble and screw, and I'll see to it they do both," said June. Then she put away her marked calendar. "Any broad coming here for a legit career has to be off her goddamned rocker. Las Vegas is where the money is, and in huge piles. I'm gonna grab some of it before it goes into those little black boxes under the gaming tables. The idiots who gamble here dropped $300 million this past year. Junie's gonna cut herself in for some of it."

That was the end of the discussion. She got up, and I thought, hell, this isn't exactly copy for a home newspaper. I didn't really believe she'd get what she wanted. So I promptly forgot that whole incident the moment I left her in the hotel. I'd heard such ambitious talk from other girls in the shows, but it wasn't long before these aspiring femmes were gone from Las Vegas and back slinging hash or selling trinkets in a five-and-ten-cent store.

In the following months I ran into June Blackman several times. She was always in the company of a substantial gent, and both were rushing off to a Strip hotel casino to gamble. Then I lost track of her.

On the morning of June 16, 1963, the phone rang around

eight o'clock in the morning. "Ralphie, this is June. How about you and me having coffee this morning in the Sahara? I have a scoop for you."

Once again we were sipping coffee together. This time, however, June Blackman had the look of a conqueror. She took out the circled calendar and a slip of white paper, then showed me what she had accumulated during the past 365 days.

"I have $215,640, three mink coats, a Bentley motor car, and a bagful of diamonds, rubies, and emeralds."

Christ, our Junie had been a busy girl!

Today she's a happily married woman in a fine Beverly Hills home. Her show-girl friends and her high rollers would never recognize her, because she's not blonde or flashy any more. Her hair is dark and she has a fancy nose job, which she had promised herself back in Toronto if she ever struck it rich. In June Blackman's case, the wages of sin were very lush.

I almost choked over the buttered bagel I was chewing on as I saw the figures. It sounded like a page out of a sordid Mickey Spillane paperback novel. June had gone way over her $150,000 estimate of a year ago. It certainly showed what hard work and dedication can accomplish. Late to bed and late to rise had made Junie not too healthy, but awfully wealthy and wise!

An hour after our talk, June Blackman took a plane for New York, where she would meet her mother. They went on a lengthy shopping spree on New York's Fifth Avenue, and then on a thirty-day cruise to the Orient. What did her orthodox Jewish mama think about it all?

"I told my mama that I had made a stock investment that had paid off handsomely. Maybe she didn't believe it, but she didn't ask questions," said June.

A WASHINGTON BY ANY OTHER
NAME . . .

Her name was not really Ruthie Washington, but during the Fifties she was the most affluent madam in all Las Vegas. I liked the lady because you would never have figured out her profession when you met her. Not only did she conduct herself flawlessly, but she dressed modestly and in fine fashion.

Whenever I ran into Ruthie, she usually had a "pigeon" in tow. And before he got away, Miss Washington would have separated him from many valuable yards of Uncle Sam's currency.

One night at the Frank Sinatra opening at the Sands, Ruthie and her male escort, a prominent lobbyist from the nation's capital, walked by on their way to a ringside pew. Later during the show, a captain brought me a note from Ruthie asking to talk with me after the show.

So, later that night we sat in the coffee shop. Ruthie had a problem. (That kind of problem I would gladly have for the rest of my life.) "I'm getting ready to take a four-week vacation in Europe with a good friend of mine," and she looked toward the other end of the room, where her "good friend," the distinguished guy from Washington, D.C., was talking with one of the hotel bosses.

"So, maybe you can help me, Ralph," said Ruthie. "I have a fourteen-room house overlooking the Desert Inn golf course, but I'd like to rent it while I'm in Europe. I see where Eddie Fisher and his new bride, Liz Taylor, are coming to Las Vegas about the time I'll be on vacation. Could you ask Eddie if he wants to rent it? There are six bedrooms, two sitting rooms, two swimming pools, a den, a playroom, and a sauna bath. And all I want is $5,000 for the six weeks Eddie'll be working at the Desert Inn."

I told Miss Washington I'd call Eddie the first thing in the morning. "The only thing is, Ruthie, if I can rent it, what happens if you return from Europe sooner than you expect?"

"No problem," she answered. "I have another house, this one's twelve rooms, also on the Strip, where I can stay."

The wages of sin pay off heavily, baby, in case you ever doubted it. Ruthie's long gone—retired and independently wealthy in Switzerland—but her boudoir exploits live on.

No, she never did rent that $400,000 house of hers to Eddie and his Liz. However, the gallant bosses of the Desert Inn gave them the Presidential Suite overlooking the gaming casino. It was a honeymoon Eddie would never forget.

He blew more than $300,000 at the dice tables, half of that sum in markers which stayed unpaid for several years. At this writing Eddie, now a bankrupt, is trying to make a comeback and get booked here again. No one has booked him yet, but good luck, Eddie!

CONFORTES, CLIPPINGERS, AND CO.

A man by the name of Joe Conforte one day invited me to visit his Mustang Bridge Ranch eight miles east of Reno off Highway 80. It was a unique ranch—one which had fillies who wore bikinis instead of saddles and who were in the upper brackets working as prostitutes for Joe and Sally Conforte. The girls earned in the nice neighborhood of $30,000 annually while working only three weeks every month.

Joe and Sally Conforte conduct a legal house of prostitution in Storey County, which happens to be about the size of Manhattan's Central Park. Joe, who got rebuffed the year before when he tried to erect an "annex" in prosperous, flourishing Clark County, which boasts a bustling town known as Las Vegas, took his defeat philosophically, contenting himself with writing indignant letters to the editors in Las Vegas.

A short gent about fifty, he wears flashy diamond rings, one on each hand, and is a jolly sort of guy. And why not?

After paying his annual license fee of $18,000 to Story County, and the big wages to his thirty girls, a couple of secretaries, and a chauffeur, Joe is more than happy to bring home the bacon to wife Sally, really the legal operator of Mustang Bridge Ranch, to the tune of half a million dollars yearly.

But about my visit to Joe's "Ranch."

It was a ranch as unlike the Cartrights' Ponderosa spread of TV's "Bonanza" as George Wallace is unlike Sammy Davis, Jr. After you pass what looks like a "graveyard" for broken, battered automobiles, you came upon a railroad crossing and a rickety wooden bridge. It reminds me of that Chappaquiddick bridge. This one creaked loudly as I crossed it.

Parking in a huge lot, I walked across to a chain-link fence, which had a couple of German shepherds on the inside. Joe came rushing out of a small mobile home, which served as a reception office and led to several connecting mobile homes. This, he told me, is where all the action happens. There are luxurious bedrooms in each of the trailers, TV, expensive carpeting, and almost everything to make "customers" feel right at home.

Since it was early in the day, the girls were merely lolling about the grounds, hair in curlers, dressed in comfortable slacks, blouses, and sweaters.

Conforte, who had been in Reno for the past fifteen years, steered me out into the open. "Legalized prostitution is the greatest thing that can happen in a gaming state like you have in Nevada. We run an orderly house. The girls all do well financially and only work three weeks every month. There's also a doctor on the grounds, who sees to it they don't have, whadd'ya call them, oh yeah, communicable diseases."

The base fee for a gent seeking this kind of carnal pleasure starts at $10, but Joe quickly explained, "They can have other services that run a bit higher." I didn't ask him to explain the "other services." And though the Mustang Bridge Ranch is open for business around the clock, mornings are relatively quiet. Only a handful of girls were "on duty" to take care of the stray males. The others were writing letters home, shopping in Reno, or just lying under a tree enjoying the sun.

"Come back around six tonight," urged Conforte, "and you'll see all our girls—about twenty of them—in action." I declined reluctantly. "Gotta catch a plane back to Las Vegas, Joe, at two this afternoon. But thanks anyway." I was too embarrassed to tell him that my ever-loving wife had warned me earlier that morning, "Look, you little bastard, but don't touch the merchandise!"

As a most enterprising, tax-paying citizen of Storey County, Nevada, Joe has great faith in "the oldest profession in the world." He tersely predicted, "It'll be here long after these bluenoses who are always screaming to put me out of business are dead and buried. And usually those bluenoses belong to women whose husbands are my best customers. So, go figure it."

He was driving me back to the Reno Airport. "What really busts my balls is the attitude of some of the county commissioners back in your neck of the woods. If ever a place needed a legal house of prostitution, it's Las Vegas. Christ, on any weekend in the year, you fall over the whores standing around in the hotel casinos and bars waiting to grab a pigeon. How's the poor sonofabitch gonna know if the broad who picks him up isn't loaded with VD, or that she won't fleece him once she gets him in the hay?" A good point.

Now at the airport, several porters, a sheriff's deputy, and the man who runs a store in the airport greet Joe warmly. Grinning almost shyly, Joe darts a quick look in my direction to see if I have caught the local reaction.

166

"You might make a note of this point," observed Conforte. "We are always getting letters from girls who want to work for Sally and me. They write from almost every state in the nation, and nine out of ten of them are girls working as legal secretaries, typists, clerks, or just plain housewives. Too bad you couldn't have stayed around and met some of them."

Now I was running for the plane, and Joe Conforte, one of the better businessmen in Reno, yelled, "Say hello to Martha when you see her."

Martha, of course, was another story all by itself.

She was a lady in her early sixties who had spent most of her life as a public-spirited citizen heavily involved in charitable affairs in Nevada. Despite the fact that she had lived in and around Las Vegas, read the newspapers, and watched the TV news daily, she was still a most naïve lady.

Wealthy, independent, and without a family, Martha's greatest joy was trying to help the sick and destitute. She had an air of innocence that would have been much more proper in the environs of Whitefish, Montana, than here in the Show Capital of the World with its boozers, losers, lovers, and dollies as far as the jaundiced eye could see.

It was time for the annual Heart Fund campaign, and many important banking executives, members of the clergy, and the president of the university were meeting behind closed doors to pick a VIP to head the campaign that year. Naturally, no meeting would have been complete without Martha in attendance. Her suggestions and her untiring efforts were always eagerly solicited, because she had plenty of spare time to offer.

At the meeting several important names were offered as possible campaign leaders. Then Martha asked to be heard. She was beaming happily, because she had the name of a man who would probably be the next head of that year's Heart Fund. At least that's what a local press agent had told her earlier in the day when she asked for his suggestion of a big VIP name in town who might fit into that Heart Fund picture.

This wasn't one of Martha's better days, because the slightly degenerate press agent, playing a prank on poor Martha, had suggested the name of Joe Conforte to her as the next Heart Fund chairman. He explained that Joe came from a wealthy Mormon family in Nevada with impeccable family ties and unlimited wealth.

The mere fact that Martha had never heard of Joe Conforte didn't bother her. There were a lot of notables in Nevada Martha had never heard of. She was overjoyed. Not only would she have a prominent chairman, but a man who would contribute heavily to the Fund.

Now Martha was on her feet there in the luxurious offices of one of the town's bank presidents. "Yes, gentlemen," she proudly said, "I do have the name of a most prominent Nevadan who'll be the ideal person to head up this year's drive. His name's Joseph Conforte, and I'm sure you all know him."

Then she sat down hurriedly, because an enormous howl of laughter filled the room. Some of the more austere gents, who hadn't laughed in years, practically fell on the floor.

"Joe Conforte?" More screaming and laughing. However, the clergyman and the university head were not amused, and sat glowering at poor Martha, who was trying to disappear under her chair.

Yelled one VIP, "Martha, you've got a priceless sense of humor." Martha nodded and replied with a sickly, greenish look and dyspeptic grunt. She was mightily confused. No fund chairman having been chosen, the meeting was adjourned until the following afternoon. Outside the bank, a suspicious member of that meeting, an advertising agency executive, stopped Martha as she was getting into her car.

"You didn't really know who Joe Conforte was, did you,

Martha?" The look of sheer misery on the patrician lady's face was answer enough.

"Joe Conforte is one of the more undesirable people in this state," he explained. "He owns and operates a couple of houses of prostitution just outside Reno." Martha gulped, and almost fainted.

In all fairness to the practical-joking press agent, he never dreamed that she would do what she did in that banker's plush office. He thought she would have quietly checked out his suggestion, then learned the awful truth before getting up and plunging the VIP's into absolute hysteria.

She hasn't talked to that press agent since.

Joe Conforte, who heard about it all, never stops telling the story to his friends and "associates."

Back in the early Fifties, a "loving, hard-working couple," Eddie and Roxie Clippinger, owned and most successfully operated an illegal house of prostitution, "Roxie's," which was exactly four miles from the bustling Strip. Before the FBI moved in to enforce the Mann Act by charging the Clippingers with "transporting girls across state lines for immoral purposes," the Las Vegas *Sun* and its publisher Hank Greenspun had already exploded the $1 million annual operation at "Roxie's." Suffice to say, it was eventually closed down.

Eddie and Roxie had been convicted and sentenced to three years in a federal penitentiary. Before starting their sentence, Roxie talked with a newsman from Reno and complained bitterly about the "vendetta" because "Roxie's" grossed a million dollars a year.

"Those bastards never took into account that Eddie and me had plenty of expenses running 'Roxie's.' All the money didn't come just from the girls. We also operated a legitimate bar at the motel, cigarette machines, and a car rental agency on the grounds. We also took in rent money from the girls who worked for us and stayed at our dormitory."

But investigation revealed that, of the annual million-dollar gross, $2,000 came from the bar, $200 from the cigarette machines, $1,500 from the dormitories, and $600 from the car rental.

A mathematically inclined newsman, calculating rapidly, came up with the figure that "only" $995,700 came from the girlie operation, instead of a million dollars as recklessly revealed by the press. Of that $995,700, approximately one-third went to the girls, leaving a comfy, cozy $660,000 less $100,000 a year "payoff money" to former Sheriff Jones and several others promoting the cause of the Clippingers in those early Fifties.

You're probably asking if there happens to be a moral to this sordid tale of the Clippingers and the Confortes. You can bet your bippy there is. The Clippingers resorted to "the muscle" and stayed in business as long as they greased the proper palms by handing out about $2,000 a week. Not so the Confortes. They're as legal as you possibly can get in Storey County. They have a yearly license, pay taxes, and contribute regularly to the annual fund-raising drives, while giving off a fresh, medically pure daily image.

And should you run into the Confortes either by accident or in availing yourself of Joe's "wares," he'll tell you what he tells everybody casting a jaundiced eye at his operation.

"Listen, this is a business like any other. If you haven't tried it, don't knock this oldest profession in the world. It'll be here long after you and me is gone."

6. Burglars, System Players, and Slot Addicts

Danny Glass is no longer working as a blackjack dealer in a Strip hotel. But when he was here he was one of the most popular guys ever to don a gaming apron. In his late thirties, Danny was a veteran of the Korean War, and, when he returned to his chores dealing the pasteboards, the hotel and all its employees were very happy to see him again.

Unfortunately Danny came back from his service in Korea with a piece of shrapnel in the back of his neck. It was a slight injury, but it had affected a nerve in his neck. So Danny had to scratch it whenever the nerve acted up. But he was cheerful about it all. "Listen, I came out of it a lucky guy. So what's an itch in the neck when many of my buddies never came back?"

Danny was probably the most personable dealer in the entire casino staff. He always chatted with the players, which didn't hurt his paycheck at the end of the week. He got more tokes (tips from winning players) than the other dealers got. And he didn't do too badly on his days off. The girls were just as wild about Danny as were the players and the hotel employees.

Then one day a new pit boss was hired for the casino. He was a veteran in the business and trusted nobody, not even the boss who had hired him for the job. One day, while watching the players as well as the dealers, to keep both sides honest, he noticed poor Danny Glass scratching at his neck. So, he counted all the times Danny did that during his six-hour shift and found it to be roughly fifteen times.

The pit boss checked out Danny Glass's itch and was told about the shrapnel wound which caused it. He also learned that Danny was a five-year veteran at the hotel. The pit boss didn't sleep well that night as he dreamed of Danny's itching neck. And he continued to sleep badly for the next week.

Bright and early one morning the pit boss came up with a solution for Danny Glass's itch at the back of his neck. But he waited until Danny was ready to quit his shift. Then he asked him to come into the office. "I wanna talk with you."

Imagine Danny's shock and annoyance when the pit boss closed the door, then said, "Okay, Danny, I think I know how to cure you of that itch in the neck. Take off your shirt." Danny resisted until the pit boss brought in a couple of security guards, who promptly helped Danny take off the shirt.

It was a shirt like he'd never seen because it had a special band *which contained ten $25 chips!* For five years, personable Danny Glass had been palming $25 chips in his hand, one at a time of course, and, when he rubbed the back of his neck, he skillfully slipped the chip down into the fake neckband.

The pit boss roughly calculated that Danny Glass, who lived in a modest $125 apartment in town and drove an economy car, must have put away about $1,000 a week, or about $250,000, during that five-year work period of his.

The bosses at that hotel were so shocked by their favorite blackjack dealer, Danny Glass, that they merely fired him and told him to get out of town and never return. It was more than all right with Glass, who now lives in a small Mexican town which has a beach that rarely caters to American tourists. He can live there like a millionaire for the rest of his life, which he is now doing. But other gaming dealers caught in such a caper haven't been so lucky if caught. Need I say more?

Before you start getting notions that Danny Glass was an oddity, let me tell you about a pit boss in a Strip hotel whose name wasn't Sam Martin. But let's call him that.

Sam Martin was a special pet of the two bosses at that Strip hotel. They watched him come up the ladder from a dealer, then a pit boss, and finally a shift boss with a two-point ownership interest in that hotel. Many a night Sam Martin dined at the home of one of the owners or played golf with them. He was like one of the family. He got long vacations, big bonuses, and expensive gifts from the bosses.

But not everybody in the owner's family was sold on Sam Martin. The owner's son, also prominent in that hotel, went to his father one day and told the old man, "Pop, I know how you and mom and Charley feel about Sam Martin. But I think he's stealing from us."

The old man turned pale, then purple, with indignant anger. "You gotta be crazy. I trust Sammy with my life. Why should he steal? He has everything he wants. Would he grab a few bucks here and there and take a chance to lose a deal that earns him $75,000 a year? And that's not counting bonuses and gifts. No, George, you gotta be crazy. Forget it."

But George, who shared the shift with Sam Martin, didn't forget. He merely kept a closer watch on Sam Martin's actions in the gaming pit. After two weeks, George got to feeling that maybe his old man was right—that Sam Martin was honest. So he decided to watch one more week, then give him the benefit of his suspicious doubt.

One afternoon it was very busy in the gaming pit, so George decided to put our Sammy Martin to the test. He sauntered over to Martin and said, "Hey, Sam, I'm gonna take twenty minutes to get something to eat. Take charge, willya?"

Then he walked out of the casino, dodged behind some people playing at the roulette wheel, and sat himself in the lounge which overlooks the casino. Grabbing a newspaper, George put it in front of him, then with the lighted cigarette in his mouth, burned a hole in the newspaper so he could have a clear view of the entire casino, including Sam Martin.

Heavy money was being wagered, and the pit bosses were moving fast in the pit to keep up with the activity. Sam worked diligently with the others. Ten minutes had passed, and Sam's actions were above reproach. Just as George decided to give up and go back into the pit, he noticed Sam coming toward him and the roulette table that was only ten feet from where George sat hidden.

Sam took some chips as he stood there with his back to the rest of the casino. Then, when he wheeled around, he cleverly put the chips in his pocket with one deft motion. That was all George needed to see.

Rushing out of the lounge, George was in the pit in three jumps. Grabbing Sam by the arm, he hustled him into his father's office, then hurled him against the wall. His father, completely dumfounded, looked on as George snarled, "Okay, you honest sonofabitch, you may have fooled my father and his partner, but you never fooled me! Take out the chips in your left pocket!"

Caught with his "duke in the tambourine," Sam Martin emptied his pockets of folding money, also the thefted "chips," which were silver dollars! Larcenous Sammy had put a $75,000 annual salary on the line, then "crapped out" for petty cash. He wasn't prosecuted, but he was a beaten man who could never get a job in Vegas again. He earned a meager living in Los Angeles until he died of a heart attack two years later.

The good customers in Las Vegas, and I'm not referring to those who play dollars on the blackjack table and nickels and dimes in the slot machines, have to be treated like spoiled kids. Give them everything they crave, from broads to champagne parties in their suites, and they'll break their necks getting to the hotel's gaming tables at one time or another before going back to the wife and kiddies and a prosperous business.

Take this case of John "X," a prosperous lawyer from a midwestern city. For several years he'd been a steady customer at the Desert Inn Hotel. At least five times a year he would fly in, check into his regular $14 room on the second floor, then have himself a ball for at least two days. The records clearly indicated that Johnny "X," who insisted vehemently on paying for his room, would leave approximately $50,000 behind in the Desert Inn gaming casino every year. One year he got lucky and was only nabbed for $20,000.

Now he was back in the Desert Inn in 1962. I know because I sat with one of the owners, the late Ruby Kolod, having coffee in the nearby coffee shop facing the front door. In came Johnny, and Ruby told me all about him and how he insisted on paying that $14 daily rate for his room while shunning free food or booze or broads. He brought his own broad and paid for everything.

"We should have a thousand customers like that," beamed Ruby. "He gives us absolutely no trouble, loses his money, and then can't wait to come back to visit us."

Suddenly Johnny began pulling away from the front desk with his one piece of luggage. Trouble! Ruby jumped out of his chair and grabbed Johnny just as he was going out the front door toward a cab—and probably another hotel.

Ruby and Johnny spoke heatedly for several minutes, with Johnny, the Windy City barrister, pointing angrily toward one of the desk clerks at the front desk. Ruby finally overcame Johnny, and they both returned to the front desk.

Johnny checked in and was soon escorted by a couple of hotel "good-will" gents to his room—the same one he stayed in every time he came to the Desert Inn.

Ruby Kolod came back to the coffee shop, plumped down heavily in his chair opposite me, then began rubbing the beads of nervous perspiration off his brow.

"Jesus Christ, we almost lost the guy. That stupid, fucking desk clerk, who shoulda known better, told Johnny 'X' his $14 room was now $15.75. So Johnny said 'screw you' and started to walk the hell out of here. It took a lot of fast talk to tell Johnny that his room on the second floor would always be $14 a day even if he came back ten years from now."

Get the point, Mister Howard Hughes and executives?

Not only are big bettors illogical, they're also superstitious as all hell. So, is it bad business to give away booze, room, and chow to a guy who spends an average of $35,000 a year?

The Las Vegas gaming economy, I'll tell you again, is unlike any other of its kind in the world. And the most qualified operators, regardless of their unsavory pasts, are the "boys" themselves. Over the past twenty years I've seen too many "qualified industrialists" come to Las Vegas to operate gaming casino hotels and lose their asses in the process.

The next time you visit Las Vegas and want to see what a system player looks like, watch for anyone sitting at a blackjack table or standing at craps and roulette with a paper and pencil close by. He'll take notes after every hand of blackjack and every roll of the dice and the little white ball at roulette. Then, after an appreciable amount of time when his paper is all filled with curious hen scratches, he'll start wagering with his money. That's a system player, who believes that even hazardous games of chance can be beaten.

So, here's how the gaming casino bosses feel about system players: If you can convince them you have a substantial bankroll to back up your particular system, they'll gladly fly you to Las Vegas for free, put you up in their hotel, and maybe even throw in free meals and a glamorous doll in the bargain. The system to beat the honest, well-run games in Las Vegas casinos hasn't been conceived yet, if that species of gamer will abide by the regular rules of the house.

Those who frequent race tracks try beating the nags by poring over the daily "dope" sheets. A few succeed, while many others take the gas pipe or go on city welfare. So systems exist even away from Las Vegas. As a matter of fact, there's even a system used among inveterate slot-machine players.

I remember one elderly lady well. It seemed I couldn't walk into a Strip hotel around show time without seeing her cuddling up to three nickel slots at one time. An unsuspecting slot-machine player, innocently walking over to one of her machines and attempting to play it, would instantly be attacked by the seventy-year-old curmudgeon.

When not playing her machines, the gray-haired lady would expound by the hour on the art of playing slots. "You just don't put a coin in and pull the handle. Never play a machine unless someone is already there. Then watch that player and see if his machine is paying off. If not, and the guy walks away, you jump in because it's probably ready to pay off. Lots of people can't just stand there and play without getting tired. So they sit on stools supplied by the house. But not me. I stand there and get a firm hold, spit on my palm before each pull to lower the electrical contact, then yank slowly—like a mama dragging her infant teaching him his first steps."

On the other hand, I remember an elderly gent who worked as a porter in one of the Strip hotels. He, too, had a system for beating the slots. He believed that the 99-percent standees playing slots all over Las Vegas were being "duped" because, by standing, they immediately set up electrical impulses favoring the machine. So, he never played a machine without sitting down.

Then there was the lady player who always managed to get away from the family early in the afternoon "because I told them I had to take a stroll in the park for my health." Instead, of course, she hastened to the corner market, which had several slots near the check-out counter, to play her favorite dime slot.

"I always hold the machine at the side with my left hand, while pulling the handle with my right hand. In that way I control the lemons, cherries, and pears from jumping away from last-second payoffs."

A sympathetic market clerk scoffed at the lady later when I talked with him. "She puts about $5 in that machine every time she plays here. Sure, once in a while she hits a couple of jackpots to keep her happy. Otherwise she helps pay my rent."

Though it may look like petty cash, watching coins being dropped into thousands of machines all over Las Vegas, don't you believe it. Many a small operation on or off the Strip has kept its doors open with "bread and butter" slots that paid the rent, the employees, and still returned a profit.

Although some gamblers walk away from the gaming tables with big winnings, that never happens on the slots. A slot machine player never knows when to stop playing until he has put every available coin into that machine. If you think I'm kidding, the next time you're in Las Vegas walk up to a slot with five dollars in dimes, then start playing. Even if you got $20 ahead of the game, you wouldn't realize it until that and your original fin had vanished into the mechanical jaws forever.

I was having a chat with one of the casino bosses one afternoon in the Dunes Hotel when suddenly a mighty roar swept through the hotel followed by a shower of plaster and broken wood falling from the ceiling onto the heads of the slot-machine players. All of the slot players ran screaming for cover, but not a fragile old lady on a stool. As the plaster and splinters fell lightly on her white hair, she brushed them off and continued to feed the machine with coins.

An employee of the Dunes rushed over to her and said, "Better get away from here before you get hurt, madam." The elderly lady continued to play. So the worried employee tapped her on the shoulder and repeated his warning to evacuate that area. Stopping her play, she faced the man and said, "Say that again, bub—only louder this time."

The steady army of slot players, armed with their paper cups to hold the coins, have to be the most optimistic players in all creation. One lady, a habitual dime slot player, invested $10 a day for almost a year and always came back for more. What amazed the slot-machine employees who knew her well, she wore rags over her skinny frame, existed on scraps of food, and would stand in front of a slot as long as her dimes held out.

Then, as quietly as she came in, she'd leave, empty-handed but determined. Sure enough, she'd be back the next day. And that's the way it went for at least six months. It got to the point where I couldn't sleep well at night wondering how a poor old lady could play at least ten dollars a day endlessly and still come back for more with a fresh "bankroll" of dimes.

One afternoon, while driving with some friends in North Las Vegas, which is about ten miles from the Strip, I spotted this little old lady wearing the black and red coat and hat symbolic of the Salvation Army. And that was the answer! She collected on behalf of the Salvation Army during the early hours, kept at least $10 for herself, and turned in the rest.

I resolved never to reveal my findings. Unfortunately, a

month later a Salvation Army official, new to the Las Vegas office, became suspicious of this delightful old swindler and tracked her down from her favorite corner to her slot-machine rendezvous. He then advised her that the Salvation Army didn't need or encourage fund-raisers who worked on "partnership deals" as she had been doing.

I haven't seen that toothless old crone since. I often wonder if maybe she didn't join the Mafia. Her unique talents that went unnoticed for almost a year would have been useful to that organization.

A typical system player checked into the same apartment house where I lived early in 1955. He had a dedicated look on his face, like a guy going to the chair but sure he'll get a last-minute reprieve from the governor.

That was Joe Geis, a New Jersey truck driver with the all-perfect system to beat the craps tables. We became good friends, so he told me about his system. "I read about it in Walter Winchell's column," said Joe furtively. After all, such invaluable knowledge on how to become a millionaire at the dice table couldn't be blabbered around.

In his heart and soul Joe never expected to go back to Passaic and that twenty-ton diesel truck he jockeyed practically every morning of his life, whether it rained, snowed, or got blisteringly hot. After years of such labors, Joe was ready for instant prosperity. Furthermore, he was single, had lived in an $8-a-week room, and saved all his money. Otherwise, how could he have saved $12,000?

Now his retirement dream seemed to be just around the corner, especially after Joe had worn out the dice trying out that Winchell system. Every night, after getting off work, Joe would roll up the scatter rug in his room and throw the dice for hours. He kept a record of his winnings and losses for fully thirty days and now could boast that he started with a mythical $1,000 and wound up the thirty-day period a $42,690 winner!

Okay, so that kind of winnings sounded unreal. But Joe Geis wasn't a pig. He would gladly settle for a cool and comfy $25,000. That should be more than enough for his Florida retirement. And as he jockeyed his king-sized truck through the bitter snows of a New Jersey blizzard, he kept comforting himself with the thought that he was going to Las Vegas at the end of the month.

On the thirty-first day, Joe had rushed down to his bank and withdrawn all his $12,000 in savings. He had notified his boss that he was going on his regular two-week vacation. After all, he reasoned, there just might be a hitch in that Winchell system that might leave him high and dry. Then he bought himself some clothes, an airline ticket, and went off to Las Vegas, the land of milk and honey and winning streaks for system players named Joe Geis.

Now he was in Las Vegas with his $12,000 and raring to try out the "infallible system on the dice tables." It would have been utterly foolish for me to try to dissuade him from his do-or-die campaign. I didn't tell him that gaming casino bosses here would have gladly flown him for free to Las Vegas from New Jersey if they had known he wanted to gamble with his $12,000, and on a system yet!

Joe went off gambling that first night, and I didn't see him until the next afternoon at the swimming pool. He was all smiles as he sat at the pool with a couple of show girls driving him out of his square mind by showing their titties through their skimpy swim suits. I got a sinking feeling. He had won money with that ridiculous system—$800 as a matter of fact.

Joe was now in the laps of the gods who look down kindly on such system suckers, but never do a goddamned thing about helping them to get the hell out of town, winners, when they're ahead. But then, not everybody who gambles in Vegas loses. Just ninety percent.

Never a gambler myself, I had a fleeting moment or two of doubt. Maybe that damned Winchell system was a natural. What was the Winchell item to beat the dice? Forget it. There are too many gullibles who wouldn't learn a lesson from this story and try it themselves.

Anyway, I dashed out of town for several days. When I got back I didn't see Joe at the swimming pool the next morning. So I went to his apartment. There over a mess of charts, loaded with figures, was my Joe with a large pencil. "I haven't been doing too well," said Joe. "But that's because of an error in my betting. I'm trying to straighten it out before I go back to the tables tonight."

Still enthusiastic, Joe did mention that he had dropped $2,500 from his initial bankroll of $12,000. But it would be different that night, which it was. Joe dropped another $2,000. And within a matter of four more nights, Joe, the system player, had blown his entire bankroll. But he did have his return airline ticket plus $20 which I gave him so he could eat and survive long enough in Passaic to go back jockeying his beer-loaded diesel truck.

"I don't want you to think I'm discouraged," Joe said as I saw him off at the airport. "I'll be back." But I knew differently. That was the last I would see of Joe Geis here in Las Vegas.

Not so. Eighteen months later I got a call from Passaic, New Jersey. Joe was coming back to Las Vegas with a much smaller bankroll of $4,000, which he had saved by cutting down on his corner-diner daily food. He had even put in backbreaking overtime to be able to save that $4,000.

Joe could be identified as a "dice-hard," who was going to go along with that Winchell "system" even if it killed his newfound bankroll. There was nothing I could do to persuade him about the futility of that system, because he would come right back with the crack, "Listen, it's gotta work. I spent hours rolling the dice on the floor of my apartment, and it worked for me."

That, unfortunately, is the eulogy of a busted dice player. Or am I being redundant? You know the rest of the story. It was just a matter of days before the truck driver from Passaic dropped his $4,000. But he didn't "die" easily. There were moments when Joe had winnings up to $9,000, but he never gave up on the system.

Now he was out $16,000. At six o'clock the next morning he called to tell me he was broke. "But I'm not giving up," said the system-happy Joey. "I'm not going back to Passaic, gonna get an apartment, a job, and live here. I'll still show you that system works."

"But, Joe," I moaned, "you dropped a small fortune which you earned working like a bastard. Doesn't that prove anything?"

"Sure, baby. Easy come, easy go," cracked Joe. And what was the use of telling him to look at the multimillion-dollar hotels all around him that were built from the money of losing system players like himself?

I see Joe now and then during my wanderings on the Strip. Don't ask me what he does to make a living here, but he has a determined, slightly hungry look every time we stop to talk to each other. And I don't doubt that Joe's saving his dimes, quarters, and dollars so that some day he'll try again—and—again—and again.

7. Herman Milton "Hank" Greenspun, "Man in My Life"

Back in the mid-Thirties I attended the St. Johns Law School in Brooklyn for want of something better to do in those days when the whole country was strangling from a depression. I've had many experiences that I can look back on with much nostalgia and pride. Unfortunately the years I spent in law school were far from being nostalgic and proud moments in my life.

One of my classmates in those hectic, depression years was a guy by the name of Herman Greenspun. He sat at my left and, many an afternoon, when I came to class totally unprepared for the lecture, he would slip me his paper on torts or domestic relations or contracts in case I was called upon.

Fortunately, my school days at St. Johns Law didn't last past the second year. I was heavily in debt to the school, not having paid my tuition for the past and present semester, and now I was on the "carpet" in the dean's office. Not only was I in debt, but my grades were all marked in red ink.

Later that afternoon St. Johns Law School and I parted company, but I never forgot the strangely dedicated guy with the burning eyes who had been my "left arm" when I needed him. That Greenspun would one day be my boss, the publisher of the Las Vegas *Sun,* seemed utterly ridiculous, incomprehensible.

Yet, if I had gotten an inkling of what was to come, possibly I might have slipped him a poisoned tuna fish sandwich when we ate in the downstairs cafeteria between classes. Herman stayed, and I went into an entirely different occupation.

I decided to celebrate my good fortune, getting out of law school in such an unorthodox way, by treating myself to a round-trip vacation to Miami Beach via Greyhound bus. More dead than alive three days later, I gallivanted among the palm trees in Florida away from the bitter cold and snow of Brooklyn.

Then I met Damon Runyon. And my whole life was to undergo a drastic change, the first of two such transitions. The second one would come about ten years later in Las Vegas.

Strolling in downtown Miami, I saw a sleek black limousine with the license plate, "DR-I, New York," and hoped it would be the famous nationally syndicated columnist and author, Damon Runyon. Ten minutes later out came Runyon. I introduced myself and explained that I was on my way back to New York City, and could he recommend me to a local newspaper editor in Brooklyn for a job writing sports?

He did just that by going to a phone and calling the Brooklyn sports editor then and there. I went back to New York via Greyhound, loving every moment because it was drawing me closer to the job I'd always wanted, writing sports.

There were several jobs on newspapers after that. And one April morning in 1945 I found myself in Los Angeles. The editor of the Hearst feature service asked me to fly out to Las Vegas and do a piece about a new hotel going up there owned by one Bugsy Siegel.

And there I was, in Las Vegas and walking down a lonely highway, which would one day be the celebrated Las Vegas Strip with numerous hotels and broad highways instead of two isolated hotels and one more going up "almost out of town."

I visited the skeleton that would one day be the Flamingo Hotel and talked with several people on the site, then went back to my hotel, the Last Frontier, where I proceeded to gather up my toothbrush, a pair of jockey shorts, and that extra shirt to fly back to Los Angeles and write my story.

There was still some time left, so I hung around the hotel talking with the manager, a couple of bored bellhops, and a lady who had just lost all her money and was wondering how the hell she was going to get back to Minneapolis. As a guy holding a return airline ticket to L.A. and $6 in his pocket, I certainly wasn't her answer.

Now I was ready to head for the front door and a waiting car that would take me out to the airport. Instead, a strange force took over. Whether I knew it or not, now was the time for that second transition to take place. Several times I made for the front door and my waiting car, but I always delayed it for one petty reason or another. A drink of water, two unsuccessful visits to the men's room, and a long walk to the coffee shop to buy a Hershey bar.

Somehow I had a nagging feeling that it just wasn't the time to leave for the airport. I couldn't explain it. Now, after stalling for more than twenty minutes, I finally made for the front door. As I opened it, a party coming in on the other side collided heavily with me. Crashing to the floor, we lay there wondering what the hell had happened. Then we recognized each other. The guy on the floor with me was none other than my "left hand" in law school, Herman Greenspun!

It was now more than perfectly clear that fickle fate had reached in and knocked him and me on our asses at the same time. It also explained why I had been stalling in that Last Frontier Hotel lobby and not understanding why.

Greenspun and I hadn't seen each other since that day

when I had been bounced out of St. Johns Law School, and now he was fresh out of the army, and visiting here in Las Vegas for the very first time. As I think back to that afternoon, when he and I met so forcibly, I wonder why couldn't fickle fate have decreed that I leave that afternoon by a side door? Or that Greenspun might have stopped off at the El Rancho Vegas Hotel down the street?

Herman, who was on his way to New York to pick up his fiancée, Barbara, then get married, decided to stay in Las Vegas so we could have a three-day holiday and reminisce about "the good old days." We did more than that. We decided to publish a weekly entertainment magazine here in Las Vegas. I wasn't able to change his mind that Las Vegas was strictly for gophers, lizards, and guys and gals pursuing the polished ivories and the pasteboards in their own inimitable manner.

"But remember I warned you," I cautioned him. "You'd be much more successful operating a kosher delicatessen in Butte, Montana, than publishing a magazine in Las Vegas." As things turned out, it was one of the rare predictions I would make over the years that would hold up.

Greenspun was insistent, however. "This will be the greatest resort town in the whole world within fifteen years," he prophesied. Yeah, I said to myself at the time, and Bing Crosby and Bob Hope will one day apply for welfare.

But I went along with him—for the time. Our magazine venture, titled *Las Vegas Life*, lasted six months and folded with a squish like a deflated balloon. One of our biggest, if maybe the only, major advertiser at the time was Bugsy Siegel's Flamingo Hotel. When Bugsy got done in, the magazine folded.

Later that week I helped Herman Greenspun, whom I had named "Hank," bury the little literary mess, then prepared for my immediate flight the hell out of there. We shook hands solemnly and I remember telling him, "Don't be a schmuck, Hank, take Barbara and Susie," a year old at the time, "and get out of here while the getting is good."

It was early in May, 1947. As far as I was concerned, Las Vegas was for cowboys, hookers, and craps shooters, and I was none of the above. Hank laughed at my advice. "You go ahead, but I'll guarantee that you'll be back soon."

I proved him a goddamned liar. I wasn't back "soon." It took all of six years before I came back. By now the amazing Greenspun had started his own daily newspaper, the *Sun,* which proceeded to make waves in the entire state. Over the years I've feuded with Greenspun because of our difference of opinions. He wanted to sell newspapers while I wanted to write fearlessly, the hotel advertiser be damned. And that also went for the temperamental star who resented my muscularly critical opinions.

We no longer carried on as affectionately as we did back in the late Forties, because there has been a world between us. He's a multimillionaire with a dozen projects going at once, while I'm a slightly solvent columnist who still doesn't see eye to eye with him editorially.

Today you'd never know we once sat elbow to elbow at the St. John's Law School in Brooklyn weaving fancy dreams, while pledging undying loyalty to each other no matter what. Greenspun will gladly tell you that on numerous occasions he has been harassed by big-name café stars to "get rid of that little pain in the ass, Ralph Pearl." How much more loyal can you get than that? he'll tell you.

He'll also tell you, not only stars but top hotel executives and a few owners felt the same way. Somewhere early in this book, I made mention of the fact that some temperamental stars and executives don't see Las Vegas in the same light as they would Miami Beach, Cleveland, or New York.

Las Vegas is really a vast, ornate personal playground for them, an "electrically charged high fence" that should keep out objectionable, critical columnists who tend to get too nosy.

Right now I'm trying to arrange a meeting with Howard Hughes in several foreign countries, also in motels and in the back seat of cars, to get him to finance me in establishing another newspaper. An afternoon newspaper that won't compete with Greenspun's *Sun*.

Strangely, he doesn't answer my letters. But if I get that newspaper, I can write my fool head off and not have to worry about the spoiled darlings of the café circuit, sensitive hotel owners and the "privileged citizens" who only want nice things written about them. I'd even be willing to write nicely about Howie.

8. Potpourri

I won't be silly enough to dare compare a dazzling Hollywood movie premiere with the opening-night show in a Las Vegas hotel. Very little can compare to a movie "preem" when the street is illuminated with spotlights that light up the sky for miles, and hundreds of movie and celebrity addicts line the bleachers and streets to get a quick look at their cinema gods and goddesses as they enter or exit the theater.

However, in Las Vegas, gaming bosses in the hotels aren't too happy about the sightseeing, autographing mobs that turn out for an Elvis, Tom Jones, Humperdinck, or Sammy Davis, Jr., opening night. These eager addicts not only crowd the entrance to the showroom, but they crowd into the gaming area, making it difficult for the gamblers to get to the tables.

That's where they stay for as long as the show lasts in the showroom. Then they clutter around the showroom to ogle each and every person exiting. After all, at those kinds of openings there are usually a couple of dozen big-name stars in the audience. For the average patron or newspaperman to

The author and his charming wife, Rosalyn.

Footballer Joe Namath and the author help the Roger Smiths (Ann-Margret) celebrate their third anniversary.

The author and Barbra Streisand hold hands in her dressing room at the old International Hotel back in July of '69. She's telling him almost tearfully why he was the only newsman she would talk with during that month-long engagement.

HAPPY 3RD ANNIVERSARY
ANN and ROGER
FROM JOE AND THE GANG

FLAMINGO
HOTEL

Cary Grant and the author breaking bread at the Sands Hotel.

The late and great Joe E. Lewis, receiving a plaque from the author in the Copacabana in Manhattan where Joe was the guest of honor at a testimonial dinner.

Tiny Tim and his Vicki run into the author on their way to open a two-week engagement.

Frank Sinatra and Ralph Pearl, smoking an invisible peace pipe in the lobby of Caesars Palace after having been at each other's throats for more than fourteen years.

The author and his house guest, Jack Benny.

fight his way through that waiting throng is as easy as opening a can of sardines with his teeth.

And like their Hollywood prototypes, they come armed with autograph books and pencils, also a keen instinct for identifying the celebrities as they come from the showroom.

Also, the VIP's of the world gather here in Las Vegas from time to time, either to shoot a bit of craps, catch a show, or maybe indulge in a secret love affair in some nearby motel, far from the prying eyes of their press agents, wives, managers, and other authority figures.

Café stars love opening nights because it inflates their already blown-out-of-proportion egos. Instead of having to play just to ordinary people, they are delighted to look over the footlights and recognize not only celebrities from their own craft, but possibly a world-famous author, jurist, or athlete staring back at them. Add a few of the not-so-glamorous denizens from the world of industry and the crafts, and you'll find a hubbub of excitement at some of the more important opening nights here.

If a Milton Berle, Jack Carter, Don Rickles, or Joey Bishop was opening, he'd look searchingly into the front row of seats, then crack, "It's so nice to see so many fathers sitting at ringside with their lovely daughters."

But enough about the fathers and their lovely "daughters," let me now chronicle some of the VIP's and other stars as yet not written about here.

LBJ

Then a ripsnorting U.S. senator from the state of Texas, Lyndon came roaring into Las Vegas one July night in 1958 with some of his lawmaking cronies from Washington and a couple of pals from his home city of Austin, Texas. They came into the Sands Hotel to catch the Frank Sinatra show, and, while waiting for Francis to make his stage appearance, they proceeded to consume much of the hotel's supply of Scotch whiskey.

I know because I sat at an adjoining table and marveled at their capacity. Francis Albert Sinatra came and was soon gone, but Johnson and his cronies continued at their merry pace downing the spirits as rapidly as they were served up.

But the most astonishing part of it all came when they got up to leave the showroom. Lyndon was the only one of the party who didn't stagger. Walking straight as a ramrod, he went past my table like a man rushing to catch a plane. Hurrying after him, I confronted the future president of the United States, asked a few meaningless questions about his stay in Las Vegas, then said I marveled at his capacity to down so many whiskeys without falling on his face.

Lyndon Baines Johnson, a towering specimen, smiled and said, "Young man, if you think that was drinking, you should attend one of our barbecues on the ranch back in Texas. Now there's where we really do a bit of drinking, not this 'soda-pop' piddling like you saw back in that showroom."

JUDY GARLAND

Come what may, this lady will always be my absolute, un-equivocal choice as the greatest entertainer I ever saw in Las Vegas or any other café in the entire world. Tattered, broken, and utterly spent a couple of years before she ended it all via booze and drugs, Judy nonetheless was always able to start my motor working furiously by her mere entrance onto a stage here in a Las Vegas café.

Talk about charisma, she invented the word. And it should have been removed from the English language as soon as she died. Not only could Judy make the blood run cold, hot, and straight up with her magical brand of singing, but she also wreaked havoc with the rest of the anatomy as the tears would well up and the heart pound wildly when she began singing the opening strains of "You Made Me Love You."

Judy never cultivated any columnists during her hectic stay among us mere mortals. Even though I was one of her greatest fans and wrote endlessly about her talents, even when she was a mere shell of the once superb Garland, she seemed to ignore it during her visits to Las Vegas.

Playing her last date in a Strip hotel, Judy was not only terribly sick, but she was taking a fierce beating from her ex-husband Sid Luft, who wouldn't let her be. It was bad enough for Judy to make supreme efforts every night just to make that first show without Luft plaguing her constantly.

Naturally, upon learning of her nightly tortures, I castigated Luft in a column the following morning. Later that night I attended the show, sitting ringside and dying inside as I watched a once magnificent Garland struggle helplessly against overwhelming odds. Had she seen the column? Had she not?

Now she had the hand mike and was walking toward the end of the stage where I sat numbly but strangely joyous. Smiling wanly, she leaned toward me and whispered, "Sid's gonna hate you for that blast you gave him this morning."

JACQUELINE KENNEDY ONASSIS

The first time I ever laid eyes on Jackie, her husband was a U.S. senator from Massachusetts and she was a most attractive lady who had been born with a whole set of platinum spoons in her mouth. The mere fact that she had come to Las Vegas was startling news in itself, but when the press agent at a Strip hotel phoned excitedly to say she was attending the dinner show of "Casino de Paris," I dropped everything and headed for the Dunes Hotel.

Sure enough, there she sat with several hoity-toity friends, each with that inimitable Southampton, Palm Beach bored look on their quizzical kissers. Jackie watched the nude gals parade before her, but the nudies seemed to be getting a bigger charge watching her. All through the show she gave the impression she was sniffing at a most disagreeable odor—and that odor was Las Vegas. Undoubtedly, she and her friends considered a visit to any of the show palaces here as "slumming."

I still remember that night she spent at the "Casino de Paris" show. During it, she suddenly got up and headed out of the showroom. I followed her, but stopped dead in front of the ladies' room, where she was going. Later that night, on my way out of the hotel, I asked the matron in the ladies' room about Jackie.

"I know the lady you're speaking about," she said, "because she tipped me two dollars. If ever I saw a broad who peed icicles, she was it."

PROPHET OF PEEK: WALTER WINCHELL

The death of this internationally known gossip columnist from cancer early in 1972 brought back many memories when Walter was jumping from New York to Hollywood and Las Vegas between ocean hops to London and Rome. He always treated Las Vegas with disdain. Yet early in 1957, the owners of the Tropicana Hotel asked Walter if he could put together a revue and play their showroom for two weeks. Salary: $35,000 a week.

Winchell suddenly lost his disdain. He was enormously interested, because he had started back in 1910 as a song-and-dance man with the Gus Edwards Revue. Now he was given a chance to play one of the more popular hotels here in the Show Capital of the World. And for a tidy sum of Uncle Sam's filthy lucre.

Walter signed the contract, then asked me if he was right in playing a night club. I told him he was foolish, because he wasn't equipped to play a club. He stared me down, then crisply told me to mind my own goddamned business.

Within sixty days Winchell signed a couple of variety acts and a group of boy and girl singers and dancers. And since he was the star, he would not only do a dance or two and sing a couple of songs but he would set up a small desk center stage, put a mike on the desk, and give out toward the end of the show with several legitimate news items like he did on his once-popular "Jergens Journal of the Air" in the Thirties and Forties.

Needless to say, the show was an absolute disaster. Café-goers stayed away in droves. Even more harmful to Walter, I ran a most critical review of his nitery debut in Las Vegas.

A terribly vain man, Winchell not only screamed in agony at the very poor business, but he screamed even louder when he read my review. As far as he was concerned, I had committed the cardinal sin in daring to oppose a Winchell effort of any sort.

He didn't talk to me again. As a matter of fact, he vowed to gouge out my eyes with a salad fork if I ever came near him again. He had been almost mortally wounded. Sure, it was all right for him to belt someone, even a newsman, in his column, but heaven help the guy or gal who did it to him.

Yet, with all of that, he was a remarkable luminary in gossip journalism during that wonderful era (1930–55) of nonsense in America.

JAYNE MANSFIELD, A "CHILD OF DESTINY"

It was a simple nickel picture postcard mailed from Biloxi, Mississippi, June 26th by Jayne Mansfield. She had written, "Working a trap down here, but am not giving up. I'll be back in Las Vegas before you know it. Jayne."

Three nights later, after her second show, Jayne, her attorney and new boy friend, Sam Brody, and her three children, Miklos, Zoltan, and Marie, got into a chauffeured car and headed for New Orleans. She was going to appear on a television show. Their car ran into a truck. Jayne was decapitated, Sam and the chauffeur were instantly killed. The children in the back seat sustained injuries.

And so ended the life of a spectacular thirty-four-year-old woman, and not by her own hand as she had been trying for the past year when she discovered that stardom was slipping away from her. The sensationally bosomed Dallas girl had suddenly become old hat, with her contrived, phony publicity stunts, and the newspapers as well as the public were getting thoroughly fed up, especially with her on-and-off marriages and "love affairs."

A combination of tranquilizer pills, frequent and heavy doses of straight Scotch whiskey, and little or no sleep at all had almost done her in several times. It seemed she was determined to end it all.

Jayne had started out a great career on Broadway with *Will Success Spoil Rock Hunter?* then appeared in it on the screen. She attracted one of the owners of the Tropicana Hotel, who signed her to come in with ex-Mr. Universe, Mickey Hargitay, a strong boy who had worked with Mae West for a couple of years. Sure, the Trop knew she had no talent, so what? They weren't paying her for her nitery skills. But in those early days in 1957, Jayne Mansfield was getting on page one regularly with one screwy stunt after another. She would be a great attraction for the curiosity seekers coming to Las Vegas.

And that's exactly the way it turned out. People came to ogle the lady with the forty-inch bust and her spectacular Hungarian with the huge biceps and barrel-shaped chest. She returned to Las Vegas, to other hotels, during the next three or four years, but she was no longer the draw she had been back in 1957.

The girl who would never touch whiskey or smoke was now getting desperate. She soon acquired those habits—and many more that would lead her down the path to her eventual destruction. The last time she played Las Vegas was at the Fremont Hotel for a fraction of the $25,000 a week she had gotten five years before at the Tropicana.

Café-goers in Las Vegas could care less about Jayne Mansfield at the Fremont. She did poor business with an act that was brutally bad. Not only that, she was shoddy with her personal life before and after she appeared onstage. It was nothing for her to pick up with men of all sizes, colors, and standing. Before she closed disastrously at the Fremont, Jayne had staggered back into the hotel one early morning at five o'clock accompanied by three weirdos.

They followed Jayne into the elevator and into her suite and didn't come down until later that morning. The management was now determined not to pick up the option on Jayne's other engagement at the hotel later that year. They, as well as many others in the theater, movie, and café business had *had* it with Jayne.

Eight months later she eagerly accepted a nitery engagement in the second-rate club in Biloxi. Though utterly dissipated and practically out of her mind, she and her lawyer, who was going to leave his wife and marry Jayne, were trying for the "new life" when they crashed into a truck just around the curve ahead at 2:30 on the morning of June 29, 1967.

I received her picture postcard the next day.

There were few if any daily newspapers that didn't feature her violent end on page one. She would have wanted it no other way. In my column, I noted in part, "She had drunk lustfully from the cup of pleasure once too often, probably to hide her obvious lack of talent in a business where she really didn't belong."

And though she had hopelessly tried being another Marilyn Monroe, Jayne Mansfield was never able to outdo Marilyn until her spectacular, shocking death.

CAROL CHANNING

Carol Channing, a dear friend and great performer, stopped off to visit with me back in the late Fifties. She had been an enormous success on Broadway with *Gentlemen Prefer Blondes* just by chanting the hit tune, "Diamonds Are a Girl's Best Friend."

As we talked, Carol said she was utterly baffled because some of the Las Vegas talent buyers had completely ignored her.

"I'd love to play a showroom here in Las Vegas," she said, "but I've already been turned down by the El Rancho Vegas."

I, too, was confused. I had been so sure that El Rancho Vegas Hotel owner, Beldon Katleman, would have been glad to buy Carol Channing when I had suggested the lady to him. But Beldon had reasoned poorly that Broadway and Las Vegas were as far apart entertainmentwise as was Wall Street in downtown Manhattan to Little Rock in Arkansas.

I didn't get discouraged. A week later, after Carol had gone back to New York, I sat down with some of the owners of the Tropicana and painted a glowing picture of the "Diamonds" lady. They signed her to a two-year contract a week later, and Carol was so delighted she popped out her eyes until they almost fell into my lap. The lady with the Mixmaster hairdo and nasal voice had finally conquered Las Vegas.

The week she played here, I was utterly delighted and didn't hesitate to write about her constantly in my column. Then she was my guest on my television show and I babbled for almost a minute introducing a "lady who has not only been the toast of Broadway for several years, but she's one of the most talented entertainers in the entire business. So, ladies and gentlemen, please say hello to Carol *Burnett!*"

I was completely unaware of that faux pas until Carol let out one of her famous guffaws, then actually fell to the floor screaming with laughter. It was only then that I realized what I had said. I sat back with the look of a schmuck wanting to crawl under the table.

It was fully a minute before order was restored and Channing had wiped away the laugh tears and composed herself. Needless to say, I limped bravely through the thirty-minute interview, which was frequently interrupted by Channing's making reference to my oral goof.

But even more disaster was awaiting me six months later when I invited Carol Burnett, now working in some TV shows in Los Angeles, to chat with me on my TV show. Remembering what a solid hit she had been on the Ed Sullivan nitery show at the Desert Inn about eighteen months before, I gave her a flowery introduction, then almost provoked myself into cardiac arrest when I introduced her as "Carol Channing."

No one in the whole wide world—except those TV viewers who were watching the show—would ever believe that I could make that mistake twice. But there are still native Las Vegans who'll remind me of that "goof" with both Carols whenever they get a chance.

STREISAND, THE "MELON ADDICT"

After only two years on Broadway, the young lady with the velvety purple eyes and prominent proboscis was now the toast of the town. As one of the principals in the Broadway show, *I Can Get It for You Wholesale,* she had attracted great reviews from the critics, and was responsible for the success of the show.

Sitting with other newspapermen in her dressing room,

which she shared with another lady principal in that show, I listened as Barbra Streisand ("remember, it's Barbra, not Bar-bara") told the press she didn't want diamonds, rubies, foreign cars, and a penthouse apartment. "All I really want so I'll really know I'm a big success on Broadway is to be able to buy as many honeydew melons as I want, then just eat the tops of them."

I remembered that aspiration of the terribly homely, terribly talented girl from Flatbush Avenue in Brooklyn. I went back to Las Vegas and raved to all the owners about that Streisand girl I'd seen on Broadway. The owners yawned and went back to counting their money. "Who the hell ever hoid of Barbra Streisand?"

Frankly, they were right at that time, because her greatness was confined to the East Coast. However, I did manage to convince one of the bosses at the Riviera Hotel, Harvey Silbert, to catch her show when he visited New York again. About six months later Harvey came back from Manhattan and quietly told me he had bought Streisand and that she'd be opening with Liberace in the summer, which was about four months away.

I then proceeded to tell my Las Vegas readers to keep a sharp eye open for that young lady's opening, that she would probably knock them all on their asses. Instead of ass, however, I used the Puerto Rican word, "tuchis."

A couple of nights later, I attended the opening at that same Riviera Hotel of *Irma La Douce*, fresh from Broadway, and hammered it into little pieces, it was that brutally bad. So the top brass, Gus Greenbaum and my old "buddy," Harvey Silbert, read the review and promptly barred me from the Riviera Hotel premises for the next two years.

Three months after being set down, Barbra Streisand came into the hotel with the star Liberace and did as I had predicted, she knocked those first-nighters on their asses even though she was an opening act and sang just four songs.

200

Since the barring didn't affect my wife, Roz, she went in my place and came back after the show in a daze. "So great, so great, so great." I worried plenty because I'd never seen the frau in such a transfixed state. She wasn't able to elaborate, just mumble endlessly, "So great, so great."

Even though I journeyed to New York City a couple of years later to catch Streisand starring on Broadway in *Funny Girl*, I wasn't able to see her in Las Vegas until the summer of 1969, when she opened the International Hotel, then owned by Kirk Kerkorian, for the record-breaking salary of $100,000 a week PLUS. The "plus" was a bundle of International Hotel stock in addition to her top salary. She took away almost a million dollars four weeks later. She could buy honeydew melon farms now.

Backstage in Barbra's dressing room after that opening-night show, she was breathless, as always, but still aware that working before live audiences in theaters and cafés "isn't exactly my idea of a lasting tribute to myself. I prefer the motion picture screen because, whatever I've done, it'll still be shown many years after in movie houses everywhere in the world."

She had a point there. Yet it didn't stop her from returning to Las Vegas a couple or three times after that so she could pick up some fat weekly checks working "live."

THE CINEMA QUEEN

Cinema queen Elizabeth Taylor, encrusted with walnut-sized diamonds adding pounds to her already generous chassis, is the regal lady in Cinemaville. She commands vast sums of money every time she sticks that classically beautiful puss of hers in front of the cameras, especially when co-starring with her hubby, Richard Burton.

But I can remember when she wasn't the toast of the international jet set. As a matter of fact, she was being blamed by many for utterly enchanting singer Eddie Fisher to a point where he divorced Debbie Reynolds and married the "widow Todd." If anything would contribute to the eventual downfall of Fisher, it had to be the pictures in the newspapers and magazines showing Debbie and the two children looking as forlorn as a snowy day in Butte, Montana.

Even though the comics and the columnists poked violent fun at Eddie, he and Liz enjoyed their brief fling. One comic sneered from a Las Vegas stage, "Eddie trying to make love to Liz is like a midget trying to flag down the Super Chief with a Zippo lighter."

They honeymooned in Las Vegas at the Desert Inn during a four-week engagement by Eddie in the hotel's showroom. Never a robust gent by any stretch of imagination, he took on a deathly pallor as he and Liz spent hours in the hay grappling in the throes of a frustrated sexuality. He got skinnier, while Liz, who had been severely shaken by the death of her Mike Todd, became as contented as a fat pussycat. It didn't take superior boudoir gymnastics to satisfy Liz in those days.

During those four weeks, Eddie's pals saw very little of him. The only diversion for both of them came late in the afternoon when they would leave the Desert Inn and walk across the street to the Stardust Hotel to play a bit of poker in that hotel's gaming parlors.

Except for his two shows nightly, attended religiously by Liz, who sat at ringside, Eddie didn't see the press or mingle in the hotel with his pals. However, he did make an appearance on my TV show one evening. It had to be a mighty sacrifice on his part because he looked all during the interview as if that would have to be the last time he would be seen anywhere. His complexion was spotty and as green as the outfield grass at the Yankee Stadium in November.

My first question to Eddie Fisher: "Gosh, Eddie, I haven't seen you since you opened at the Desert Inn. Whadd'ya been doing that's interesting?" My cameraman, director, and floor man immediately broke up, but Eddie remained stoic. He probably didn't have the strength to participate in anything as strenuous as robust laughter.

Liz, watching the interview from their suite with several mutual friends, broke up instantly and rolled all over the fancy carpeting howling at the top of her lungs with glee.

Eddie overlooked my facetiousness, then went on to chat amiably about how happy he was with Liz and that they looked forward to a lifelong marriage "with about six kids, at least," said Eddie with a weak smile.

But no matter how hard he tried being a blowtorch, Eddie just couldn't rise above his "Zippo lighter" rating.

JOHNNY CARSON

"You have to be completely out of your mind," I snapped at Del Webb, the hotel tycoon, when he told me he had just signed television emcee Johnny Carson to a contract to appear at the Sahara for the next three years.

"The guy's a television personality, and that's all," I argued. "He'll bring in a few curiosity seekers, some school teachers on their sabbatical, and elderly television viewers who'll probably play the nickel slot machines, nothing more."

Now, after several years as a top headliner in Las Vegas, Johnny Carson rates with Elvis Presley, Frank Sinatra, Dean Martin, and Tom Jones as one of the all-time, constant sell-out attractions in Las Vegas.

Unlike his cohorts in the talk-show business—David Frost, Merv Griffin, and Mike Douglas—who've played Las Vegas showrooms in the past with less success, Carson had the touch that brought café-goers flocking to his shows at the Sahara.

Johnny has the unique ability to dish out equal shares of corn, nostalgia, and TV reminiscences in a most personable, professional manner. Audiences love it and him. The losers, lovers, and boozers come from far and near to hear Johnny poke fun at his TV bosses, his boss Del Webb, and the nude shows on the Strip.

Not only does the Omaha pride and joy have himself a ball playing Las Vegas, but he drags down top money from Del Webb for playing there about eight weeks a year.

As Johnny says during his show, "Christ, I'm embarrassed to tell you how much Webb pays me to work here. I'm almost tempted at times not to take the money. But I do." Much laughter.

JACK BENNY

Always a polished, skillful performer, Jack Benny lost his aplomb late in the Fifties when he decided to play a night club in Las Vegas. As he was already a veteran in show business for more than thirty-five years, all his pals reasonably assured Jack that playing the Flamingo Hotel would be a snap.

Jack felt differently. He was plenty scared. Came the night of the debut and Jack stood in the wings waiting for an opening-act, $500-a-week singer to get the hell off. He could hear a restless muttering out in the showroom. It reminded him of the bloodthirsty denizens of the Coliseum waiting for a Christian to be thrown to the lions in the arena.

Suddenly a flock of butterflies began dive-bombing inside the Benny belly. "Believe it or not," remembered Jack a couple of years later, "I suddenly felt faint and my legs began to buckle under me. Me, a veteran of thirty-five years behind the footlights.

"My first thought was to get the hell out of there and head back to the coziness of our home in Beverly Hills and leave café entertaining to Sammy Davis, Jr., Danny Thomas, Buddy Hackett, and the others. Then I remembered I would be getting $35,000 a week, and that was enough to straighten me out and shoo away those miserable butterflies in my stomach."

Suffice to say, the gent from Waukegan was a most determined performer that night. But he was far from funny. However in the years that followed, Jack developed a nitery act that is a crowd-pleaser in Las Vegas.

What makes Jack's presence here all the more interesting these nights is the fact that he has gotten into the $70,000-a-week class over the past several years. "And for that kind of money," says Jack, "who worries about butterflies?"

DANNY THOMAS

The Lebanese "camel jockey," as he has been affectionately tabbed by the columnists over the years, has become a legendary figure on the Las Vegas show scene. He would have to be included in any poll taken of the five greatest Vegas performers.

Born Amos Jacobs in Deerfield, Michigan, he appropriated the first names of his brothers, Danny and Tommy, and thus became Danny Thomas. At the peak of his career, Danny began more and more to spout sanctimoniously while behind the footlights. Some of the columnists began ribbing him.

Soon they had Danny sending "St. Thomas" medals to St. Christopher. His mightiest contribution, however, is not to show business but to mankind. His St. Jude Hospital in Memphis, which cares for needy kids suffering from various types of blood-cancer diseases, has indeed earned him a "St. Thomas" tag.

In thinking about Danny, I have to remember that day back in the early Fifties when he was appearing at the Sands Hotel. Charging through the lobby like an Arab chieftain atop a charger, Danny headed for the gift shop. He didn't look well. As a matter of fact, he was sporting a large lump in his cheek. So, after hearing him tell the girl behind the counter that he wasn't going to work that night, I rushed away and noted in my column that "Danny Thomas missed his shows at the Sands last night because he was suffering from a swollen gland in his cheek."

When the screaming died down, Rosemarie, his lovely wife, told me that Danny had gone to Los Angeles for the night to do a TV segment of *Make Room for Daddy*. She also informed me that Danny loved chewing tobacco—Red Eye Chewing Tobacco.

NICK THE GREEK

Probably the greatest man of mystery in all of Las Vegas for many years was the fabulous Nicholas "Nick the Greek" Dandolas, a supreme, cold-blooded gambler who once told me, "The next best thing to playing and winning is playing and losing." We sat in an off-the-Strip coffee shop. Nick chewed away at his favorite repast, an American cheese on white bread.

And though he wagered more than $500 million in casinos all over the world during his forty years, Nick died flat broke on the West Coast instead of in his native village of Heracleum on the Isle of Crete. Chewing on an unlit cigar because his doctor told him smoking was bad for his health, Nick took me back to his room at the Dunes Hotel just a year before he died.

There on the table near his bed was a stack of letters a foot high from people seeking handouts and others wanting to know more about Nick's gaming system. On another table were several philosophy books, also a couple of cartons of lemon and vanilla wafers. Several thoroughly chewed-up cigars filled an ashtray and gave off a sour smell that mixed with the odor from a half-eaten, rotting banana.

Now we were back in the lobby of the hotel, and a couple of tourists sauntered by. One of them recognized Nick and got bug-eyed. "Hey, Nick, tell me how I can beat those goddamned crap tables, will you?" The lady with him, however, was more realistic. She dragged him away from Nick, then whispered loud enough to be heard all over the casino, "That ain't Nick the Greek, stupid. Nick wouldn't be wearing a lousy, unpressed $50 suit with all the millions he's won over the years."

It sounded most reasonable to the gent, and he and his wife sauntered off, leaving Nick and me chuckling.

Now we were out on the Strip, which was all aglow with millions of neon lights popping off in our faces. We started walking. It was a cool autumn evening, and almost every fifty feet we walked, a cabbie would honk his horn in recognition of Nick, or yours truly.

The Greek, a frustrated philosopher, was in a talkative mood. And such an occurrence was as rare as a snowfall in Clark County. Nick talked about people in gaming.

"You watch people gambling all around you and you see how they waste their lives. The people in need want to get independently wealthy so they can quit their jobs and become another Nick the Greek. The other people with money gamble because they want more material things in their already cluttered up lives. I've never advocated gambling, because to me it's nothing more than a game. I want nothing from it."

Now we were in front of the Stardust Hotel. Nick was going to play a bit of craps there, so he said goodbye and walked off. He was so right about gaming having absolutely no importance to him. Considering the huge amounts of money he must have won during his many years as a professional gambler, he didn't own blue-chip stocks, fancy homes, or foreign motor cars, because money was of no value to him other than as legal tender at his favorite craps table.

As I walked away from Nick, I reflected that old gamblers never die. They just crap out . . . and fade away.

LORNE GREENE

The white-maned rancher from TV's *Bonanza* was healthy, wealthy, and very wise until that day back in the late Sixties when I convinced him to make his night-club debut in Las Vegas at a fleabagger titled, believe it or not, the Bonanza Hotel. He signed a contract with the Bonanza Hotel bosses, then came to town to look over the hotel.

The place looked like a poor trading post instead of one of the luxury traps Greene had thought it would be. Then Lorne saw the phone-booth suite given him by the owners, and went gunning for me.

The three-weeker that followed in the showroom was equally disastrous. Lorne was a famous TV personality, but he lacked a night-club show.

He still blames me for getting him involved in what he says were "the most uncomfortable moments in my entire professional life."

EDWARD G. ROBINSON

The once fearsome hoodlum of the silver screen was just a pussycat when I saw him for the first time in a Las Vegas hotel. Even more disillusioning, he talked art and literature instead of Capone, Lansky, and Mafia. Still more startling, Edward didn't talk from the side of his mouth or chew ferociously on the stump of a cigar as he had done so many times on the screen.

Neither did Robinson swear, kick elderly ladies, or try to muscle into the gaming industry in Las Vegas. The bearded art collector did, however, display a weakness. He couldn't keep away from the nickel slot machines. Not only that, but

208

the last time I saw him he was heavily engaged in figuring out his sixty-cent KENO ticket.

ZSA ZSA GABOR

This preening, busty lady, whom I affectionately call the "Hungarian Patriot," has never really overwhelmed café-goers with her questionable nitery skills—even though she draws $35,000 a week when playing Las Vegas.

This professional collector of costly baubles and husbands didn't always get that kind of money for her act. I can remember when she was glad to settle for maybe a handful of $25 chips from a grateful pit boss in a gaming casino. Back in the early Fifties, even though Zsa Zsa was already well known in Hollywood, she loved to come to Las Vegas as a tourist.

Spectacular in her skin-tight gowns that showed lots of breast, Zsa Zsa always shook up the crowds gathered around the tables at the old El Rancho Vegas Hotel, long since defunct. One of the brainier pit bosses, sensing her value in the casino, gave Zsa Zsa four $25 chips and asked her to play some blackjack as a courtesy from the house.

Never one to look a gift horse or chip-giving pit boss in the mouth, Zsa Zsa grabbed the chips and began playing three-and four-dollar "21," while shooting quick, nervous glances at the nearby pit boss. It was as if she expected the guy to call in his four chips at any time.

As she began winning, which isn't too frequent an occurrence at blackjack, Zsa Zsa began stuffing some of the chips into her more than ample cleavage when the pit boss had his back turned. Being thoroughly engrossed in grabbing off some winnings (as if the pit boss gave a damn) Zsa Zsa didn't realize that she had attracted a couple of high-betting blackjack players to her table.

The shrewd pit boss may have gotten "cheated" by Gabor

209

for a couple of hundred dollars, but the two gents blew $12,000 at that same table.

JULIET PROWSE

The shapely lady with the million-dollar legs and the orange hair (I found out it was a wig) will never forget her debut at the Riviera in the late Fifties. The lady, a big draw in the East, had come to Las Vegas with the Broadway show, *Irma La Douce.*

I never saw a worse opening-night show. In my column the next day, I said so. "If Juliet Prowse is such a great talent from Broadway, she certainly hid her talents remarkably well last night at the *Irma La Douce* premiere at the Riviera. For some strange reason, the producer of *Irma* had Juliet doing lots of singing and a minimum of dancing, which is akin to Sammy Davis Jr., doing a juggling act and Jimmy Durante a pantomime routine. Juliet sings in a raspy, most annoying manner. . . ."

The lady Juliet threatened to shoot me on sight after she read the column. And as I noted earlier, the bosses at the Riviera barred me from coming into the hotel for the next two years.

About seven years later, after Prowse had played at the Flamingo with far more skill, she opened at Caesars Palace with the smash Broadway musical, *Sweet Charity.* It was one of the greatest musicals ever to play Las Vegas. As for Prowse, she was magnificent in the role of the dance-hall hostess with a maniacal craving for matrimony.

I not only screamed her praises in my column, but from several adjoining housetops. I then went backstage one night at the Palace and told her how superb she was in *Sweet Charity.*

Prowse smiled happily. The feud was over.

PERRY COMO

For many years, while he shared the spotlight with the greatest stars in show business, Perry kept turning down lucrative offers to play a Las Vegas café. He reasoned that life in a Las Vegas club could be far more rugged than the peace and quiet of his life as a top TV star.

Actually, Perry feared working in front of "live" audiences, since he worked only in a studio before his immediate crew when turning out his TV shows. The land of booze, broads, and blackjack offered too muscular an image for him. However, after taking a verbal pounding from his pals who were earning fortunes as regulars in Las Vegas, Perry one day decided to start playing Vegas.

And now that he has played the Hilton International, which is feared by the average performer because "it's like playing in the Grand Central Station," Perry's terror of the tough Las Vegas audiences has diminished considerably.

Whenever Perry played Las Vegas, he was constantly on the lookout for hazards, actual or imaginary. So, it was ironic that Perry wasn't looking when he did an NBC Special in New York City in the late summer of 1971 and broke his leg getting offstage.

MIKE DOUGLAS

Every summer I would be a guest on Mike's popular syndicated talk show, which he taped in Philadelphia. Naturally, Mike and I would discuss Las Vegas and show business. Mike, a congenial Hibernian with a huge daily audience in many cities around the nation, was more than casually interested in the happenings in Las Vegas the last time I guested on his show.

He was going to bring a show into Las Vegas for the first time in a couple of months. Of course, one of the first questions Mike asked was, "How d'ya think I'll do in Las Vegas with my show, Ralph?"

"Simple, Mike," I answered in my usual blunt manner. "If you bring in a good show, you'll go over well. On the other hand, you can easily die there if you bring in a bad show. And should that happen, Michael," I said as ominously as I could, "then I would have to be most critical in my column. As a matter of fact, I'd probably take a couple of layers of your skin off."

The audience in the studio and Mike's guests laughed. Surely I must be kidding Mike. The only one who didn't laugh was Mike himself. He got the idea I would do just as I had said. So he got off the subject hurriedly.

"Tell me, Ralph, in all the years you've been in Las Vegas, have you ever been mistaken for one of the stars?"

I thought a moment or two, then truthfully answered, "Yes, Mike. A couple from Los Angeles once approached me in the lobby of a Strip hotel. The lady rushed over and screeched, 'Captain Kangaroo! Can I have your autograph?'"

It brought a howl from the studio audience because in those days, when I was terribly overweight, especially in the face and the haircut, I really did look like Captain Kangaroo.

Now the show was over. Mike and I said our goodbyes, and I was happy to notice that the twinkle in his Irish eyes had returned. "I'll see you at the Riviera, Mike." Then I was off and winging back to Las Vegas.

However, I stopped off in Chicago for a few days before continuing my homeward flight. And when I finally got home, one of the many messages awaiting me was from the Riviera Hotel boss. The message read, "Have a Mike Douglas item for your column. Please call."

That I did and the Riviera Hotel boss, Eddie Torres, said, "What did you do to Mike Douglas? He has just canceled out of his show by telling me he didn't think he was ready for Las Vegas."

Later I learned that I had really scared Mike. Or, better still, I had made him aware of the fact that one doesn't come to Las Vegas with any old show.

A year later, Mike made his debut in Las Vegas, but not at the Riviera. He opened at the Sahara, and did fairly good business.

PHYLLIS DILLER

This remarkable comedienne started a show-business career at an age when most ladies in her age bracket were busy marrying off their children or attending daily Mah-Jongg sessions. She cashed in by coming into a Las Vegas café looking like she had just been hatched from a giant "goofer" bird.

One night, after opening on the Strip, she sat in her suite, moaning that she was getting the wrong kind of publicity.

"I know I don't look like a Mitzi Gaynor, or even a half Gaynor, but I'm tired of getting all that silly crap about being a weirdo. I want some sexy items."

Giving Diller a sexy image in a column or out of a column was like trying to sell a red-blooded male on the idea that it was better to curl up with a good book on a rainy night than with Raquel Welch. However, I tried—in my own psychopathic manner—and ran a Phyllis Diller item in my space the next day, "Phyllis Diller never looked sexier than the other night when she had a howling mob of guys from the L.A. Rams ogling her stunning 21-21-21 chassis hungrily."

Diller hasn't talked to me since.

"What got me mad at the little sonofabitch," howled the lady, "he wasn't too far off in his measurements."

MARLENE DIETRICH

The glamorous grandmother from Hamburg was the first star to play Las Vegas for a record-breaking sum of $35,000 a week back in 1954. Though veteran café stars, getting far less, howled with rage, it was the best deal the Sahara Hotel, then owned by Milton Prell, ever made because the hotel, Marlene, and Las Vegas got a couple of million dollars' worth of publicity in the national magazines and the newspapers, not to forget television, from it.

Marlene, a shrewd entertainer, added to it all by coming out that opening night with a dress that was positively shocking. That same dress today wouldn't even get a line in the columns. But then it was a shocking "see through" beige job in lace and silk.

You had to know the key men at the Sahara in those days to grab a reservation to Marlene's show. As always, she sang in a raspy baritone voice that reminded no one in the room of either Judy Garland or Doris Day. But what did it matter? The fashion-conscious ladies from all over the nation flocked to Las Vegas to catch her.

Today in Las Vegas, several comics and singers get $35,000 a week in an economy which has Presley, Streisand, Tom Jones, and a few other stars getting in the cozy neighborhood of $100,000 a week. Marlene? She could get maybe $25,000 a week if she wanted to play Las Vegas again. You see, she doesn't have the appeal she had in 1954.

CARY GRANT

Sitting with the once-fabulous movie star, now a top executive at Fabergé, at the Palace one night watching the Tony Newley show, a few elderly people strolled over to get Cary's autograph. Cary gladly obliged. It was not an unusual chore for a movie hero who had been one of the top box-office attractions for many years.

The pretty lady sitting with her husband next to us couldn't stop staring at Grant. More people came over for Cary's autograph. Now the show was over and the lights came up. People filing out of the room suddenly started making a mad dash toward us. Grant was in for a busy time.

Then something strange happened. The large group of people dashed right past us and gathered at a table just behind ours. They completely blocked the aisles while surrounding a man with an enormous mop of hair. It was Johnny Cash!

He had been wearing dark glasses all through the show, and that's why the autograph seekers hadn't recognized him. Evidently, Johnny had watched that steady stream of fans getting Cary Grant's autograph, then decided to do something about it.

Removing his dark glasses when the lights went up was all Johnny Cash needed to start a mob scene. As for Cary Grant, who was smiling. "Mind? Not the least bit. As a matter of fact, I'm also a fan of Johnny Cash. I might just get his autograph myself."

TONY CURTIS

A poor kid from the Bronx ghetto, Bernie Schwartz, became a famous movie star by the name of Tony Curtis, who made a colossal error when he let his manager and press agent talk him into doing a night-club act at Caesars Palace in the summer of 1967.

Surely it couldn't have been the money that persuaded Tony. He had been a star for many years, and had saved a goodly portion of his huge movie salaries. But, comes that moment when a star begins to believe his publicity. A night club? Why not? "I'll sing a couple of songs, tell a few funny stories about my life in Hollywood, and maybe even do a dance or two."

215

Tony Curtis sang a few songs and told some terribly un-funny stories. He spared the café-goers further agony by leaving the dance numbers out of his nitery act. However, it all added up to being one of the worst night-club shows I'd seen in years. Single-handedly, Tony Curtis had almost suc-ceeded in killing off the entertainment industry here in Las Vegas. His only consolation, about two years later, was that a movie colleague of his, George Hamilton, came into the Hil-ton International Hotel with an even worse act.

It must have made Tony Curtis feel much better.

But here's the funny part of it all. Tony as recently as 1971 was still encouraging his agent to book him back into a Las Vegas showroom. Tony and Roger Moore were the stars in a TV series, *The Partners*, and Curtis figured that the television exposure might help him in Las Vegas. Not so. TV exposure only helps when you have an act.

CAROLE AND BERNIE

Back in the summer of 1968 I sat at a blackjack table in a Strip hotel trying to kill about a half hour, also $20, waiting to catch the dinner show in the adjoining showroom to the casino.

A nice couple from California sat next to me. They were as lovey-dovey a pair as I'd seen in weeks, especially at a gam-ing table. Generally the boy friend or the husband considers his mate hard luck and would rather gamble by himself. But in this case they played as a team. She was Carole and he Bernie.

Watching this bit of kissing and hand-holding was my wife Roz, who didn't hesitate to tell me about the lovebirds. "When's the last time you held my hand, you little rat?" she whispered in my ear. "Look how attentive he is to his wife. It wouldn't hurt you to take a lesson."

Finally it was time to go into the show. I'd blown my $20.

bankroll, so I got up, said a few meaningless pleasantries to Carole and Bernie, then escorted my wife into the show.

Two days later, I picked up the *Sun* and there they were, the lovey-doveys themselves, Carole and Bernie, on the front page of the *Sun*. They'd been picked up by the sheriff and were being charged with the death of Bernie's wife back in California! They were Carole Tregoff and Dr. Bernard Finch.

My wife Roz was strangely quiet for the next month, especially when she spotted a couple in a showroom or a movie house holding hands and making love.

WOODY ALLEN

The wispy gent with the enormous talents never fails to emphasize the fact, while he works at Caesars Palace, that he's an absolute "despoiler of women." It's a great line, especially coming from an emaciated lad who looks as if it would take a major effort on his part to despoil a butterfly. The Brooklyn-born "Walter Mitty" gets a warm response from café-goers, if only because they're so relieved not to look like Woody.

The scrawny writing and acting genius has gotten lots of yardage from kidding his parents and ex-wife Louise Lasser, who were brave enough to have stayed with him. Woody, a nonconformist in every sense of the word, is probably the only performer to play Las Vegas who could come on a stage wearing the kind of clothes one wears when attending a football game in rather crisp weather.

However, Woody appealed only to those appreciating the cerebral type of humor. The others stayed away or, if they did attend, would look on puzzled as he went into elaborate detail about how such lovelies as Faye Dunaway, Elke Sommer, Sophia Loren, and Kim Novak were always chasing him in Hollywood because they wanted his body.

Woody loves to tell about the time he was loitering near a slot machine one afternoon at Caesars Palace when he was approached by a hustler. "Wanna have a good time, buddy?"

Said Woody, "I'm already having it just watching the slot-machine players hitting jackpots."

DAVID FROST

The saucy, award-winning TV talk-show host from the United Kingdom strolled on the beach at Malibu with this author and thought for a moment or two before answering the question I had just put to him, "Would you play Las Vegas for $20,000 a week?" Frost had just started his new TV talk show.

Said David, "You bet your American ahss I would." Three years later, riding the wave of his popularity in America, Frost signed to play the Riviera Hotel for $55,000 a week.

Erudite as well as charming, yet always with a male eye peeled for any femininity that might be straying by, David Frost prepared for his nitery debut in a Strip Hotel. It was afternoon, and he would be opening that night. I strolled by the showroom to watch rehearsals.

The first coffee break that was called, Frost relaxed and joined me just off the stage in the vast, empty room. "I like that shirt you're wearing Ralph, and I know just where you bought it—at Aquascutum's in London. Right?" I was flabbergasted. "How'd you know?"

"Simple. I bought one there just before leaving for Las Vegas. Only mine's in a white and blue stripe. Cost seven pounds, right?"

I answered in the affirmative. Then the coffee break was over and Frost went back to his rehearsing. But about that shirt I was supposed to have bought in London for $17. I bought it at a sale in a small, going-out-of-business men's shop in downtown Fremont Street. It cost me $3.95, and the reason I didn't tell him the truth, he would have torn up his own, very expensive, white-and-blue striped one immediately.

TALLULAH BANKHEAD

Back in the summer of 1955 I got at least one phone call a week from Tallulah, who was then appearing in a Broadway play in Manhattan. She, like me, was a long-suffering New York Giant baseball fan. The team was in a bad slump, so "Tallu" would call and we'd try to find a way to get them out of the doldrums.

One afternoon the call came again from the lady. We were convinced that Bill Terry, the Giant manager, was not rotating his pitchers in proper order. For more than a half hour we ran up and down the line-up, making suggestions to each other about what the manager would have to do to get the boys back on winning ways.

As Tallu was getting ready to hang up, she suddenly let out a screech. "Dahling, I just remembered. Those silly old bosses at the Sands Hotel have signed me to open there in two months for a three-week engagement. And those silly asses are going to pay me $10,000 a week. Imagine that!"

There were no more calls from Bankhead until she came out to work at the Sands. Obviously the talent buyer at that hotel had bought Tallulah Bankhead merely because he felt she'd be a draw on that marquee. Certainly she didn't have an act for a night club. And she proved it twice a night for the next three weeks. However, what did it matter? Tallu and I talked New York Giant baseball every evening, just before she did her first show.

Now it was her closing night. I sat in her dressing room in a state of utter despair. The Giants had dropped six straight ball games. The future looked bleak. Then Tallu came up with the solution—so she insisted.

With a fierce gleam in her eyes (actually a normal expression on that lady's face), Tallu grabbed me by my insecure lapels, then hissed, "Listen, don't flinch. I've got to do this because it may just be the ticket to stop our Giants from losing." Then she spat fully on the front of my sport shirt!

She was still holding on to my lapels. "Now, do the same to me," she hissed. I stammered and stuttered, "You crazy or something? I can't spit on a nice lady like you."

"You want the Giants to stop losing, don't you?"

"Buuuuuut, Tallu."

"Stop stuttering, you little bastard, and start spitting."

Out came a slim bit of unwilling saliva, and right on her pretty blue dress—the one she intended to wear that night onstage for her first show.

Believe it or not, two things happened. First, she did wear that dress onstage, but nobody could see the saliva because it was hidden by a flock of sequins on the dress.

Second: The following night the Giants broke their losing streak and won the next four games!

NAT KING COLE

A supreme song stylist, who never failed to jam the Sands Hotel every performance, Nat King Cole commanded a reverence from even the southern bigots, not to mention hecklers who instantly clammed up when Nat began singing. No other Black entertainer could make such a claim—not even one of the greatest performers of our time, Sammy Davis, Jr.

Hence I was thoroughly awed one night at the Sands when told that the florid, black-haired man coming into the room at that moment with a party of four was none other than George Wallace of Alabama. And though his party of "rednecks" were far from impressed, Wallace was. They sat quietly, even applauded at the end of each Cole ditty.

The group sat in a booth away from ringside, but Nat was

told before the show that the Wallace party would be in to catch his show. Throughout his act, Nat had a merry twinkle in his eyes. He was in top form that night, even more superb than usual. Toward the end of his show, I began wondering whether or not Cole would introduce "the celebrities" in the room. Besides the Wallace party, there were Mitzi Gaynor and her husband Jack Bean, also Hollywood movie actor Ronald Reagan and his wife.

Cole introduced them. Now, would he rib Wallace before introducing him, or just ignore him? I would have figured that Nat would overlook him and his party.

Instead, and simply, Cole introduced "Governor Wallace from Alabama." The smattering of applause, but appreciably more boos from those losers, boozers, and lovers that night, was Cole's way of proving a point without getting himself involved.

EDDIE FISHER

The dark-eyed, curlyheaded South Philadelphia singer probably enjoyed the greatest days of his life when he was the husband of movie actress Liz Taylor, in the mid-Sixties. They were wined and dined wherever in the world they went —Eddie as one of the top singers in cafés and TV, Liz as a seductive movie actress.

Little did the gent know that a few years later he would hit the bottom of the barrel and declare bankruptcy in a Puerto Rican court. He had two ways to go—one completely out of show business, the other, a heartbreaking climb back up to regain at least a portion of his glory as a high-priced singer in Las Vegas showrooms.

He's trying for the latter, but it isn't easy.

Talk about a successful star having been waylaid by booze, broads, and blackjack, Eddie was a living, breathing example of the "bad" life. He still owes a small fortune to a couple of

Las Vegas Strip hotel gaming casinos for excesses at the tables. And his flair for women is well known.

That's why, when we met and he told me he might try writing a book, now that he was on the comeback trail, I promptly asked if I might give it a title.

"Sure," he grinned. "What's the title?"

"How about *Eddie Fisher: Where Did I Go Wrong, and What Was Her Name?*"

Eddie immediately turned to his current fiancée, one Barbara Hayman of Beverly Hills, and glowed, "That's one helluva title, isn't it, dear?"

As I write this, Eddie and Barbara Hayman are contemplating marriage. And Eddie is solemnly declaring once again, "I'm really in love this time!"

THE SWEDISH PUSSYCAT

In the summer of 1960, George Burns, wagging his Havana cigar as if it were a small-sized golf putter, came onstage at the Sahara Hotel with his own revue. As radiant as an Alabama sharecropper with a picture button of George Wallace pinned on his tattered overalls, George told the first-nighters that among the entertainers with his revue was a pretty and sexy young lady by the name of Ann-Margaret Olsson.

"She sings and dances and has a very attractive set of 'moving parts,' " Burns announced. Then he brought on the youngster, and I had to agree with George, though not entirely. She was pretty and sexy, but couldn't dance or sing well enough for a night club, especially a Las Vegas night club.

Naturally, in my column the next day I noted that fact, and added that, ". . . if Ann-Margret would take my advice, and there's no reason to believe she will, she'd leave show business and get herself a husband, then raise herself a nice

222

family. She just doesn't have the talent to cut the mustard in show business."

Within three years, Ann-Margret was to prove me a cockeyed liar. And she has continued to do so, while turning out starring movies, playing major cafés around the world and making sure to waggle her Oscar at me whenever I drop over to her house in Benedict Canyon out Hollywood way.

Instead of being furious at me for almost drumming her out of the business, Ann-Margret has made it her life's work to see that I never forget that rotten piece I wrote about her when she made her debut with George Burns back in 1960. She has noted it from the stage of any night club she plays in Las Vegas—if I happen to be in the room that night.

On those occasions, in a most meticulous way, she outlines in detail what she intends doing the rest of the year in pictures, on TV, and in cafés. Twinkling her baby-blue eyes, she then minces, "And that's not bad, Ralphie, for a girl who was supposed to quit show business, get married, and raise babies. Right?"

One morning at seven I got a phone call from a mutual friend in Beverly Hills alerting me to the fact that Ann-Margret and her fiancé, Roger Smith, had suddenly decided to drive to Las Vegas and get married. As it was a spur-of-the-moment decision by Ann-Margret and her Roger, they didn't even bother to change clothes as they drove from Palm Springs and checked into the Riviera Hotel early in the morning.

The ceremony was performed by a local judge in the Riviera Hotel suite, and only a handful of press attended, I being among that minority group of fourth estaters. As soon as the lovebirds faced the judge, Ann began whimpering and crying. And she couldn't stop all through the brief, five-minute ceremony.

Instead of the traditional flowing white-lace gown and the

223

bouquet of lilies clutched to her bosom, Ann-Margret wore tight-fitting pants of a brownish-red color, an equally tight-fitting yellow blouse, and sandals. As for Roger, he wore a pair of greenish, rumpled slacks, a tan sport shirt that had two top buttons missing, and a pair of scuffed, slightly frayed loafers.

Maybe that's why she was crying. It wasn't exactly the kind of ceremony a girl dreams about one day having. Before she knew it, the wedding was over, and both were sitting on a chaise longue while the press boys asked their usual asinine questions. "Are you happy?" "How big a family will you have?" "Will you quit making movies and start making Roger's breakfast and mending his shirts and socks?"

I listened to it all, then decided to ask Ann-Margret my own kind of question. She was still weeping quietly and repeating, "If only my mama and papa could have been here." I noticed she was dabbing at her eyes with the same piece of Kleenex I'd given her when the ceremony began and she first began making with the weeps.

But about my question to Ann-Margret: I got up and handed her another piece of Kleenex, then whispered in her shell-like ear, "My prediction of 1960 may still come true, Annie. Now if you can start raising a family and just possibly retire from pictures, you'll make me look good."

It took several moments for the whispered comment to sink in. But when she finally realized what I'd said, the tears stopped flowing and the mere suggestion of a smile began edging over her countenance.

Several minutes later, the newlyweds jumped into their convertible and drove back to Palm Springs. And to this day I regret that I didn't save that piece of Kleenex she discarded. I could have bronzed it, along with my baby shoes, and put it on my dresser beside an autographed picture of my hero of the Thirties, baseball's behemoth, Babe Ruth.

Now in the summer of 1972, Ann-Margret, my little Swedish pussycat, is still happily married to her Roger, who's also her manager. But they don't seem any closer to raising a family than they were back in 1960 in that Riviera Hotel suite. As for retiring from pictures, TV, and cafés, Ann-Margret keeps threatening she will any day now.

SUSAN HAYWARD

Don't ask me why, but the biggest stars of Hollywood, television, and the Broadway stage yearn to round out gratifying professional careers by playing Las Vegas too. It has to be more than mere money that makes them long for a sojourn on a Las Vegas stage. The fact that they might not be qualified to play a night club doesn't enter into their thinking.

The "ham" in them is enough reason for their debuts in Las Vegas. After all, aren't they the reigning stars in the nation, even the world? But go tell a tourist and his wife, coming all the way from North Dakota, to plank down $35 for dinner just to see Suzy Shithead, a great TV star, who has had big Neilsen ratings on her show all season long. They couldn't care less. The Durantes, the Frankie Laines, the Danny Thomases, and the Mitzi Gaynors are the people they want to see and spend their money on, not Suzy Shithead.

However, it becomes easier for Broadway and Hollywood stars to make the trip into Las Vegas niteries if and when they play in a Broadway musical. And that's what Susan Hayward decided to do when she got that Las Vegas feeling. She signed to play Caesars Palace as the star in *Mame*, and everybody glowed among the fourth estaters and the public.

I was pessimistic. After all, Hayward had been a movie star for many years. Those endless sessions, year in and out, must have taken a severe toll. Playing two vigorous shows a night for a couple of months at the Palace could knock her on her glamorous fanny. And that's what I wrote in my column.

However, despite my obvious concern for her welfare, the lady and her people rebelled violently and scoffed at such nonsense. Hayward released a story, via her press agent, that it would all be a breeze. "Has it been easy working all these years before cameras in numerous parts of the world? Why should it be any harder working here at the Palace in *Mame?*"

Then *Mame* opened. It wasn't the best or even one of the better musicals I'd seen in Las Vegas, though I had to admit she tried awfully hard. But Suzie H. had bitten off too much for proper and pleasant digesting. After the second week, Hayward was starting to breathe heavily, like a lady walking uphill dragging a dinosaur behind her.

For a while, she wouldn't give up. Then, on the morning of February 18, 1968, some twenty-three days after the *Mame* opening, the top brass at Caesars Palace called a press conference and announced that the star, Susan Hayward, had something to tell the press.

We all assembled that morning and awaited the entrance of Susan Hayward, who strolled in, head high, slightly fatigued from her chores in the show. In a faltering voice, trying desperately to hold back the tears, Miss Hayward told the assembled fourth estaters, "I find myself in poor health and am forced to leave the show." Thanking everyone in the cast, and giving me several embarrassed glances, she sat down.

Silence! Nobody, not even the owners, the assembled press, or her managers, uttered a word. It was then most fitting that I rose and proposed that the people in the room "give Susan Hayward a hand for showing us all that she's really a champion all the way."

More tears by Susan, several members of the press, and her staff.

Unlike some earlier occasions, when my predictions had come true, I was strangely deflated by my "scoop."

It took the nice Hollywood lady more than a year to get over her Las Vegas debut in her home in Fort Lauderdale, Florida.

HAROLD MINSKY

Though frequently identified in the classier journals for many years as the "number one girlie show provocateur in the nation," many in Las Vegas are prone to refer to Harold as the "guy who puts on the best tit-and-ass show in Vegas." He had done just that for more than a quarter of a century, following his Uncle Billy Minsky, who started burlesque shows back in the early Twenties in the East. It would be safe to quote a figure in the hundreds of thousands in estimating how many "tits and asses" Minsky has had to look at since then.

Harold Minsky probably counts tits and asses instead of sheep when he tries sleeping on insomniac nights. But in happier moments he can always remember the roster of star names who first started working for him in burlesque—Lou Costello, Phil Silvers, Bob Alda, Red Buttons, and Pinky Lee.

Harold's prize tale is about one of his most famous discoveries, ecdysiast Lili St. Cyr who titillated many a male café-goer all over the nation with her striptease and provocative bathing number onstage. Way back one year in New York, Harold Minsky had just signed Lili to star in one of his revues. Since they had never met, Harold went backstage to Lili's dressing room to introduce himself. Lili's door was slightly ajar, and Harold could see that Lili was clad in just panties and a bra. He pushed into the room and, before he could introduce himself, Lili gave him a savage tongue-lashing for being a "peeping Tom."

It didn't matter that in a few minutes Lili would be onstage wearing only a smile and a G-string, nothing more, and ogled by a houseful of male wolves. All she knew was that her privacy had been invaded.

The same rule holds true for many other ecdysiasts. What they do on a stage has nothing to do with their private lives, which in some cases are more prim and orderly than the life style of the lady next door to you.

9. Tall but True Tales

THE LADY AND THE TIGER

I can remember days here in Las Vegas in the Forties and Fifties when a tourist didn't have to float a bank loan to come to Las Vegas for a weekend. A guy and his missus could catch a Joe E. Lewis, a Danny Thomas, or a Jimmy Durante dinner show and still walk away with change from a sawbuck. It was a happy era for the gaming bosses because "the less a guy spends on food, entertainment, and booze, the more he'll have to spend on the dice tables and blackjack."

No Thoreaus, these gaming guys, but so elemental.

I remember the day a couple of friends of mine drove in from Los Angeles just for an overnight outing before driving back to Los Angeles and their Monday morning jobs.

They had $30 to spend, so $6 went immediately for gas and oil and a snack on the road. They hid another $6 for the return trip, then recklessly flaunted the remaining $18 for the twelve hours ahead of them. They would fun all through the night, then drive back about three in the morning in time for a quick shower and a change of clothes.

Remembering that the Last Frontier had a great menu and low prices, they made a dinner reservation to catch Marilyn Maxwell and her live tiger, who had been generously publicized in the Los Angeles newspapers.

Both ate high off the hog, had a couple of drinks and a fancy dessert, then sat back burping pleasantly waiting for the show to start. It occurred to them to be a bit apprehensive sitting so close to the stage, wondering if the live tiger might wind up in their laps.

Many other diners in the room were just as worried. The newspaper publicity had called Marilyn's "pussycat" ferocious, a "man-eater." But the management explained there was no need for alarm. Not only would the beast be tranquilized before every show, but a net would be drawn onstage to protect the people from the tiger.

Last Frontier Hotel owner, Jake Kozloff, was a happy gent from all the national publicity he'd gotten from the tiger and Marilyn. However, Jake did complain that the tiger was eating him out of the hotel. All the beast would eat was raw filet mignon, nothing else. He turned up his nose at horsemeat.

But Kozloff wasn't going to argue with the tiger about a hundred pounds of raw filet mignon a week as long as the customers turned out for this widely publicized Maxwell and her tiger show.

So, that opening night, the Los Angeles couple sat with the rest of us in the showroom, full of expectations. Many of Marilyn's pals from the movie industry had also shown up, but they refused to sit too close to the stage.

And even though Marilyn had taunted me earlier in the dressing room about sitting center ringside, I sat in a booth near the door. Everybody in town was talking about the tiger, and word of its danger had spread among the hotel's waitresses working the showroom that night. Three quit rather than take a chance on the tiger jumping over the footlights and devouring them. The other waitresses, who were getting ready to walk out also, were persuaded to stay on for double salary that night.

Jake Kozloff, at the back of the room, bit his nails anxiously as he figured the added cost of the filet mignon and the extra salaries. However, he'd get it all back at the gaming tables—he hoped.

More than a hundred people had to be turned away at the door for that first performance, but they'd stay and see the second show—and maybe gamble a little while they were waiting. One of the items on that special menu for the Marilyn Maxwell show featured "Tiger Soup."

The show started and little Joel Grey, in straw hat and cane, opened with his song-and-dance routines. That he would some day develop into an international star on Broadway and in Hollywood never entered my mind.

Joel took his bows and introduced Marilyn Maxwell, who came slithering out in a "see through" gown. The "live tiger" gimmick had done wonders for her. Never a show-stopper, she could push her way into the heavy money if the show was successful. If the tiger clawed a few at ringside during the course of the evening, Marilyn might even become a national figure.

I noted that a couple of Hollywood's cowboy stars sat at that ringside table once reserved for me. They shared it with a couple of the town's hookers, who were so excited they wet their panties. Busty Maxwell glowed up there behind the footlights.

Then she announced to the opening-nighters that she would bring out the main attraction, the tiger. She walked into the wings, and came out almost instantly dragging a long leash, which had to have the tiger on the other end.

But the leash went so far and no farther. Maxwell began yanking away with all her might. The suspense was fearful. Maybe the tiger had just feasted on a couple of prop men in the wings?

231

Suddenly the "man-eating" tiger made his appearance, while the audience let out a fearsome gasp. He was flat on his back and being vigorously pushed out onstage by a couple of sweating prop men. The beast, old and mangy and almost toothless, was half asleep from the tranquilizer shot. He gave off a rancid odor of age and fear.

He looked about as ferocious as a bunny rabbit in heat! Maxwell, working quickly, managed to get the tiger to its feet. Now many in the room were tittering. Some were betting it would never live long enough to get offstage.

And as the tiger wobbled feebly toward the footlights, a couple of boozed-up ringsiders jeered noisily at the animal, causing him almost to fall down from the scare. He had two discolored teeth, no claws, and that terrible smell. Maxwell aged considerably during the first show. Finally it was over.

But she didn't give up. The prop men backstage doused the tiger with cold water and tried to get him ready for the midnight show. By then, of course, the newsmen were having a field day with their "ferocious tiger" and Marilyn Maxwell. She got publicity, but not what she expected.

It turned out to be the howl of the town, and Marilyn had to do the show with a very tired tiger for several nights before Jake Kozloff called a halt to the farce.

The poor beast was eventually returned to Los Angeles, and Jake swore up and down the hotel that he would never bring in another animal even if Sabu went along with the deal. And it didn't help his disposition any when he learned the tiger, nicknamed "Peaceful Pussy" by the Last Frontier backstage employees, had defecated all over the place before they could get him out of there.

Our Los Angeles couple? They had a weekend they never forgot.

ELEANOR ROOSEVELT IN VEGAS

The greatest slot-machine story of all time concerns the late Eleanor Roosevelt, who made her one and only visit to Las Vegas a most memorable one for the employees and boss, Beldon Katleman, of the now defunct El Rancho Vegas.

It happened in the summer of 1958 just two years before El Rancho Vegas burned to the ground. Returning from the West Coast to New York and her post with the United Nations in that city, Mrs. Roosevelt had decided to stop over in Las Vegas on her way home, just long enough to visit Hoover Dam.

So, her trip to Las Vegas was cloaked with much secrecy and cloak-and-dagger protocol from her entourage. Unfortunately the selfsame entourage hadn't anticipated that a certain bright, young stewardess would be on the plane taking Mrs. Roosevelt to Las Vegas.

The stewardess called her friend, Beldon, just as the plane was ready to leave the Los Angeles Airport for Vegas. So, when the plane landed here, there was Beldon with a swanky limousine and an overwhelming charm that completely captivated the former First Lady. She was offered a huge cottage on the grounds of El Rancho Vegas for as long as she would stay.

Mrs. Roosevelt agreed to stay there overnight and leave the next morning for New York. She was whisked away with a minimum of publicity. Fortunately for me, the stewardess on that plane had more friends than just Beldon Katleman. She was also my friend, so I knew all about Mrs. Roosevelt's visit here, and her staying at the El Rancho Vegas Hotel.

But I guarded that information well and arranged to be at El Rancho Vegas the following morning "just by accident."

Having retired immediately on arrival because of the lateness of the hour, Mrs. Roosevelt was up bright and early the next morning, eager to get in some sightseeing. She had already made plans to visit Hoover Dam, the state capitol in Carson City, and other points of scenic interest going and returning.

Since it had been a surprise visit, none of the state's top brass knew about her visit to Las Vegas. Mrs. Roosevelt had a quick breakfast at El Rancho, then started out of the coffee shop toward the waiting limousine. That's when she became aware of a shiny group of slot machines all over the gaming casino, which was totally deserted at that early hour.

At her side and eager to carry out her slightest wish, Owner Beldon Katleman began to explain those miserable "one-armed bandits" which have been the lifeblood of many a gaming hotel not doing too well at the tables. Slot-machine revenues never vary except in steadily increasing profits.

In those days, the gross slot-machine take of El Rancho Vegas on normal months was in the comfy neighborhood of $150,000 a month. Slot-machine players always seemed to be enchanted, maybe even mesmerized, by the strange clanging noises the one-armed bandits gave off.

And Eleanor Roosevelt was no exception, as she looked at a quarter machine with more than casual interest. Suddenly she began groping in her purse for coins, and that's when Katleman jumped in gallantly and gave her a Dixie cup filled with quarters.

As the stately, utterly mystified lady began inserting the quarters with the same gingerly, awkward motion she might have used to put her fingers into the mouth of a cobra, Katleman dashed away to find the slot-machine mechanic. There was a hurried consultation with the man, who then quietly stepped behind another machine about ten feet away from Mrs. Roosevelt and began adjusting little wheels at the back of the machine while Katleman watched Mrs. Roosevelt drop quarter after quarter into her own slot machine without success.

234

Unfortunately no photographer was in sight to record an image of sheer incredibility: the dignified, internationally famous Eleanor Roosevelt putting quarters into a slot machine, then grimacing disappointedly when the little cherries, lemons, and oranges whirled about maddeningly without landing in a payoff position for her.

"Mrs. Roosevelt," apologized Katleman, "that machine seems to be cold. Why not try the quarter machine over there?" Then he skillfully guided her to the machine that had just been tampered with.

She was utterly astounded by the results of her new slot machine. It paid off three times out of every five. As a slew of quarters cascaded down into the mouth of the machine, Mrs. Roosevelt squealed with delight. And as her pile of winning quarters mounted, so did her spirits.

Eleanor Roosevelt never did get to visit Hoover Dam or Carson City. After cashing in her horde of quarters for six crisp one-hundred-dollar bills and four twenties, the gracious lady called over Katleman and said, "Please see that this money is given to the local charities here, would you, Mr. Katleman? Anonymously, if you don't mind," she hastily added. Beldon K., a man with a professional eye for good will, took the money, then told her, "I'll add an equal amount, Mrs. Roosevelt."

As much as it grieved Katleman that she had firmly requested no publicity on her quickie visit to Las Vegas and her successful encounter with a slot machine, he went along with it.

In my column the next morning I revealed her presence in town at the El Rancho Vegas Hotel. However, I have never printed her experiences with a "fixed" slot machine until now.

Several weeks later Beldon Katleman received a gracious letter from Mrs. Roosevelt thanking him for making her unexpected stay in Las Vegas at El Rancho Vegas a "most pleasurable, rewarding one."

Katleman may have missed out on getting a wire-service story and picture, especially showing her at the slot machines, but she told him in that note that every time she attended a United Nations function or a charitable affair, she never failed to tell her friends about her "fabulous success with a quarter slot machine at the El Rancho Vegas Hotel." She also wrote Katleman that President "Harry Truman was most envious of my success at that machine. He wants to come to your hotel, providing you'll let him play that lucky quarter slot machine."

The great lady went to her death never suspecting that she had played a "fixed" slot machine.

THE HEIST

Many a tourist or local with a smattering of larceny in his soul has had his eyes pop out an inch as he ogled the thousands of dollars in chips lying conveniently stacked up in neat little piles against the casino tables. A fortune was his for the taking—provided he could win all the chips via the dice, blackjack, or roulette route. And maybe he could if he lived long enough and his bankroll was the size of Howard Hughes' and J. Paul Getty's.

But to separate the casinos from all those chips illegally would be another matter. The burly security guards who roam about the tables with steely, piercing looks and guns in their holsters keep the customers fairly honest.

To burglarize either the casinos or the cashier cages, where a million dollars and more are kept to redeem the chips, is just about as practical as a one-man raid on Kentucky's Fort Knox.

One bright and early day on April 21, 1955, the first high rise in Las Vegas opened wide its doors, and the bosses of the brand-new Riviera Hotel stepped back gingerly to avoid the rush of humanity that jammed the hotel. Hysteria set in as people attacked the gaming casinos, the coffee shops, and the bars. It must have looked to a casual observer (if there was one in the hotel that day) that money, food, and goodies were being given away for free. Of course, they weren't, but the slot machines are loose and more generous on opening day, and little gifts are usually given away.

The one place where it was quiet was a suite on the sixth floor. Three men and a lady sat around a large table with pencils and much white paper and made copious notes. They could have been the school board members in your small American hamlet jotting down topics to discuss at the next Chamber of Commerce meeting when they got home.

Actually the three men and lady were burglars plotting to rob the casino of precisely $60,000—no more, nor less—during the next eight or ten hours.

The three men were dressed like the male supervisors in the casino below. Such employees were better known as pit bosses. They wore somber black silk suits, white on white silk shirts, and somber black ties. The lady wore a loose-fitting dress over a specially constructed bra. The dress had a large "pocket" across the middle, with an opening about sixteen inches long and a foot deep. She wore a large shawl that covered her shoulders and reached down to her knees.

One of the men and the lady left the apartment suite and headed for the crowded casino below. They knew exactly what had to be done, as they stepped out of the elevator on the lobby floor and mingled with the mob.

The man went directly to the gaming pit, which was in slight turmoil as pit bosses went about their chosen tasks. Since he was dressed exactly as they were, he passed unnoticed. Then he walked over to the desk in the gaming pit, reached for one of the "order books," and began filling out a requisition for "two trays of $100 chips." He scribbled his initials at the bottom, then walked briskly out of the pit and toward the casino's cage. It was not unusual. The real pit bosses had been doing that since the casino opened for play.

Shoving the order for two trays of "hundreds" under the wicket, he snarled in his nastiest pit-boss manner, "C'mon, c'mon, table six is all outa blacks."

He got his two trays just as quickly. Holding them in a death lock, our man headed in the direction of "crap table six." But he never reached that table, because his dowdy lady associate was hurrying toward him through the crowd. Pushing and shoving to get through the mob, they almost met head on. He deftly dropped both trays and the chips into her "pocket apron." She, of course, immediately covered her new-found treasure with the shawl and proceeded in the opposite direction.

Ten minutes later they met in the sixth-floor suite, where their other two associates were idly playing gin rummy for a quarter cent a point, drinking coffee, and chewing on stale hamburgers. The lady emptied her treasure on the bed—two hundred black chips that could be redeemed in the Riviera or other Las Vegas hotels for the going price of $20,000.

One down and two to go!

And as the "dowdy lady" freshened up a bit before making another sortie to the casino area, the gent who had safely made the first heist briefed the second "pit boss."

"Listen, all went well. Just be careful not to stay too long at the cashier's cage. Push in your order and demand the chips. They're knee deep in shit, sweat, and steam, and too goddamned rushed to stop and think. Okay? Good luck."

Two more trips followed with equal success. Then the three gents and the dowdy lady sat around on the floor counting the chips for the third time. It came out to $60,000—just what they had planned.

A grand premiere in a Strip hotel doesn't happen every

238

month in Vegas, so the fast and furious festivities continued for the next three days.

But they weren't out of the woods. The hard work was still ahead—cashing in the six hundred beautifully shiny chips during the next forty-eight hours before the shortage of black chips would be noticed by the Riviera Hotel gaming tycoons.

The "dowdy lady" now became a most attractive lady with elegant measurements. She was handed a hundred "blacks," then went below to wine and dine and, from time to time, cash in some of the chips until all hundred had been redeemed. The three gents did likewise, each toting a bulky one hundred "blacks" for redemption below.

On the following day and evening, still more chips were redeemed, but to make it look "kosher" the boys dabbled a bit on the tables, cashing the "blacks" into quarters ($25 chips) before trying their luck at "21" and dice.

Exactly ninety-six hours after checking into the hotel, the four heisters left for parts unknown, each pocketing $15,000, greatly heartened by the fact that they had outsmarted Las Vegas society.

It took almost a week before the hotel's gaming auditors discovered "three questionable order slips for $60,000 with unknown initials!"

But the top brass at the hotel were too overjoyed by the $1,300,000 the hotel had grabbed off during the festive three-day-premiere holiday to fret about a "lousy" sixty grand.

Unfortunately, in spite of their $1,300,000 windfall, the owners were poorly equipped to operate a gaming hotel. After almost a year of "hit-and-miss" operations, they sold out to a gambling syndicate.

FIG NEWTON

The apple-cheeked youngster with the all-American well-scrubbed look was phoning from the lounge of the Fremont

Hotel downtown. He and his brother, Jerry, were a low-priced combo working in that lounge from early evening until the wee hours of the following morning. And they were pretty tired of such a backbreaking routine even though Wayne, the younger of the two, was only eighteen.

Wayne was calling me to say that they wondered if I would mind giving up the glamorous Strip one night to come downtown to the honky-tonk clubs and gaming-club stores that dotted Fremont Street.

Yes, I did mind leaving the Strip, because I had an aloof attitude about anything in show business that wasn't good enough for a Strip hotel showroom. However, to please the lads, I went downtown one night, sat in the tiny lounge, and heard Wayne Newton sing a couple of dozen songs in a pleasurable manner while his brother, Jerry, sat on a stool off to one side of the stage and heckled him.

Wayne not only wanted me to catch the act, but if I liked what I saw, he wanted me to be their manager. Now that was a laugh. Me, a columnist, managing a couple of young lads who sang! Bob Goulet, yes. Tony Newley, yes. Even Don Rickles, yes. But a couple of kids named Wayne Newton and brother Jerry? NO!

However, I sat through part of their act, listening to Wayne sing endlessly while brother Jerry piped up cutely from time to time for the benefit of a handful of disinterested beer drinkers in a room that didn't hold more than forty people. What made it hard for the boys was that they were on for thirty minutes and off for fifteen, so they were working many sets nightly. But they were young, fearlessly determined, and in possession of a certain amount of saloon talent.

Back on the Strip I suddenly felt guilty for not staying around for the complete show, then going backstage to talk with the lads for a moment or two. So I went to a phone, got Wayne, and explained that I had very much liked what I saw on that tiny lounge stage. I wasn't prepared for Wayne's

240

spontaneous reply, "So, why don't you handle us, Mr. Pearl?"

I began sputtering and stuttering, all the while thinking of an answer to get out of this embarrassing situation.

"Wayne, I would love nothing better than to handle you kids as an act. You'll probably hit it really big one of these days." But who was I kidding? I didn't really and truly believe what I was telling young Wayne Newton.

Four months later, the Newtons, Wayne and Jerry, worked with Jack Benny on a stage in Phoenix, then with Jackie Gleason on "fatso's" TV show in New York. Wayne took off in a hurry toward stardom. The theater audiences in Phoenix as well as the enormous TV audience watching the Gleason show sang his praises. Next thing I knew the columnists and feature writers began touting Wayne Newton as America's next star.

Late in 1971, Jerry Newton left the act, but he left a very rich man because Wayne had been earning upwards of a million dollars a year for the past five years. As a single in 1972, Wayne would pay taxes on about $1,750,000.

And every time I begin figuring what 10 percent of that kind of money would have netted me, I start throwing up wherever I happen to be.

"MY WHOLE LIFE FLASHED
BEFORE ME"

An inquisitive radio interviewer in New York was giving me a bad time as he threw question after question at me about "the mob boys in control of gambling in Las Vegas." This was back in the late Fifties before Hilton, Hughes, and company.

I cracked, "It certainly isn't controlled by IBM or the American Tobacco Company!"

That seemed to placate him for the moment, so he went

into another series of queries, "Is there much whoring around in Las Vegas by the hotel owners and the stars?"

Answer: "No more than you'll find here in New York among the industrialists and radio commentators."

Now the radio interview was at an end, and I straggled out into the broiling July sun of a typical Manhattan scorcher. As I walked slowly back to my hotel, I tried to remember the many items in my column that dealt with who was creeping into whose pad and where.

I'd been threatened many times by outraged (but guilty) boy friends, husbands, wives, and girl friends, but it had never reached a serious point where my life was threatened— except once at the Stardust Hotel when I was sure that my number had finally come up. And at high noon yet!

Before I had taken more than a couple of steps into the hotel one afternoon, a burly gent who looked at least eight feet tall rushed over and grabbed me by the tie. Then without a word, he began tightening it before trying to lift it over my head.

Talk about your whole life flashing in front of you when you're faced with pending doom! I really ached. A big eight-foot slob with steel claws for hands was about to choke me to death in the lobby of a Strip hotel. And all because of a lousy column item. There was no point in appealing to the guy. And even if I could, he would never understand the croaking, wheezing noises I was making. Strangely, all I could think about was the kind of obit my publisher would give me. Probably he'd hide it in the back pages.

Anyway there I was dangling at the end of my taut tie and making like a Jewish Yo-Yo when suddenly I spotted a couple of laughing gents off to one side in the Stardust lobby. They were getting an enormous charge out of the "hanging party."

Since one of them was Milt Jaffe, a bigwig in the Stardust gaming casino, it all came to me in a flash. He had been a boxing manager back in Pittsburgh before reforming and joining the Stardust. The guy he managed? None other than the muscular guy who was dangling me: Billy Conn.

At that moment Billy set me down. He was giggling like a happy schoolboy who had just been informed that the schoolhouse had burned down. I should have recognized Billy, but have you ever tried reading a book while standing on your head? Or dangling from a thoroughly stretched neck while the toes barely touched terra firma? Billy, Milt, and the others were having a big laugh at my expense as I tried straightening out my bent tie.

"Go ahead laugh, you bastards," I snarled in my fiercest falsetto tones. Then, turning to Billy Conn, I said, "Sure, you can laugh now. But I knew all along it was a gag. You're lucky you put me down when you did, because I was getting ready to deck you with my right at any moment."

Unfortunately the hoax "lynching" spread all over the Strip. I was the laughing stock of the town. Cabbies honked their horns at me as I roamed from hotel to hotel screaming, "Hey, Pearl, look out for Billy Conn. He's out to get you." That night I escaped into the Sahara showroom to catch Judy Garland, who has never had an equal as a café performer.

Sure enough, Judy spotted me sitting off in the corner of the room, hidden behind a tall soft drink. She stopped singing and told her audience, "Ladies and gentlemen, the late Ralph Pearl, who was accidentally throttled this afternoon by Billy Conn, the ex-fighter, is in the room. Ralphie, if you're not too stretched out, will you get up and take a bow?"

It went on like that for three months. Don Rickles, when he played the Sahara lounge, made a nightly note of the incident on his show. I vowed that I'd get back at Billy if it took the rest of my life. Two months later I got a tip from a Pittsburgh sports writer that Billy Conn was going to go to work for Milt Jaffe at the Stardust as a host. Glory be! My chance had come.

The day that Billy went to work at the Stardust I ran an item in my column, "The pride and joy of Pittsburgh, Billy Conn, joins the 'Lido de Paris' show today as a chorus boy. He'll also moonlight as a host during his spare time."

The roar Billy let out when he read that item could be heard all over the Strip. It was a human sonic boom. I went on my vacation the next day and, when I returned a week later, Billy Conn had calmed down. In fact, the first night we met after my return, Billy came forward, hand outstretched and a pleasant smile on his face. We shook hands, and it was ten days before I could move my fingers.

FATHER TONY

Back in 1962, religion came to the glamorous Strip in the form of a dapper little fifty-five year-old Catholic priest, Father Richard Anthony Crowley, whose church, a small storefront house of worship, was about five miles from where all the show-biz action was taking place. Father Crowley would travel nightly to the Strip, in the wee hours of morning when most of the entertainers had done their final shows for the night, and try to persuade them to return with him for a special entertainers' 4:30 ayem mass.

He wasn't succeeding that first year, except for a few stray performers. But Father Crowley didn't give up. If he brought a couple of showgirls, a comic, and a juggler—maybe also a couple of blackjack dealers—back with him, then he'd enlist their support in getting them to talk to their friends and colleagues about that 4:30 mass.

One day the boss at the Stardust Hotel (Moe Dalitz, who was of the Jewish faith) decided to help Father Crowley. He let him hold his 4:30 mass in the convention hall adjoining the Stardust and right in the center of all the glamorous hotels. For the first time since he had come to Las Vegas, Father Crowley had a "sellout" crowd for his early morning mass. It was a roaring success.

Father Crowley became popular with the gaming bosses, and the collection plates benefited mightily from the friendships. Then one day Father Crowley was gifted with a $6,500 Mercedes-Benz sports job. It was white and had green leather seats. From then on you could see Father Crowley behind the wheel of his sports car at all hours of the day and night.

Crowley's favorite crack about holding mass in a gambling town such as Las Vegas was, "Didn't they gamble for the Robe at the foot of the Cross?"

One day, while he was driving along the Strip in broad daylight, he was spotted by a prominent tourist member of the clergy and reported to the Monsignor in Reno. Shortly after, Father Crowley put an ad in the daily newspaper: "1960 Mercedes-Benz for sale. Only five months old and being sold at a sacrifice."

A week later the good and Reverend Richard Anthony Crowley was given notice that he was being transferred to another church in an eastern city. The day before he left he was given a farewell party at the Convention Center, which saw a turnout of almost seven thousand people, many of them from show business and of other faiths. It was the kind of night Father Crowley would never forget. Many of the acts working in Strip hotels entertained the crowd, as well as the good Father, for the next four hours.

He got a scroll from the performers, but not before he did a soft-shoe dance routine and a chorus or two of "Harrigan, That's Who." Several Strip hotel producers offered him contracts to stay and work their showrooms. But the Father shook hands all around, shed a couple of tears of gratitude to an "unruly mob" of performers, croupiers, horse players, and out-and-out parole violators in the hall that night, then departed for other shores, other churches, but none that would ever match his parish in Las Vegas.

PINKY LEE

Little Pinky Lee, a bundle of nerves all his life, doesn't play Las Vegas any more. As a matter of fact, the last time Pinky played Las Vegas was in 1959 at the Dunes Hotel, when he shared billing with an animal act of trained ponies and monkeys.

A shrewd vaudevillian and pioneer on early TV, Pinky capitalized on a stutter, a lisp, and those crazy checkered pants and pea cap. Also on an act that was a combination of burlesque and old vaudeville. But that's what the customers wanted in the late Fifties in Las Vegas.

I sat at ringside one night watching the little one introduce Gautier's ponies and monkeys, who proceeded to gallop about the stage while doing tricks. There was no chance of the ponies' littering the stage, because all eight were tranquilized before every show.

Pinky had just done a couple of routines with a busty blonde, brought on the ponies, and retired to his dressing room to put on his "trick suit" for the closing number with that same blonde. It was an old burlesque routine where on a given cue the blonde grabs Pinky's lapel, then pulls, leaving him standing there only in a pair of large checkered shorts. It never failed to get laughs.

As Pinky sat in his dressing room adjusting that suit, he suddenly heard a commotion out front. Grabbing a robe, he dashed out into the wings and saw pandemonium onstage and in the showroom.

A pony had thrown off the effects of the tranquilizer while galloping about the stage. So he decided it was a fine time to drop a load right there in front of a huge audience of boozers, losers, and lovers.

246

The other ponies, still tranquilized, kept on circling, kicking the horseshit all over the stage and among the dining ringsiders. I was just in the process of mouthing a piece of lamb when the shit hit the fans. If you've never tasted horseshit with lamb, don't bother. It has a flavor unlike any steak sauce you ever tried.

The other diners shrieked as the pony crud hit their food. The more sensitive ones vomited, then swooned. Women were trying to get it off their clothing, hair, and faces. The bosses stood petrified watching the turmoil as the curtain finally came down to block off the flurry.

Finally the debris had been cleared and a certain order had been restored. Out came a spokesman for the hotel to tell the diners that all checks for that show were being picked up by a terribly apologetic management.

Backstage, Pinky Lee had been fainting every five minutes when he wasn't sobbing bitterly. But now he pulled himself together and returned to his dressing room to put on that trick suit, because the show was continuing.

Pinky and the blonde threw some lines at each other, then she found Pinky's lapel and yanked away vigorously. Off came the suit, leaving Pinky standing there without a stitch of clothes on! In all the excitement, Pinky had forgotten to put on those floppy checkered shorts.

MERV GRIFFIN

Once a band singer, Merv Griffin is now one of the more popular TV talk-show hosts in the nation. He comes to Las Vegas five or six times a year and tapes his television show from the showroom of Caesars Palace. Since it's an afternoon affair for the whole week, the tourists and locals come flocking, filling the showroom to overflowing and then brimming over into the lobby, gaming casino, and even into the coffee shop.

The gaming top brass don't mind, because afternoons aren't the best time of the day to bring out the gambling customers. Hence, if the hotel casino can snare even ten percent of those afternoon throngs to try their hands at the games, they're still ahead.

Unlike a couple of his colleagues who ventured into Las Vegas with nitery shows, then came away slightly scarred and muttering to themselves, Merv is bright enough to merely get his toes wet in the Vegas waters by taping his shows from there.

Late one afternoon, after taping a show at the Palace, Merv walked out into the casino and unwound by dealing blackjack to his horde of fans who flocked around the table when they saw their idol make like a dealer. Merv dealt for fully fifteen minutes, letting the players win as often as possible as the gaming bosses looked on in a strangely benevolent manner. The players were only playing dollars, so what could the house really lose while getting lots of publicity?

Suddenly the voice behind Merv said, "Griffin, you're a natural blackjack dealer. You should have made it your life's work instead of television."

It was Mike Douglas.

Epilogue

It's time to put away the portable and head for the Strip. Time and opening nights in Las Vegas showrooms wait for no man, especially columnists. It has been a blistering hot August day and my air conditioning is wheezing. That means it must be at least 110 degrees outside, and it's already seven in the evening. Making it still more uncomfortable, a sandstorm howling outside my window makes it almost impossible to see more than a couple of feet out the window.

The gaming bosses like to see sandstorms, but not in the evening when the tourists are making ready to catch the shows and do some gaming. They prefer the sandstorms at high noon when those tourists "waste" their time lounging around the swimming pools or shopping.

Unfortunately, neither sand, infernal heat, nor rain can keep this appointed courier of show-biz happenings from his appointed rounds. And right now there are several hotels to visit, several rumors to check out and, much later in the evening, a chat with Jack Benny in his Sahara Hotel dressing room.

Right now I'm in the gaming casino of a Strip hotel and

chatting with my old friend, Ike, the guy who claims he rarely has a winning shift in his casino. Remember, he always insists his shift just "breaks even." Tonight, however, Ike is beaming, which is a rarity for that dour-faced gent. I'm in luck. Ike must be going to tell me that he has had a winning shift after all. Otherwise, why would he be so jovial?

Unlike a chameleon, however, Ike doesn't change his complexion or close-mouthed attitude about what has gone into those little black boxes under each gaming table. Behind that familiar cigar and those yellowing teeth, Ike is still his pessimistic self.

"Don't be fooled by all the people around the tables, Ralph. Christ, I never seen so many winners like tonight. Every sonofabitch and his brother is beating us. No, we won't break even tonight, we'll lose our asses."

Spoken like a true gaming boss. I leave Ike to his cigar and head for the front door. The sand is still blowing, but not as badly as before. I begin walking down the Strip and, as I stroll, I indulge in my favorite outdoor sport—dreaming.

Will this be the night a long, lean figure of a man will emerge from the shadows, identify himself as Howard Robard Hughes, then lay an exclusive story on me that will break on page one in every newspaper in the world? Even in Biloxi, Mississippi.

A screeching sound snaps me out of my reverie. A cab has narrowly missed knocking me into next Tuesday. Slamming on his brakes, the driver lets go with a series of oaths that clear my clogged sinuses. I'm no longer dreaming. There are things to be done, stars to be visited. I make a mental note to pick up that dream within the confines of my bedroom later tonight.

It's now about three ayem. Bone-weary and a bit grimy from the sand, I notice the creosote bushes have started to descend since the sand has stopped blowing. My little notebook is crammed with juicy items, but, even more gratifying, my chat with Jack Benny will give me half a column tomorrow.

Yet, I'm not a happy columnist this early morning. As a matter of fact, I'm in a reflective, depressed mood. Off in the distance the brooding black mountains seem to be trying to tell me something. Sooner or later I know I must look toward those mountains for the sign I've been waiting for since early 1952. And when it comes, I know I'll have to leave everything and run for my life.

Myron Cohen was most prophetic in his story about the traveling salesman who told the irate husband, "Everybody's gotta be some place." That's why, when my sign comes from those brooding, black mountains all around me, I hope it'll have arrows pointing the way to my new destination.

I can't explain my disloyalty. I just know that I've never really been convinced of the durability of this huge gaming city in the desert, this Utopia of constant fun and pleasure in shifting sands—even though Bugsy Siegel's words keep hammering at the back of my skull, "This town'll be woild-famous one day."

As far as I'm concerned, Las Vegas still belongs to the reptiles and rodents, who merely subleased the town to the gamblers and the Mormons. I vow I must one day give these little creatures the recognition they so richly deserve but never really got.

Now I'm home. I head for my typewriter and put a piece of paper in the machine while my croupy air conditioner starts wheezing again. I have a more important chore right now than just writing another column. That can wait till morning.

I start banging away on the keys. My sequel, *Son of Las Vegas Is My Beat*, is starting to unfold in front of my jaundiced eyes.